FROM LIGHT
INTO
DARKNESS

THE EVOLUTION OF RELIGION
IN ANCIENT EGYPT

FROM LIGHT
INTO
DARKNESS

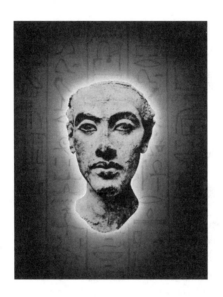

THE EVOLUTION OF RELIGION
IN ANCIENT EGYPT

STEPHEN S. MEHLER

ADVENTURES UNLIMITED PRESS

From Light Into Darkness
The Evolution of Religion In Ancient Egypt

Published by
Adventures Unlimited Press
One Adventure Place
Kempton, Illinois 60946 USA
amphq@frontiernet.net
www.adventuresunlimitedpress.com

Cover design, book design and layout:
Robert W. Taylor Design, Inc.

Cover photo by AMORC

CONTENTS

DEDICATION

Dedicated to the loving memory of:

Sol and Freida Kalski Goldstein.
Bill (Tajalli) Wichman.
F.R. "Nick" Nocerino.
Dr. Albert H. Doss, F.R.C.
Parsifal, Persephone Sue and Ting Li.

LIST OF FIGURES

Figure 9: Giza. Great Pyramid. Scorch/burn marks in ceiling of Grand Gallery. Photo by author 2003. Page 36.

Figure 10: Giza. Great Pyramid. Cracks in granite beams in ceiling of King's Chamber. Photo by author 1992. Page 38.

Figure 11: Giza. Great Pyramid. Cracks in granite beams in ceiling of King's Chamber. Photo by author 2003. Page 38.

Figure 12: Abu Roash. Pyramid in ruins. Photo by author 1997. Page 39.

Figure 13: Dahshur. Bent Pyramid showing corners severely damaged. The damage may be from ancient cataclysm. Photo by author 2003. Page 41.

CHAPTER FIVE

Figure 14: Mother Goddess Figurine. Found in Egypt and dated to ca. 4000 BC but is probably much older. Page 47.

Figure 15: Mother Goddess Figurine. Also found in Egypt and dated to ca. 5000 BC but may be as old as 8000 BC. Page 47.

Figure 16: Abydos. Temple of Osiris. Djehuti (Thoth), masculine lunar Neter of wisdom. Djehuti was the principle of the sacred sounds that led to writing. Photo by author 1998. Page 53.

Figure 17: Dendara. Temple of Hathor. Seshat, the Neter of sacred geometry and writing. Seshat provided the forms for the sacred sounds to produce the symbols for the first written scripts. Photo by author 2004. Page 53.

Figure 18: Hieroglyphics, known as the Suf language to the ancient Khemitians. Page 54.

Figure 19: Sakkara. Step Pyramid. Dated by Egyptologists to 2700 BC, Third Dynasty of Old Kingdom Period. The structure was built in several stages and may actually have been started ca. 4000 BC, is predynastic, and is not a true pyramid but a symbolic tomb. 1999. Photo by author. Page 61.

Figure 20: Abydos. Temple of Osiris. Dated by Egyptologists to 1200 BC, 19th Dynasty of the New Kingdom Period. The temple may be as old as ca. 4000 BC and was dedicated to the Neter Wizzer (Osiris), and not constructed for any king. Photo by author 1992. Page 62.

CHAPTER NINE

Figure 44: Luxor. Valley of the Kings. KV 47, the tomb of Yuya. Photo by author 2004. Page 118.

Figure 45: Giza. Stele in front of Sphinx attributed to King Tuthmose IV, ca.1450 BC. Photo by author 2003. Page 115.

Figure 46: Cairo Museum. Profile of mummy of Yuya, possibly the Biblical Joseph. Note distinctive Semitic features. Page 121.

Figure 47: Sakkara. Tomb of Horemheb. Relief depicting Amen Priest and subservient "captives," ca.1310 BC. Scene may show oppression of Hebrew/Atenites, the followers of Akhenaten. Photo by author 2004. Page 122.

Figure 48: Sakkara. Tomb of Horemheb. Close-up of scene possibly depicting oppression of Hebrew/Atenites before The Exodus. Ca.1310 BC. Photo by author 2004. Page 122.

Figure 49: Cairo Museum. Israel Stele, ca.1210 BC. Attributed to reign of King Merneptah. Photo by author 1997. Page 126.

Figure 50: Cairo Museum. Close-up of Israel Stele of Merneptah. Glyphs in second register from bottom mentions "Israel" as both a people and a place, ca. 1210 BC. Photo by author 1997. Page 126.

Figure 51: Luxor. Medinet Habu. The Ramasseum, the Temple of Time and Timelessness. Relief depicting a sea battle ca.1200 BC. Scene depicted is victory of armies of Amen over the "Shasu," the Hebrew/Atenite followers of Akhenaten, The Exodus. Photo by author 1998. Page 128.

Figure 52: Luxor. Medinet Habu. Temple of Time and Timelessness. Another relief depicting armies of Amen in victory over their enemies, The Exodus from "the Egyptian side," according to Abd'El Hakim. Ca.1200 BC. Photo by Theresa L. Crater 1999. Page 128.

Figure 53: Amarna. Tomb of Ramose. Scene showing images of Akhenaten and Nefertiti defaced by Amen priests, ca.1350 BC. Photo by author 1998. Page 130.

Figure 54: Amarna. Tomb of Ramose. Another scene with images of Akhenaten and Nefertiti defaced by Amen priests, ca.1350 BC. Photo by author 1998. Page 130.

Figure 55: Aswan. Elephantine Island. The Neter Hathor depicted with cow ears. The worship of the golden calf mentioned in the Book of Exodus of the Old Testament by the Hebrew followers of Moses was an image of the sacred cow, a symbol of Hathor. Photo by author 1999. Page 134.

Figure 56: Relief with the glyph Nesu, a stalk of wheat. The term also indicated cooked food utilizing the sense of smell and may be where the word nose originated. Page 137.

Figure 57: The Hebrew letter Aleph, "A" in English. The Khemitian sign for Neter can be seen in the Hebrew letter. Photo by author 2005. Page 145.

Figure 58: The Hebrew letter Shin, "S" in English. The Khemitian sign for Neter can be seen used three times in the Hebrew letter. Photo by author 2005. Page 145.

Figure 59: Aswan. The Temple of Isis at Philae. The Khemitian glyph Neter-Neteru, the "triple Neter," The Neter of Neters. The triple Neter was utilized in the Hebrew letter Shin, a letter representing El Shaddai, a Kabalistic name of the Jewish God. Photo by author 2004. Page 145.

Figure 60: Abydos. Abd'El Hakim pointing to glyph of Mesu, the three jackal skins meaning rebirth. Photo by author 1998. Page 146.

CHAPTER TEN

Figure 61: Rosicrucian Park, San Jose, California. The author and Shawn Levin standing in front of AMORC Administration building constructed in the style of the Temple of Horus at Edfu in Egypt. Photo by Diane Hardy 1997. Page 150.

Figure 62: Rosicrucian Park, San Jose, California. One of the many depictions of Akhenaten found at Rosicrucian Park. Photo by author 1997. Page 150.

Figure 63: Dr. H. Spencer Lewis, Imperator of AMORC 1909-1939. Photo by AMORC. Page 154.

Figure 64: Rosicrucian Park, San Jose, California. The author pointing to one of the many sphinxes found in RC Park with the face of H. Spencer Lewis. Photo by Diane Hardy 1997. Page 155.

Figure 65: Rosicrucian Park, San Jose, California. Rare photo of the first administrative staff of AMORC in 1927. H. Spencer Lewis is seventh from the right in the third row. Photo by AMORC. Page 156.

Figure 66: Cairo Museum. King Tuthmose III. Considered to be the traditional founder of the mystery school that became the Rosicrucian Order. Photo by author 1997. Page 158.

Figure 67: Men-Kheper-Ra, one of the titles of King Tuthmose III. The title was used by AMORC in the *Rosicrucian Digest* to indicate the tradition of this king being the founder of the RC Order. Page 160.

Figure 68: Giza. First modern pilgrimage to Egypt of Rosicrucians led by H. Spencer Lewis in 1929. Photo by AMORC. Page 161.

Figure 69: Rosicrucian Egyptian Museum, San Jose, California. Painting by H. Spencer Lewis depicting Nefertiti sitting for her portrait bust for the sculptor, Tuthmose. Photo by AMORC 1935. Page 162.

Figure 70: Dr. H. Spencer Lewis at Rosicrucian Park, San Jose, California 1934. Photo by AMORC. Page 165.

Figure 71: Dr. H. Spencer Lewis in his office at Rosicrucian Park 1936. Photo by AMORC. Page 165.

CHAPTER ELEVEN

Figure 72: Edfu. Temple of Horus. Glyph for *Per-Wir*, the House of the Wise Man or Teacher. Represents the first university. Photo by author 1999. Page 171.

Figure 73: Giza. Abd'El Hakim Awyan in his home in the village of Nazlet el Samman, near the Giza Plateau. Photo by author 2004. Page 178.

CHAPTER TWELVE

Figure 74: Ushabti, ca.1400 BC. Page 186.

Figure 75: Ushabti, ca.1400 BC. Page 186.

Figure 76: Figurine of Akhenaten. Created by priests of Aten to replace ushabtis in tombs of his followers. Ca.1350 BC. Page 186.

ACKNOWLEDGMENTS

There are many people who have contributed to and aided in the research and preparation of this work. First and foremost, the biggest thanks and appreciation goes to Theresa Crater, my life partner and closest friend. Theresa and I have spent many hours editing the drafts and discussing the topics of this book. Having accompanied me to Egypt twice on tour, she has experienced many of the facets of Khemitian knowledge and wisdom personally. Theresa and I have taken and renewed vows to each other on two occasions in the presence of Hathor at the Temple of Dendara in Egypt, and this book could never have been accomplished without Theresa's love, support, energy and wisdom. I also want to thank our feline children Wizzer and Arwen.

This book could also not have been accomplished without the love, wisdom, patience and collaboration of my beloved teacher, Abd'El Hakim Awyan. I have often stated that Hakim is a walking library and I have been blessed by his sharing some of the knowledge of the indigenous oral traditions of the ancient Khemitians with me. The great love and support of his family must also be recognized, especially that of his eldest daughter Shahrzad (Shahira), who is a living testament to and embodiment of Khemitian wisdom. Her sisters and brothers; Reba, Maryann, Awyen, Bora, Moses, Haroun (Aaron), Haman, Yagoob (Jacob), Yusef (Joseph) and Sadat have always treated me with love and respect and are my Egyptian family. I also mention and give thanks to Maryann's daughter, Hakim's granddaughter, Yazmine (Jasmine) who has the potential to be the Hemeti, The Woman of Power, the future head of the family.

My great appreciation and thanks again to my brother and sisters,

Bob Mehler, Sunny Goldstein Mehler and Layne Hackett, always there for support and love. Thanks to the two people who are my biggest supporters, Phyllis Goldstein Hoffman and Ron Hoffman. Thanks also to Joni Mehler and Mike Taylor, Rick Mehler, Steve and Kristine Mehler and Daniel and Zachary. Thanks also to Raquel Hoffman Lebish for her continued support.

The support and contributions to the research by several key people must be noted. Christopher Dunn, whom I am honored to count both as a close friend and esteemed colleague, has provided incalculable ideas, energy, insight and inspiration for me for many years. Jeanne Dunn, Geno, Alex and Peter have given support and love for both Chris and I. A special mention of gratitude to another dear friend and colleague, Dr. John DeSalvo, Director of The Great Pyramid Of Giza Research Association, and his family. John has become a precious friend to me and is an enormous conduit and resource for alternative researchers.

The research efforts of Dr. Fred Alan Wolf, Barbara Hand Clow, Dr. Volodymyr Krasnoholovets and Ahmed Osman have provided important contributions to the ideas of this book. I must also mention and give thanks to Mark Amaru Pinkham, David Hatcher Childress and Edward F. Malkowski, whose excellent research also contributed greatly to this work.

There are many Rosicrucians who I would like to mention who have aided greatly in this effort. Julia Jordan Catlin, a dear friend who has accompanied me on several tours to Egypt, has been a great source of love and support for many years, and was personally responsible for introducing me to the Rosicrucian tradition. Daniel H. Schmidt, an extraordinary mystic and scientist, has been another good friend for many years and a source of wisdom and spiritual understanding for this book. Françoise Beaudoin, another very dear friend, as owner for many years of Ram Metaphysical Bookstore provided the first opportunity for me to teach these ideas and supplied a meeting place for many mystics and metaphysical people to share and meet in the 1980s and 90s. Rosicrucian friends such as Shasta Bates, Anne Santos, Diane Hardy and Cherie Bersok have provided great support for me. I must also mention Lamar Kilgore, Guy Dickinson, Hank Bersok, Dr, Erwin Watermyer, Dr. George Buletza, Olive Asher, Ed Lee, Don and Dee Walker and Hugh Sims as profound Rosicrucians and mystics who have had great influence upon me.

Special thanks to dear friends Shawn Levin, Eddie and Georgette Gale, Ama Fox, Olga Peck, Susanne Gillen and Elizabeth Lamar. Once again there is a special place in my heart for Wilma Faye Moore, my spiritual "Mom" and a long ago daughter of Akhenaten who has my deepest love and appreciation.

I also want to thank Joe and Marylee Swanson, JoAnn and Carl Parks and Max, Khrys Nocerino, Mac McCrary, Tom Krupa, William Stevenson, Jonathan and Andi Goldman, George Noory, Jeff Rense, Dr. Bob Hieronimus, Laura Lee, John Cadman, Dennis Balthaser, Joe Parr, Jim Rodger, Ted St. Rain, Mark Flett and family, Rob Arlinghaus, Adrienne Taylor, Karen Degenhart, Jonathan Boyd, Tamsin Elliott, Mandi Sanders, Nancy and Jannel Kuhta, Jean Smith, Bennie LeBeau/Blue Thunder and Standing Elk/Golden Eagle/Spotted Horse.

Special love and thanks to Andrea Mikana-Pinkham and Body Mind Spirit Journeys for great support and for providing me the opportunity to return to Egypt to teach and share my work with many people.

My gratitude and appreciation to Robert Taylor, my former neighbor and owner of Robert W. Taylor Design Inc., for the wonderful cover, design and layout of the book.

I am again deeply grateful to David Hatcher Childress for his friendship and research, and for publishing this book, and to Jennifer Bolm and all those at Adventures Unlimited Press for their help and support.

Lastly, my eternal gratitude and love to the spirits of Akhenaten and Dr. H. Spencer Lewis, without whose life experiences and influence this book could never have been possible.

INTRODUCTION

THERE IS A STORY that has always fascinated me which seems quite appropriate to begin this book with. The story concerns the founder of the Chinese system of Taoism, Lao Zi (also written Lao-Tse or Lao-Tsu) who supposedly lived in the sixth century BC. I say supposedly because many scholars consider him to be a mythological character rather than an actual person, but many followers of Taoism are certain he was a historical figure.

There are many versions of the story, but the one that appeals to me most concerns Lao Zi as an old man. Lao Zi was part of an ancient oral tradition of wisdom keepers in China and was a great teacher with many followers. He taught a system he called The Tao or Dao, loosely translated into English as The Way or The Pathless Path. Lao Zi insisted true knowing or understanding can only arise through experience and cannot be transmitted through words, either spoken or written. Therefore, Lao Zi was skeptical of written texts and never wrote any of his teachings down. As he was getting older and approaching death, his younger disciples begged him to write down his basic teachings for the benefit of future humanity. Lao Zi patently refused and said it could not be done. His disciples would not relent and kept at the master day and night. Finally, feeling death near, he acquiesced and wrote what became the standard text of Taoism known as the *Dao de Jing* or the *Tao Te Ching*.

But to maintain his essential belief in experience, the first line of the text is often translated as follows: "The Tao that can be told is not the eternal Tao."

That first line has also been translated many different ways, but I would add to the translations in this way: "The Tao that is spoken or written is not the True or Eternal Tao." This reflects a bias of those who are involved with preserving ancient oral traditions and who maintain a natural distrust of written records and histories. I feel somewhat in a similar position as Lao Zi, not at all comparing myself to the great sage, but perhaps more like one of his students—having to record teachings in words that must be fully experienced to be truly understood. This is a major paradox that I will expand upon and attempt to illuminate in this book.

Since 1992, I have been privileged to be a student of a master of the oral tradition of the indigenous people of Egypt, Abd'El Hakim Awyan. My first book, *The Land of Osiris*, was an introduction to these traditions, providing a framework for the theory of a much older, advanced civilization that existed in Northern Africa known as Khemit in the indigenous tradition. I provided empirical archaeological, geological and engineering evidence as well as retranslations of hieroglyphic symbols to support the contentions of the prior existence of the ancient Khemitian civilization existing well over ten thousand years ago.

My reconnection with Hakim in early 2003 and again in late 2004 has now provided the impetus to further record his tradition in a more detailed exposition. This treatment, although supported by archaeological and historical evidence, will deal with subjects much more philosophical than scientific. The topics of God, soul, religion and spirituality have been addressed by hundreds of authors worldwide and are subjects that, in our current state of knowledge, cannot be determined by physical means, although recent research in quantum and theoretical physics is inexorably heading to a fusion of physics and metaphysics.

Since there are many academic disciplines that address the subject of religion, such as cultural anthropology and comparative religions, the material presented here will once again challenge some of the major paradigms of academia. The one major paradigm to be challenged is the idea that human evolution and culture have continually moved in a straight line from the primitive to the complex. There are researchers currently arguing against all the theories of Darwinian evolution, that there is no real evidence of evolution at all. I tend to support the idea of microevolution, that species do evolve over time, but that of macroevolution, that is, one species evolving into a totally different species, has never been demonstrated or proven at all.

The replacement idea for linear, straight-line evolution is that of cycles. I presented the indigenous Khemitian concept of cycles in *The Land of Osiris*, and I will expand further on that concept in this book this time dealing with the topics of religion and spirituality. I will present a definite distinction between these concepts, religion and spirituality, and how they have developed in a cyclical framework. Religion in ancient Egypt, which I will refer to as dynastic or historical Khemit, arose from previous ancient Khemitian wisdom teachings or spirituality. Those elaborate practices, rituals and written texts of dynastic Khemit evolved into the modern religion of Judaism, which subsequently led to the rise of Christianity and Islam. I will also expound on the idea that all modern metaphysical systems, especially the Western Mystery Schools that led to Rosicrucianism, Freemasonry, the Knights Templar, Theosophy, and Anthroposophy, are descended from the wisdom teachings of prehistoric Khemit. I will conclude by explaining the ancient system of Khemitian wisdom as given to me by Abd'El Hakim and the great paradox these teachings present for us today.

I fully realize I am biting off a major chunk of what makes us distinctly human in this book—spirit, God, soul and religion. That what I will state within these pages might elicit much more criticism, anger and misunderstanding in the next few years than my first book will come as no major surprise to me—Hakim has already predicted as much to me—

3

but still it must be done. The major theme of *The Land of Osiris* was that we have come to the end of a major cycle of darkness, to be addressed in greater detail in this book, and have arrived at the Awakening, a new Dawn of Consciousness. This is the major reason for this effort—to provide a further foundation for those actively interested and involved in this great shift.

CHAPTER ONE

SPIRITUALITY AND RELIGION

The Tao that can be told is not the eternal Tao.

The name that can be named is not the eternal name.

The nameless is the beginning of heaven and earth.

The named is the Mother of ten thousand things.

Ever desireless, one can see the mystery.

Ever desiring, one can see the manifestations.

These two spring from the same source but differ in name:

This appears as darkness.

Darkness within darkness.

The gate to all mystery.

—Lao Zi, *Dao de Jing*[1]

Figure 1: The glyphs for Khemit—KMT-The Black Land.

T HE ILLUMINED CHINESE SAGE, Lao Zi, presented the great paradox, the difficulty of explaining in words for intellectual processes that which can only be experienced for true knowing— the great mystery of life. And that mystery concerns the primary question, what is life and the human condition. That contemplation has always led to the realms of what we have labeled spirituality and religion.

Many scholars have often equated the two terms, spirituality and religion, as being the same. Since both deal with the supernatural, or with unseen worlds beyond the physical, and with some sort of a sense of the divine or Deity, they are often lumped together as one understanding. However for the purposes of this work, I will state that spirituality and religion are not the same, although they deal with similar themes. I will present definite, distinct differences and definitions of the two and how they have evolved over the last ten thousand years or more.

Spirituality deals with spirit, a word that has multiple definitions. Spirit is concerned with essence, a basic quality of something. However according to Dr. Fred Alan Wolf in his book, *The Spiritual Universe*, quantum physics can establish that spirit (or soul) can be a basic quality of nothing also. The great paradox that Wolf discusses is how "something," the material universe, apparently arises out of "nothing"—known in religious texts as *The Void*. I will return to Wolf and the theories of theoretical quantum physics often in this work as they provide a new scientific approach to this subject.

Religion is a term that also has multiple definitions and has been an area of concern for many academic disciplines. Many of these disciplines arose in the nineteenth century, such as comparative religion, cultural anthropology, sociology and psychology. All these disciplines have their own definitions of religion and their own version of the history of religion based on those definitions. Present throughout all these academic fields is the one pervasive, enduring, but eroding paradigm that all humans have progressed in a straight, linear progression from the primitive to the complex in all aspects. This view holds that past humans were underdeveloped as per abstract thought, and religion has progressed from the primitive to the complex.

Since religion is said to deal with the concepts of Deity, soul, spirit, possible existence after death or afterlife, rules of behavior, etc., it is an accepted paradigm of those aforementioned academic disciplines that so-called "primitive" people had (and have) primitive, simplistic belief patterns based on fear, ignorance and observed natural patterns not fully understood. This is a bias of academia—that humans over ten thousand years ago could not possibly have had the complex thinking patterns or levels of understanding that we have today.

As I severely challenged the accepted paradigms of academia in my first book, *The Land of Osiris*, so do I strongly differ with the whole incorrect concept of evolution occurring only in linear, straight-line activity. Everything in nature progresses in cycles, not in a straight line, a theme I presented in my first book. I will elaborate on this theme in the next chapter.

The overriding bias evident in academic presentations on the subjects of spirituality and religion is that all ancient belief systems were primitive and underdeveloped. Since most people who have researched these subjects in academic settings have been part of or greatly influenced by the three major Western religions, Judaism, Christianity and Islam, it is clearly assumed these modern religions, and also to some extent Hinduism and Buddhism, are the apex or highest levels of this type of thinking, and ancient beliefs or "religions" were conceived of by less evolved beings. I contend this paradigm of linear progression from primitive to complex is not only unfairly biased in approach, but is blatantly wrong in actuality.

Spirituality is not the same as religion. Spirituality can be seen as practices or beliefs concerning the essence or "spirit" of all things, speculating on the invisible domains or worlds behind the visible. It may deal with the topics of Deity, soul, an afterlife, or it may not. As I will discuss in more detail later, certain religions, such as Buddhism, do not discuss

7

the subject of Deity or God at all. The "first" time any human began to contemplate the wonders of the earth and nature, and began to realize there was an essence or spirit behind what was visually observed, that was the beginning of spirituality.

Religion, I believe, involves a whole other ball game. There is not even a universally accepted definition of the word "religion." Robert Crawford in his book *What Is Religion?* questions whether religion can even be defined. Crawford provides an array of possible definitions from many varied authors, but the following, written by religious scholar John Hick, is my favorite:

> *Religion is one thing to the anthropologist, another to the sociologist, another to the psychologist (and again another to the next psychologist!), another to the Marxist, another to the mystic, another to the Zen Buddhist, and yet another to the Jew or Christian. As a result there is a great variety of religious theories of the nature of religion. There is, consequently, no universally accepted definition of religion, and quite possibly there never will be.[2]*

However, even using Hick's quote, I will endeavor to define religion for the purposes of this work. I will also state my belief, based on my studies and tutelage with my Egyptian indigenous wisdom teacher Abd'El Hakim Awyan, that formal religion has only evolved in the last six to ten thousand years and that the spiritual practices evident before that time were not "primitive" nor the result of lesser evolved minds or consciousness of human beings.

Before that, we will examine other examples of the pervasive bias of the religious paradigms of academia. Emile Durkheim is considered one of the founding fathers of sociology. He has defined religion as "an integral system of beliefs and practices that unite in a single moral community called the church all those who adhere to it."[3] While the Judeo-Christian bias is quite evident by the use of the word "church," I find this definition useful, but for very different reasons than Durkheim intended.

Durkheim also stated that there was a predisposition among humans towards religion, that it was found universally. Other authors have stated that we are "hard-wired" towards religion, statements I completely disagree with. We may be predisposed towards spirituality, but not religion.

The origins of the word religion have even been debated. It is based on Latin, but may be from several different Latin roots. The word "religio" is said to mean "a kind of superstitious awe," but that certainly is not enough.[4] The great Roman orator Cicero connected the Latin root *relegere* meaning "to assemble" to religion, but that is still not enough.[5] Finally, the Roman writer Tertullian, writing in the third century AD, said the word "religio" derived from the Latin verb *religare* which means "to bind together."[6] This, I believe, is closer to the heart of what the true meaning is. This root verb, *religare*, is how Abd'El Hakim traces the origin of religion. He has stated many times that religion means "to bring together, to bind together," but he has also added, "that means we were no longer together," meaning that religion attempts to put people under one belief system, that people have gone astray, lost contact with spirit and must be united. This is a central point in the wisdom tradition Hakim espouses and one I will greatly elaborate upon in this book.

Therefore, I define religion as a body of beliefs and practices, in a formal institutional setting, usually accompanied by a text or writings considered sacred, with specific rituals and behaviors. With this definition, I obviously suggest that religion did not fully exist before the advent of writing and while derived from spirituality or spiritual practices, is not the same thing.

In the academic approach, particularly in the fields of comparative religion and cultural anthropology, in accordance with the paradigm of linear evolution, a straight line from the primitive to the complex, religion is seen to have evolved in three distinct stages. These stages are called animism, polytheism and monotheism. Further distinctions are made according to what are labeled "horizons," spheres of influence, according to standard paradigms of cultural evolution.[7] It is then said the animist religions developed during so-called primitive times in a tribal horizon, early ancient civilizations developed polytheistic religions and the later monotheistic religions were developed within the agricultural horizon— all this following a neat, straight line of progression. The indigenous tradition of Abd'El Hakim would disagree with these "horizons" and state these systems have risen and fallen in natural cycles and we have always been in a tribal existence, whether we are conscious of it or not.

Edward B. Taylor first used the term "animism" in 1871. It was derived from the Latin word "anima," which means soul. It was further believed primitive peoples had deduced from dreams, visions, etc. that they were inhabited by an immaterial soul that somehow survived after death. R.R. Manett further refined this theory in 1899, which suggested that primitive humans did not conceive of an immortal soul, but believed in impersonal forces that animated the world.[8]

Two other terms were included in the concept of animism. The word *mana* is a Polynesian term meaning a force, an influence, an impersonal power possessed by spirits that can be communicated to humans. This would appear to be a necessary aspect of shamanism, the ability to connect and react with spirits in unseen dimensions or worlds. The term *totem* is a word from the Ojibway, an Algonquin tribe of North America. It is related to clan or ancestor worship and represents the guardian animal of that clan.[9] Again, all the theories of animism relate to so-called primitive or pre-literate peoples.

The rise of settled agricultural civilizations, according to accepted paradigms of anthropology, around 8000 BC in the Middle East and Central Asia, saw the advent of polytheistic religions predominate. Polytheism, of course, means the worship of many gods and goddesses, and it is in this period the concept of Deity is expressed. The great civilizations mentioned in this respect are Sumer, Egypt and India, and later Babylon, Assyria, Persia, Greece and Rome. It is the inclusion of ancient Egypt in this group that I will concentrate on in later chapters.

The linear progression then leads to the advent of monotheism with the rise of Judaism, Christianity and Islam. All in a neat, nice straight line from "primitive" peoples with their "primitive" minds and belief systems, to highly advanced people (us, of course) with our well developed brains and cognitive abilities and our superior religions in which God has revealed Himself to certain outstanding individuals whose revelations have brought humanity out of the bowels of ignorant belief systems.

Do I sound too cynical? It should be obvious to those who have read my first book that I totally reject the linear evolutionary paradigms of academia based on too much dependence on the incorrect theories of Charles Darwin. But reading the thoughts and ideas of those supposedly objective scientists who have written about the history and origins of religion has really fueled my cynicism. A prime example is Julien Ries, who wrote the book *The Origin of Religions*. There was no biographical information on Ries in his book, so I am unaware if he is a professor of comparative religion, anthropology or whatever, but the book was originally written in Italian for a presumably predominantly Roman Catholic audience. Listen to these supposedly objective thoughts: "A first category comprises what are called **natural** religions, those of the peoples of central Asia who were still without writing. Next came the religions of the **great** world civilizations, which are based on writing (emphasis mine) . . . followed by the world religions: Buddhism, Judaism, and Islam. Finally there is Christianity, a religion that embodies complete originality."[10]

Complete originality? Obviously, Ries is a Christian as he subtly attempts to separate Christianity even from Judaism and Islam. But original? Any objective analysis of the origins and practices of Christianity would reveal no originality whatsoever, neither the teachings of Jesus nor the rituals based on decidedly "pagan" practices borrowed from the Hebrews, Egyptians, Babylonians, Persians, Jews, ancient Italians, Romans, etc. It is this type of thinking that permeates so-called objective, academic theories of religion.

The bias that concerns me the most is that toward ancient Egypt, correctly called Khemit (see Figure 1). In this book I will concentrate on how Judaism arose from a major influence of the religions of ancient Khemit (dynastic Egypt), and how the dynastic religion arose from the even more ancient Khemitian wisdom teachings as taught by Abd'El Hakim. But first, I will address the bias that ancient peoples were "primitive" and "underdeveloped" in their spiritual understanding and practices. I will also address the bias that writing greatly separates peoples as to their intellectual or spiritual understanding. I will present a new theory as to the origin of writing in ancient Khemit, appearing thousands of years before Egyptologists believe, as taught by Hakim. The ethnocentric bias that so-called "preliterate" people were (and are) culturally, intellectually and spiritually inferior to those who developed writing, and therefore, religious texts, is nonsense and there is no other way to put it.

So for the purposes of this book, I propose there are distinct differences in spirituality and religion. Spirituality is an understanding and practice concerned with the realization of forces, essences, and qualities that pervade all things, organic and inorganic, visible and invisible. Religion is an organized institution with specific rites, rules and practices, based on the systems of spirituality. It was spirituality that evolved thousands of years before writing and was concerned with the essences behind all creation, the concepts of physical death, and a possible afterlife long before the concepts of Deity, soul, and ritual became part of organized religions.

Interestingly enough, the science today that is closest to an understanding of spirituality is not anthropology, but quantum and theoretical physics. I will discuss much of this interconnection in this book, how quantum physics has moved into metaphysics. In the next chapter I will further elaborate on the ancient concepts of cyclical evolution replacing the inadequate paradigm of linear progression.

CHAPTER TWO

CYCLES REVISITED

Returning is the motion of the Tao.

Yielding is the way of the Tao.

The ten thousand things are born of being.

Being is born of not being.

—Lao Zi, *Dao de Jing*

R ECENTLY I FOUND AN OLD VIDEO I had not seen in a long time. The tape features an interview done with me, author and independent Egyptologist John Anthony West and Abd'El Hakim shot at the Mena House right next to the Giza Plateau in Egypt. The interview was conducted by Lynn Chester in 1992 for a small cable television show she had then in Seattle, Washington. As I listened to Hakim speak on the tape, I marveled at the consistency of his teachings in the more than twelve years that I have known him. A prime aspect of his teaching then, continuing into the present, has been the key understanding the ancient Khemitians had of natural cycles. Hakim has always been opposed to the paradigm of linear evolution, maintaining that only a complete understanding of the cycles of nature, and therefore man, could lead to a full awareness of the cultural history of writing in ancient Khemit. Hakim has taught me that writing appeared thousands of years before Egyptologists believe. The idea that so-called "preliterate" people were (and are) culturally, intellectually and spiritually inferior to those who developed writing, and therefore religious texts, is blatantly ethnocentric and incorrect—this will be explained throughout the course of this book.

The first step is my proposal that there are distinct differences between spirituality and religion. Spirituality is an understanding and practice concerned with the realization of forces, visible and invisible. Religion is an organized institution—the business that has evolved out of spirituality.

Interestingly enough, the science today that is closest to an understanding of spirituality is not anthropology, but quantum physics. The latest theories in quantum and theoretical physics are speculating on the very nature of existence and the apparent illusions of the physical world. These theories also deal with cycles, the basic patterns exhibited by quantum particles. First, I will review the ancient concepts of cyclical evolution replacing the inadequate paradigm of linear progression.

The basic concept of cycles that I presented in my first book is called the five stages of the sun. I will now return to that concept for a deeper exploration of the importance of cycles on the evolution of spirituality and religion in Khemit. To briefly recapitulate, the five stages are Kheper (dawn), Ra (noon), Oon (early to mid-afternoon), Aten (late afternoon to twilight) and Amen (night-darkness). These five stages represent both stages of consciousness and epochs of human prehistory and history. Kheper, The Driller symbolized by the scarab beetle, represents the birth of consciousness, the dawn (see Figure 2). Ra, The Stubborn symbolized by the ram, characterizes the adolescent or early stages of consciousness, the sun at high noon. Oon, The Wise symbolized by a man standing upright with a staff, stands for adult or mature consciousness, the sun in early afternoon. Aten, The Wiser symbolized by an old man hunched over with his staff, is the stage of enlightenment or full flowering of consciousness, the sun at full apex heading towards twilight. Finally, Amen, The Hidden who originally had no image, is the end of the cycle where we experience the loss of full consciousness, where truth is obfuscated or hidden, the night when all is in darkness.

Figure 2: Kheper, the scarab beetle. The symbol for the first
stage of the sun, the dawn—the Awakening

Figure 3: Giza. The Sphinx, known to the ancients as *Tefnut*.
Photo by author 2003.

Actually quantifying these stages, that is what time periods they refer
to, is a much more difficult undertaking than just elucidating their meanings. As I have mentioned many times, Hakim and his tradition are
similar to many other indigenous wisdom keepers and oral traditions in
that they are much more concerned with quality—ideas, concepts, connections, experience, interrelationships—than quantity—exact numbers.
But in the more than twelve years I have been working with Hakim, he
has always been consistent with two specific dates.

When I first heard him speak in front of the Sphinx in November
1992, Hakim calmly asserted that the Sphinx, who he referred to as
Tefnut, was over 52,000 years old (see Figure 3). He has since used the
figure of 54,000 years to refer to the actual beginning of carving the figure, but this is still consistent within a range of dates. He also stated to
me early in our conversations that the current phase of Khemitian cycles
began around 65,000 years ago. Again I say "around" because an actual

date is meaningless to Hakim, but he has always consistently said 65,000 years ago.

The main purpose of my first book, *The Land of Osiris*, was to signal the end of the stage or cycle we have been in the last five thousand years or so, Amen, the last stage of the cycle. The first book was to announce the whole reason for Hakim to go public with these teachings, kept secret in his oral tradition in tight circles of initiates for thousands of years. The reason is what Hakim calls The Awakening, the beginning of a new Kheper-Dawn phase, the end of a 65,000-year major cycle.

As in the great Vedic system of cycles called yugas, it is difficult to pin down the exact time periods and lengths in years of the various cycles. My research has indicated definite trends, such as the creation of modern forms of religion that will be discussed later that show that our current cycle, Amen-The Hidden, began almost six thousand years ago, around 4,000 BC. There are some other indications, which I will discuss in later chapters, that the transition from stage four, Aten-The Wiser to Amen, goes back even further to 5-6,000 BC. Hakim has stated we were definitely in the Amen phase between 3-2,000 BC, but no exact date is part of his tradition as the wisdom keepers do not even recognize our current calendar—before the birth of Christ or after the death of Christ are meaningless to them.

One of the purposes of this book is to discuss and give approximate dates or ranges for the last two cycles we have been in, Aten and Amen. Spirituality and religion have actuated for human beings according to those cycles and the state of consciousness present in those cycles, not in a linear form of progression. Since the indigenous wisdom keepers of Egypt are telling us that people—all cultures, not just ancient Khemit— were in higher states of consciousness 20,000 years ago than we are today, it then follows that their level of spiritual understanding was much greater than it is today. So I say we need to vehemently reject the paradigm that human beings were "primitive" with underdeveloped cognitive and perceptive abilities and awareness prior to the "God-revealed" religions that began 5,000 years ago. The only way to understand the ancient Khemitians, their culture and civilization—and their material manifestations, the Great Sphinx, pyramids and temples—is to rid ourselves of the pervasive Judeo-Christian-Islamic biases that pollute academia and most scholarly pursuits into this area.

Michael Cremo and Richard Thompson have even gone so far in their books as to state that, in accordance with the great ancient cycles mentioned in the Vedas, human civilization may be millions of years old, and they do produce some physical evidence to support their claim.[1] It is very exciting to me to discover every day in the news that some archaeological artifacts, remains or evidence are currently being found to continually push back the dates for advanced civilizations on this planet—such as the finding of ancient ruins off the coasts of Cuba and India—and they are being discovered worldwide, lending strong credence to Hakim's teachings that these cycles were universal, happening not just in ancient Khemit, but also in far Asia, central Asia, and the Middle East, all over Africa, Europe and even the Americas.

So as my first book was to prepare for the New Dawn, the Awakening—happening all over the world as consciousness is unfolding (I know with current world events that may be hard to believe)—I will now discuss the past two stages, Aten and Amen, to further prepare for the new phase coming in. This will be difficult, as few of us (myself included) are in the state of consciousness that we were in so many thousands of years ago.

This is so especially when we discuss Aten (also written Iten) The Wiser. It is in this time period we are told most of the ancient stone masonry pyramids and ancient temples (most buried still under the present desert sands in Egypt) were conceived, designed and built in ancient Khemit, the exception being the Great Sphinx at Giza, Tefnut herself. According to tradition, she was conceived and carved in three stages, covering thousands of years. But she was initially carved during the previous stage of Kheper-Dawn. What better way to celebrate the birth of consciousness than to venerate the Great Mother, known by the Khemitians as *Nut*, than to dedicate the first great monument to her as Tefnut, the spit of Nut. According to the indigenous tradition Nut is the sky, the Cosmos, representing all that is unmanifested. When Nut wanted to appear in a physical form She "spit" upon the earth and where this was became the limestone outcropping that eventually was carved into the form of the Sphinx. Hakim tells us that the ancient Khemitians gathered at the outcropping to "energize" themselves thousands of years before actually beginning to carve the figure.

Some of the most exciting new work in science is coming out of the fields of quantum and theoretical physics. Theoretical physicist Fred Alan Wolf has even used quantum theory to postulate on the existence of the soul (I will bring in his work on this subject in more detail later) and has written about the Khemitian concept of cycles. Wolf traveled to Egypt in the mid-1990s and had as his guide Abd'El Hakim.

Hakim taught Wolf about the ancient Khemitian's knowledge of cycles. Wolf states, "Ancient Egyptians were obsessed with the periodic nature of life and death . . . . Accordingly, everything followed the law of the circle—the movement of the cycle of obvious visible life and secret invisible death."[2] Although Hakim has taught me a much more profound understanding of what we term "death"—no such word existed in the ancient Khemitian language—Wolf then goes on to state that quantum theory has now verified Hakim's teachings and the ancient Khemitian wisdom. He writes of the work of French physicist Paul A.M. Dirac who was the first to consolidate relativity and quantum physics. Among other things, Dirac produced complex equations to show the activity of electrons. Wolf states, "When we look at the Dirac equation-model of the electron, the vacuum vibrates and produces repetitious patterns."[3] These repetitious patterns are cycles, now shown to appear on the micro/quantum level as well as macro/physical level of existence. Also mentioning "the vacuum vibrates," Wolf marries physics and metaphysics. As the Rosicrucians have always maintained: **All is Vibration.**

Wolf also speaks of the greatest cycle of them all, the so-called Big Bang Theory. It has been estimated that this cycle is twenty billion, billion years long (how can anyone conceive of numbers like that?), that it will end in a Big Crunch and begin again. While the idea makes sense and fits in a universal paradigm of cycles upon cycles, we do not support a Big Bang Theory. The idea that an **explosion** created the entire material universe seems too modern and patriarchal. Hakim's tradition does not support the concept of an initial beginning, only the existence of never-ending cycles. Another theoretical physicist, Dr. Volodymyr Krasnoholovets of Ukraine, also does not support a Big Bang Theory, but proposes that the never-ending dance of subatomic particles produces what he calls *Inertons*, continual quantum particle collision pulses, as the source of all energy, the vibrations of the "vacuum."

With all this evidence—physical and archaeological, natural and traditional—to continue to maintain a belief in linear progression in any system, in this case human cultural evolution, seems patently ridiculous. Everything that is observable in nature, in micro as well as macro levels, exhibits distinct cycles and patterns. We know that the universe itself is curved, as in a great ellipse, not a straight line. The number zero in metaphysics represents that concept—not being **no thing** but everything, the infinite circle and cycle of life.

With this paradigm of the five stages, the great cycles, I can now discuss the last two cycles, Aten and Amen, in the next few chapters. It is my firm belief that we will never know who we are and where we are going until we know where we have been.

CHAPTER THREE

THE AGE OF ATEN

The ancient masters were subtle, mysterious, profound, responsive.
The depth of their knowledge is unfathomable.
Because it is unfathomable,
All we can do is describe their appearance.

—Lao Zi, *Dao De Jing*

G RAHAM HANCOCK, in his book *Fingerprints of the Gods*, presents evidence for the existence of advanced civilizations prior to 10,000 BC. In discussing the age of the Sphinx with John Anthony West, Hancock quotes West as saying, "My conjecture is that the whole riddle is linked in some way to those legendary civilizations spoken of in all the mythologies of the world."[1]

Indeed, almost all the known mythologies of the peoples of the earth speak of a Golden Age. The end of this Golden Age is often linked to worldwide catastrophes: "Many early memories of these world-shaking events specifically link them with the abrupt destruction of a primeval earthly paradise widely known to classical writers as a Golden Age."[2]

When and where this Golden Age existed has varied amongst the many authors who have described it. The almost global existence of this mythology now linked with both the massive archaeological evidence unearthed in the last few hundred years of previously unknown advanced civilizations and the redating of the Sphinx by John Anthony West and Dr. Robert M. Schoch lends strong credence to the belief that indeed some sort of a Golden Age existed in prehistory.

Some authors have even noted that ancient civilizations may have been more advanced than those that followed them. In her excellent book *Catastrophobia*, Barbara Hand Clow refers to archaeological researcher Mary Settegast who states that cultures of the Upper Paleolithic period (35,000 to 11,500 years ago) were more advanced than human cultures of the early Neolithic Age (11,500 to 10,000 years ago).[3] The reason for this regression according to Clow was a global cataclysmic event—a topic I will return to in greater detail in a later chapter.

According to the cycles presented by Abd'El Hakim, the five stages of the sun, the Age of Aten (The Wiser) would certainly have been a Golden Age. Hakim states that almost all people, all over the earth, were in the highest state of consciousness, the full flowering of the senses, and advanced civilizations were present all over the planet, which could explain how remnants of these highly developed civilizations are now being discovered in many different areas.

The great difficulty is in stating exactly when it was and how people lived in that distant timeframe. Again, Hakim and the indigenous wisdom keepers do not deal with exact dates, but it was certainly over 10,000 years ago. There are no written records to guide us, and we cannot date the stone monuments such as the Sphinx and Giza pyramids that may be definite remnants of that time with our current state of archaeological dating methods. We have only the oral traditions and great myths that have remained to speak of that golden time.

But an even greater difficulty that I see is trying to understand the consciousness prevailing among humans over 10,000 years ago. We would have to imagine a world made up of all, or almost all, people with the consciousness of Akhenaten, Imhotep, Moses, Gautam Buddha, Lao Zi, Pythagoras, Chuangzi, Yeshua ben Yusef (Jesus the Nazarene), Mohammed, Padme Sambhava, Boddhidarma, Guru Nanak, St. Francis of Assisi, Ramakrishna, Parmahansa Yogananda, Bhagwan Shri Rashneesh (Osho), J. Krishnamurti, Pope John XXIII, Maharishi Mahesh Yogi, Sathya Sai Baba, etc.

All these aforementioned people would have been representative of the state of consciousness and the kind of teaching that would have prevailed in the Age of Aten. As with the example of Lao Zi, the ancient masters would have stressed the importance of personal experience for direct knowing, instead of any dependence on a teacher, written texts or an institution outside of oneself. Hakim has taught that most communication during this period would have been mind-to-mind, telepathic, and the importance of direct knowing through experience would have been strictly adhered to. Even the oral tradition itself was many thousands of years in the future as there was not a common spoken language. Sound was utilized for chanting and singing and for practical purposes such as pyramid building. The teachings would be what is referred to as "Unity Consciousness" by many traditions today—that of the interconnectiveness of all things. This understanding of unity consciousness, taught by masters of the oral tradition for thousands of years, is now being demonstrated in quantum physics. This concept of Unity is primarily represented by Hakim's teachings concerning the term *Sesh*—The People. This is to understand that people in the Age of Aten saw themselves as part of the whole, but emphasized the whole, or unity, as apart from emphasizing the individual, as we do today. This is important to understand as being very different than the modern concepts of communism or other philosophies and systems that promote a "hive" or group mentality and discourage the individual. As all these masters have taught, in the highest states of consciousness one realizes that one is a "self," but this "self" is not in any way separate or isolated, as we experience today. We are all part of the whole—there is no loss of identity or isolation with this realization but the greater understanding and feeling that we are connected to the whole—all this achieved by experiencing the whole and "being in Unity."

I speculate that the Age of Aten was in effect about 20,000 years ago. I also speculate that all the stone masonry pyramids I mentioned in the grid line in ancient Egypt we call *The Land of Osiris*, approximately twenty-five square miles from Dahshur to Abu Roash, were constructed within 25,000 to 15,000 years ago. In discussing with my colleague and good friend, master craftsman and engineer Christopher Dunn the possibility of the Great Pyramid having been constructed in three stages as per the teachings of Abd'El Hakim over 15,000 years ago, we both joked that it was a group of Nikola Teslas who conceived, formulated and directed the project. Nikola Tesla was famous for visualizing the end product, invention, machine, solution he was looking for, then seeing the blueprints for how to achieve the end product in his mind. I have discussed with Chris Dunn how I believe we will never find any blueprints, diagrams or models of the Great Pyramid—that it was totally conceived of and executed in the minds of the builders, minds in full awareness, operating in full capacity.

In Chapter Sixteen of *The Land of Osiris*, I discussed a term that has become quite popular with many alternative researchers called Zep Tepi.

This term has been crudely translated by many as "The First Time" and is believed to refer to a beginning time of creation. But Hakim was adamant to me there was no "first time" to the ancient Khemitians, only a myriad of cycles.

The term "Zep Tepi" appears in the so-called "Building Texts" found on the walls of the Temple of Horus at Edfu in the south of modern Egypt. Although this temple was a late construction, built in the Ptolemaic period around 100-200 BC, the texts were obviously from a much older date. The texts describe how the "Neters walked the earth" and taught men the principles of sacred geometry and engineering, and how to construct huge edifices in stone (see Figure 4). Manetho, a Khemitian priest in the Ptolemaic period, recorded there were over 36,000 years of ancient Khemitian history before the standard "begin-

Figure 4: Edfu. Temple of Horus. Part of the "Building Texts."
Photo by author 2004.

ning" date of dynastic Khemit of 3100 B.C. Manetho mentions ancient eras when the Neters were on earth and ruled over men. While I will state later that I distrust and doubt the accuracy of Manetho's "histories" of dynasties of kings and their sons, which is the basis of academic Egyptology, it is interesting to note that those Egyptologists who strictly adhere to his patriarchal revisionist accounts totally ignore his statements of the long prehistory of Khemit.

Hakim and I have discussed these points on many occasions. We believe the idea of the Neters "walking the earth" is meant to indicate the principles that the Neters represent being the prevailing attributes of the particular time periods. The Age of Aten would be the time of The Wiser, The Golden Age of Enlightenment mentioned in so many different mythologies. Instead of translating Zep Tepi as "The First Time," it could be described as "The Primary Time," the prime time of consciousness when the Neters manifested from mind to form and guided the physical and spiritual height of the ancient Khemitian civilization with the construction of the Houses of the Neters (pyramids) and the Houses of the Spirit (temples). All of the major temple sites in Egypt today are built on top of ancient Khemitian structures that are still buried under the sand. In the course of my investigations, I have found evidences of older temple remains at many of the famous temples we visit in Egypt today. At the Temple of Hathor at Dendara, the Temple of Amen at Luxor and even the Temple of Horus at Edfu, evidences of earlier temples still remain. Dendara and Edfu are later Ptolemaic temples, but evidences of earlier Old Kingdom temples can be found there. At Luxor, the present temple was built over many thousands of years, culminating in the New Kingdom (1500-1000 BC) period, but there is an older temple underneath.

When I went to the Hebis (Ibis) Temple at Kharga Oasis in the Western Desert of Egypt with Hakim in 1998, we found definite evidence of an older temple once having been there or still under the sand (see Figure 5). Since then, in 2000, the Supreme Council of Antiquities (SCA)

Figure 5: Kharga Oasis. Temple of Hebis (Ibis) dedicated to Neter Djehuti (Thoth). Ptolemaic Period ca. 200 BC. An older predynastic temple may be underneath. Photo by author 1998.

decided the temple should be moved because of erosion from underground water damaging it. This underground water was/is from the ancient river, what I called the *Ur Nil* in *The Land of Osiris*, and the reason the tunnels were constructed was to bring water from the ancient river to the east. Could excavations there in the last few years have revealed more evidences of an older temple underneath or the ancient tunnels for water? We do not know because nothing has been publicly reported.

The point here is that there must be more physical evidence of the Age of Aten to be found. We say the pyramids of Giza, Dahshur, Abusir, Sakkara and Abu Roash are from this timeframe and there will be no written records found claiming so. But there should be many more structures uncovered that will also be from this time period of 20,000 to 40,000 years ago. I predict there will be many more finds in the next few years in areas such as India, Central Asia, the Middle East, other parts of Africa as well as Egypt that will exhibit the same type of megalithic stone construction as the Great Pyramid and will not be able to be conclusively dated to historical time periods due to the lack of any inscriptions that will be found on them.

Can we date the Age of Aten? Due to the absence of any written records, the current scientific lack of consistent dating methods for stone constructions, and the quantitative vagueness of the oral traditions, the answer would seem to be negative. We do not have timeframes for the previous ages of Kheper, Ra and Oon leading up to Aten. There also seems to be the matter of transitional periods; one age just does not slip into another overnight, but may have periods of transition of up to thousands of years. This will be a key factor in the next chapter. I would say we were in the Age of Aten 20,000 years ago and there may have been thousands of years of gentle transition from Oon to Aten, as consciousness was already high in Oon, civilization already highly advanced. Witness the Sphinx and the related structures in front of her already built. As we further develop our now emerging consciousness into The Awakening, we may be able to be more specific as to the approximate dates of the previous ages since more physical evidence will be found. But I believe the transition from Aten into Amen was anything but gentle, and seems to present a paradox that must be addressed. This transition was so important it will need its own chapter to deal with, and it lasted for thousands of years. From the years of 20,000 to 11,500 years ago, the great Per-Neters of the Land of Osiris were active, resonating with harmonic frequencies, producing tremendous amounts of energy in many forms—quantum fields, electromagnetic, sonic, radio and microwave and even forms we are yet to discover. In the Golden Age of Aten, it may have seemed the systems would last forever, but that was not to be the case and some great changes were in store for humanity—changes that were recorded in many of the great oral traditions of the world.

CHAPTER FOUR

THE TRANSITION: TWILIGHT

When men lack a sense of awe, there will be disorder.
The world is ruled by letting things take their course.
It cannot be ruled by interfering.

—Lao Zi, *Dao de Jing*

NOT ONLY is there an almost universal theme in all mythologies of a Golden Age, but there is also a prevalent theme in almost all known mythologies of ancient peoples of a global catastrophe, a deluge. Accordingly, the flood myth exists not only in the Old Testament of the Bible, but in Sumerian and Babylonian mythology—in fact, the Bible story seems directly descended from the older Babylonian version. Stories of cataclysms also abound in the oral and written traditions of many indigenous peoples, stories that are now being supported by geophysical and geological evidence found worldwide.

In January of 2003 and in November of 2004, I engaged in protracted discussions on the subject of a prehistoric global cataclysm with Hakim in Egypt. Again, without supplying a date for a specific event, he did report his tradition has passed down the story of many global catastrophes in the history of the planet. When I pressed him on the possibility of an event occurring near the end of the last Age of Aten, he agreed that it was quite possible, but that it would have been a cyclical, natural event that has occurred many times in the past. Geophysical data does indeed support the contention of many authors that numerous cataclysmic events have occurred which may have been the result of great meteor or comet strikes causing floods, tsunamis, great earthquakes and volcanic eruptions—leading to near extinction of all flora and fauna, all life, many times in the history of our planet.

One such proposed global cataclysm has interested me for many years. Allan and Delair, authors of *Cataclysm!*, state, "the calamity profoundly affected all forms of terrestrial life, early man included . . . . Accordingly, almost every nation of antiquity perpetuated the memory of it in tradition."[1] Allan and Delair and Barbara Hand Clow have given us a solid date for this global event. Clow states, "A scientific global data convergence reveals a great cataclysm occurred only 11,500 years ago, which geology calls the Late Pleistocene Extinctions and theologians call the Flood or the Fall."[2]

Clow also states that not only did this global cataclysm of 9500 BC nearly wipe out all human civilizations in the world at that time, but the event left an indelible scar on the human psyche of those who survived— a scar that promoted dramatic changes in human spiritual practices and lifestyles. Remnants of that trauma still pervade the human psyche to this day—a subject I will delve deeper into in this and later chapters.

Indeed, this widespread cataclysm could be the main reason for the paucity of physical evidence of the existence of advanced civilizations prior to 11,500 years ago. Although this is changing daily as more archaeological evidence is being uncovered, almost all traces of previous human advancement may have been destroyed in the great-proposed event.

In their book *Cataclysm!* geologist J.B. Delair and science historian D.S. Allan provide prolific evidence for the catastrophic event 11,500 years ago. Some of this includes the recent advent of mountain ranges such as the Rockies in North America and the Himalayas in Asia, the massive recent scaring of the earth's landscape such as valleys and gorges carved out by tremendous floods, caves full of the partial and full skeletons of megafauna (huge animals) smashed against the cave walls by rapid flooding, and the now famous frozen mammoths with their partially digested last meals still in their systems. Allan and Delair not only present evidence of this event occurring on Earth, but that the cataclysm affected our solar system as well. They cite the Greek myth of *Phaeton*, a celestial outsider who wrecked mass havoc by colliding with planetary bodies in our solar system or nearly striking the earth. They use the same evidence that Zecharia Sitchin used to promote his theory of a twelfth planet, called by the ancient Sumerians Niburu, one of whose moons may have collided with a former planet in our solar system in a calamitous perturbation of its huge elliptical orbit which Sitchin states is 3,600 years.

The existence of the asteroid belt between Mars and Jupiter, great clouds of gas and debris found in our solar system, comets, asteroids and meteors are cited by Sitchin and Allan and Delair as remnants of this celestial cataclysm in antiquity. In her book *Catastrophobia*, Barbara Hand

Clow goes further and postulates the events of 11,500 years ago knocked the earth into its current tilt on its axis of 23.5 degrees from vertical. Citing evidence posited by J.B. Allan, Clow states there appears to be no natural reason for the earth to have this tilt, and the characteristic "wobble" the earth exhibits in its rotation could only be explained if the planet had been acted upon by an external force, a comet or meteor strike directly or a planetary explosion in space near the earth.

Clow goes even further and offers an original hypothesis that precession of the equinox, or even the zodiac itself, did not exist before 9500 BC. She also states world wide climates would have been very different before the proposed cataclysm, before the current tilt of the earth's axis. Clow suggests there were essentially only two seasons before this event, and she relies upon the research of Alexander Marshack. Clow says, "Marshack's research and the research of many other paleoscientists indicates that early humans show no signs of being aware of the existence of the four seasons until 10,000 years ago."[3]

This information now can help provide a clearer picture of the Golden Age, the Age of Aten. With only two seasons, a warm, wet Spring-Summer and a cool, wetter Fall-Winter, without extremes in many locales of the earth, abundant food would have been available for human populations with wild game, rivers swelling with fish, wild grains plentiful, fruit and nuts also plentiful—cities or semi-permanent settlements for the rise of civilization could have occurred thousands of years before the accepted paradigm of less than 10,000 years as now believed.

I presented a scenario in *The Land of Osiris* that all of Northern Africa was vastly different over 10,000 years ago. Rich, lush and green with abundant rainfall, Northern Africa was a series of large islands with massive rivers and many tributaries. What is today the Western Desert of Egypt was once a huge river, the Ur Nil, which allowed the ancient Khemitian civilization to flower and develop from the proposed start around 65,000 years ago (see Figure 6). Abundant rainfall is attested to by the climatological models created for time periods of 30,000 to 15,000

Figure 6: Western Desert. Possible ancient riverbed of Ur Nil.
Photo by author 1998.

years ago and provides support for the indigenous traditions of the great civilizations of Northern Africa.

With moderate climate, abundant rainfall and food supplies, the ancient Khemitians of the Age of Aten were able to construct the great stone masonry pyramids, Per-Neters, the Houses of Nature, on a twenty-five square mile gridline—an already known line of earth magnetic vortexes—to produce power and energy for their physical needs, and great temples for their spiritual needs. Now I can state what exactly it was that ended this apparently idyllic existence, and when. Allan, Delair and Clow have provided the paradigm to explain when and how the Giza Power Plant of Christopher Dunn, the Great Pyramid, ended its life as a machine.

Hakim has said that the most recent global cataclysm was a natural, cyclical event that occurs with a regular periodicity to signal the forthcoming end of a profound age. The transitions from the ages of Kheper to Ra, Ra to Oon, and Oon to Aten were probably fairly smooth with some climatic fluctuations, but nothing major to dramatically change lifestyles. But the shift from the Age of Aten to the Age of Amen was significant, a distinct great loss of consciousness and understanding, and may have required a major event like the proposed cataclysm to bring on the change.

An aspect of my research, before seemingly isolated, can now be fitted into this cataclysmic scenario of 11,500 years ago. First proposed by Christopher Dunn in 1998, and investigated by myself in 1998, 1999, 2003 and 2004, there may have been an accident or explosion in the Great Pyramid in antiquity.[4] Dunn mentions that when Sir William Flinders Petrie, the great British archaeologist, first examined the so called King's Chamber in the Great Pyramid, he observed the walls of the chamber bulged out over an inch and there were cracks in the granite ceiling beams in the southeastern section of the room. Petrie explained these anomalies as being the result of an ancient earthquake, which has been totally accepted by Egyptologists as the cause, but Dunn and myself now challenge this.

Petrie had observed in the 1880's that the Descending Passage of the Great Pyramid was remarkable in its accuracy. Three feet, five inches wide and three feet, eleven inches high, the passage extends down into the Great Pyramid at a 26-degree angle. Almost 350 feet long, the first 150 feet were constructed with limestone blocks used in the pyramid, but amazingly, the last 200 feet go right through the limestone bedrock. Petrie discovered the sides of the passage only deviated 1/50 of an inch from absolute straight in the first 150 feet constructed. He was further amazed to measure that the whole passage, almost 350 feet, only deviated 1/4 inch the entire length.[5] The point here is that if the cracks in the granite beams in the ceiling of the King's Chamber were caused by an earthquake, there should be extensive damage to the walls of the Descending Passage which would have been closer to the epicenter of a quake. There is none, and there is no evidence of earthquake damage in the Subterranean Chamber, which would have been even closer to an epicenter of a proposed quake.

So the explanation of an ancient earthquake in the Great Pyramid is not supported by the evidence and should be discarded. Since becoming aware of Dunn's explosion theory in 1998, I have been in the Great Pyramid several times to investigate for myself. In May of 1999, Dunn and I were in Egypt together, and he made another startling discovery. In the process of being interviewed on video, Dunn noticed the upper wall of the Grand Gallery was made of granite, not limestone blocks as had been previously believed. The important thing that Dunn observed when the camera lights shone on the upper wall is that the granite was blackened, highly discolored, like it had been subjected to great heat, perhaps from an explosion or great conflagration (see Figure 7).

Returning to Egypt for another documentary in August 2001, Dunn

Figure 7: Giza. Upper wall of Grand Gallery in Great Pyramid. Original rose quartz granite greatly discolored by possible ancient fire/explosion. Photo by author 2003.

Figure 8: Giza. Great Pyramid. Rectangular slots along walls in Grand Gallery. Photo by author 2003.

Figure 9: Giza. Great Pyramid. Scorch/burn marks in ceiling of Grand Gallery. Photo by author 2003.

made another discovery. In his book, Dunn had discussed the rectangular slots that are to be found on the side ramps of the Grand Gallery (see Figure 8). He had speculated in *The Giza Power Plant* that these ramps had once held some devices—he had speculated they may have been Helmholtz Resonators—that acted to amplify the resonance of the pyramid and aided in its energy production as a power plant.[6] Going inside the Great Pyramid again in 2001, Dunn discovered burn or scorch marks in the ceiling of the Grand Gallery directly above or corresponding to the rectangular slots in which the resonators were fixed (see Figure 9). Dunn has thus surmised the event that rocked the King's Chamber may have caused the resonators to explode. In the last few years, Dunn, after consulting with several physicists, now believes the King's Chamber acted as a Helmholtz Resonator and the devices in the rectangular slots in the Grand Gallery were resonators that converted vibration from a solid medium to airborne sound.

Armed with Dunn's observations, I went inside the Great Pyramid in 2003 to further investigate his claims. I had first observed the cracks in the granite beams in the King's Chamber in 1992, then the Supreme Council of Antiquities (SCA) attempted to repair the cracks in 1998 (see Figure 10). The repairs failed (thankfully) and I could still observe and photograph them in 2003 (see Figure 11). I then observed that almost all the walls of the inner chambers of the Great Pyramid exhibit discoloration, as if exposed to great heat. This could not be explained away as being carbon residue from torches of early explorers or from carbon dioxide and water vapor from the breath of tourists. The discoloration went right into the stone and was not washed off by the cleaning efforts attempted by the SCA in the years of the late 1990s. In November of 2004, both Christopher Dunn and I returned to Egypt for another conference/tour and went inside the Great Pyramid together. We again observed all the aforementioned damage and I was able to point out to him my contention that **all** the walls and ceilings of the King's Chamber, Grand Gallery and Queen's Chamber exhibit discoloration and damage.

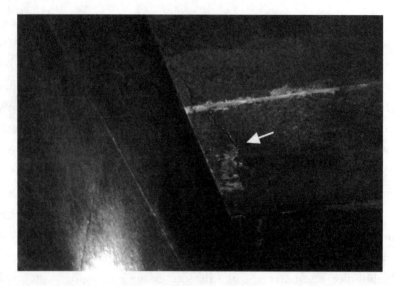

Figure 10: Giza. Great Pyramid. Cracks in granite beams
in ceiling of King's Chamber. Photo by author 1992.

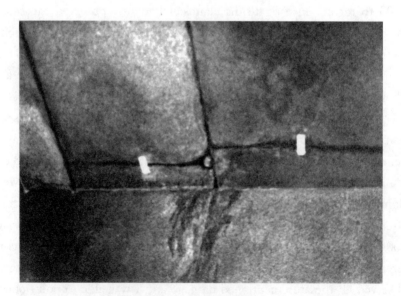

Figure 11: Giza. Great Pyramid. Cracks in granite beams
in ceiling of King's Chamber. Photo by author 2003.

We were not able to go down to the Subterranean Chamber for observation. I now state that all the walls of the King's Chamber, the famous stone box therein erroneously labeled a "sarcophagus" by Egyptologists, as well as the upper wall of the Grand Gallery, are all greatly darkened and not the original color of the Aswan rose quartz granite. Even the walls of the Grand Gallery and the Queen's Chamber exhibit discoloration from the tannish sand color of the original limestone blocks.

It then became clear to me that other anomalies observed at other sites of the Land of Osiris gridline could fit into this new explosion hypothesis. I discussed the site of Abu Roash in my first book. Located some five miles north of the Giza Plateau, Abu Roash once had an intact pyramid, all in ruins today (see Figure 12). Egyptologists have stated the pyramid there was never completed, or constructed so poorly it collapsed, or was quarried by Arabs in the last few hundred years. I had originally accepted the explanation of the pyramid having been attacked and quarried for stone by modern Egyptians, but since the visit to Egypt

Figure 12 : Abu Roash. Pyramid in ruins. Photo by author 1997.

with Christopher Dunn in 1999 and his subsequent discoveries of scorch marks in the ceiling of the Grand Gallery, I then questioned the original conclusions.

I discussed the possibility of an explosion destroying the pyramid at Abu Roash with Abd'El Hakim in the fall of 1999. He stated he would investigate this idea on his own. In 2003 when we discussed the explosion theory again, Hakim mentioned he had been back to Abu Roash and had found evidence that, indeed, the pyramid there may have been destroyed in an explosion. I plan to return to Abu Roash with both Hakim and Christopher Dunn in the next few years to further investigate the site in this respect.

It became apparent to me that with the evidence of an explosion inside the Great Pyramid and the possibility of the pyramid at Abu Roash having been destroyed by the same event, there should be more evidence to be found at other sites. If indeed, as I have suggested, all the pyramids on the gridline of the Land of Osiris were interconnected with each other by harmonic resonance and intimately connected to the earth grid itself, a cataclysmic event like the one proposed for 9500 BC should have had effects throughout the system.

I went back to the site of Dahshur in 2003 and 2004 to investigate this possibility. I discussed the two stone masonry pyramids found there, the Red Pyramid and the Bent Pyramid, in my first book. In particular, the Bent Pyramid has always interested me greatly. It was unique in the system because of its unusual construction, utilizing two angles in form producing two different sonic frequencies. The pyramid is also unusual because it shows severe loss of stone at its corners, but still has a good proportion of its casing stones intact (see Figure 13). It always has been assumed that this pyramid was also attacked and quarried by modern Egyptians in recent time, an assumption I had accepted. But after examining the pyramid more closely in 2003, it became apparent there may have been another possibility. The corners do appear to have been blown off, not quarried, and there is much loose stone lying around the missing

Figure 13: Dahshur. Bent Pyramid showing corners severely
damaged. The damage may be from ancient cataclysm.
Photo by author 2003.

corners. If the pyramid had been quarried, why did the Arabs leave so many loose blocks which could have easily been hauled off and reused? Without the possibility of considering any other reason for the blown off sides, I would never have thought of another explanation, but with the evidence in the Great Pyramid and at Abu Roash, it could be possible the Bent Pyramid, producing two different sonic frequencies, reacted to the great cataclysm by shaking so violently that the corners were greatly weakened and some stone fell off.

I realize this may sound quite speculative, but I feel strongly this is grounds for further research. If indeed a grand global cataclysmic event occurred 11,500 year ago—and the evidence presented by Allan, Delair and Clow is very convincing to me—with violent earthquakes, massive flooding and tsunamis, and the earth tilting on its axis affecting the entire grid and all magnetic fields, the Per-Neters, pyramids, of the Land of Osiris, built to be in harmonic resonance with the earth and each other, must have been affected dramatically. There remains hardly any doubt in my mind that Christopher Dunn is correct and the Great Pyramid suffered a massive explosion with concomitant release of tremendous heat sometime in antiquity.

I have proposed and designed a series of experiments and expeditions to further pursue this theory. As one of the Directors of Research (Christopher Dunn is the other) of the Great Pyramid of Giza Research Association, I am hopeful our organization will be adequately funded in the next few years to undertake this work. We would need approval of the SCA to obtain small samples of the stone box in the King's Chamber, of the upper wall of the Grand Gallery and other samples to vigorously test in chemistry and geology labs to see if it can be determined if the stone was once subjected to great heat that discolored the stone. If this proves to be so, then it would need to be determined, if possible, what caused that great event/heat.

We would also need to go inside the two other pyramids at Giza, the two pyramids at Dahshur and at Abusir and Sakkara, to determine if there are evidences of discoloration of the internal stone and any evidence of structural damage by heat or explosion. These proposals for further investigations and experiments would entail minimal incursions to the integrity of the structures—only very small samples would be needed for testing—and further observations and photographs (still and video) would incur no damage at all. As things stand now, the Supreme Council of Antiquities has been very reticent to grant any permits or permission to groups outside established academic departments, but we are hopeful that may eventually change. Our goal would be to try to get chemistry and geology professors and departments involved in these projects to make the proposals appear more "legitimate" to the SCA.

For the sake of argument, and the rest of this chapter, let us assume further testing will establish not only an explosion in the Great Pyramid, but contiguous damage to the other structures on the Land of Osiris gridline. Then let us assume this explosion and damage can be dated to around 9500 BC—I realize at present there may not be means to accomplish this dating scientifically—what would the implications be? First of all, it would obviously "prove" the Great Pyramid was older than its accepted date of 2500 BC, was not a tomb for a king, and the reality of the ancient Khemitian civilization. It would give strong credence to the work of Christopher Dunn and myself, and the indigenous teachings of Abd'El Hakim.

But more importantly, for now, we need to return to our theme in this chapter, the timeframe of 11,500 years ago. What could possibly have been the effects for the ancient Khemitians and their civilization? I speculated that the stone masonry pyramids on the gridline of the Land of Osiris, called *Bu Wizzer* by the ancients, utilizing earth resonant frequencies and flowing water through man-made tunnels to the pyramids to produce hydrogen gas for energy was a seemingly perfect harmonious system that could operate indefinitely as long as water was abundant. But the explosion evidence in the Great Pyramid clearly indicates the system was severely impacted and almost completely shut down.

If so, then many questions arise for me. The Age of Aten was in full swing 11,500 years ago. According to the oral tradition, the ancient Khemitians, indeed all humanity, were in full consciousness. Could they not see the calamity coming? Allan and Delair claim it was an alien celestial body, called Phaeton by the Greeks, that was the cause of the cataclysm. Sitchin claimed it was a moon of the twelfth planet Niburu that was the culprit. Whatever the cause, couldn't the ancient Khemitians in their great wisdom and awareness have had foreknowledge of the event, either physically or psychically? Even if they had known, was there anything they could have done about it? Apparently not.

The ancient Khemitians might have had premonitions of the event, or the event itself, as a clear signal the cycle and their civilization had peaked and humanity was going into the decline that would culminate in the next age, The Age of Amen, The Hidden. But if this event occurred at 9500 BC and the Age of Amen didn't arise until 3000-2000 BC, there were thousands of years of transitional prehistory and early history to account for. It is this next timeframe I now must address.

CHAPTER FIVE

AFTER
THE
FLOOD

The valley spirit never dies;
It is the woman, primal mother.
Her gateway is the root of heaven and earth.
It is like a veil barely seen.
Use it; it will never fail.

—Lao Zi, *Dao de Jing*

ACCORDING TO THE ACCEPTED PARADIGMS of anthropology, modern civilization began around 10,000 years ago in the Fertile Crescent—modern day Iraq—in the Middle East. This rise featured the advent of planned agriculture, domestication of plants and animals, the use of writing or symbols to convey thoughts and ideas, settled city-states with massive megalithic constructions, kingship, and modern forms of religion. The term used for the period is the Neolithic, the New Stone Age, to differentiate it from the previous period, the Paleolithic or Old Stone Age.

In the last fifty to one hundred years, archaeological excavations have unearthed great early Neolithic cultures in areas such as Turkey, Russia and Central Asia that preceded the Sumerian civilization that arose in the confluence of the Tigris-Euphrates river valleys of the Fertile Crescent around 4000 BC. These earlier Neolithic cultures were dominated by the worship of the Mother Goddess and many were matriarchal in nature (see Figures 14 and 15).

This paradigm follows the academically accepted pattern of linear evolutionary theory—before 10,000 years ago, humans existed as nomadic hunter-gatherers, had no civilization, only simple stone tools and technology, and lived in caves in Ice Age Europe and elsewhere. But the evidence of the global cataclysm of 9500 BC presents several other scenarios.

Barbara Hand Clow presents a very provocative thesis in *Catastrophobia*. Clow suggests the cataclysm not only wiped out huge amounts of flora and fauna, particularly the megafauna such as mammoths, mastodons, cave bears, giant sloths, etc, and almost all traces of previous human civilization, but it also left an indelible scar on the psyche of those humans who survived the cataclysm. A rapid change in climate and physical appearance of the earth and its rotation, massive flooding, earthquakes and volcanic eruptions would have been extremely traumatic to all who survived the rampant chaos, massive destruction and loss of life. It is this collective fear and trauma from the great

Figure 14: Mother Goddess Figurine. Found in Egypt and dated to ca. 4000 BC but is probably much older.

Figure 15: Mother Goddess Figurine. Also found in Egypt and dated to ca. 5000 BC but may be as old as 8000 BC.

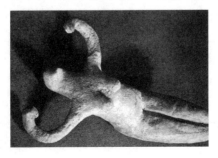

cataclysm that may have led to the necessary changes in lifestyle of the Neolithic period.

Shaken out of the reverie of the Golden Age—the prediluvian world of two consistent seasons, the abundance of wild grains, fruits and vegetables, wild game and fish, vast resources and highly advanced civilization—the world in the aftermath of the deluge and devastation was vastly different. Nature would no longer have been viewed as the ever-abundant Great Mother with never ending sustenance and harmonious life, but as a vengeful entity, no longer to be trusted. Nature would have to be appeased and controlled to prevent future calamities. Plants and animals would have to be domesticated, manipulated genetically to guarantee future food supplies and the heavens would have to be observed carefully so humans would be aware of any future "invaders" to our solar system.

So, with the rise of the matriarchal Neolithic cultures began the advent of astronomy and astrology. The Age of Cancer (ca. 8000 BC) may have been the first astrological age, or according to Clow, the next age, the Age of Gemini (ca. 6000 BC), may have been the beginning of marking precession of the equinox for Neolithic human cultures. The rise of the veneration (and fear) of nature as the Great Mother may have been the inklings of the foundation of true religious practice, which I believe culminated in the Age of Amen—corresponding to the astrological ages of Taurus and Aries (4000-0 BC).

After the great cataclysm of 9500 BC, there were, no doubt, great migrations of people seeking new beginnings after the devastation. With the major climatic shifts, there would have been long journeys to find more hospitable environments, and with the great losses in food supplies, much more primitive lifestyles than what had been previously enjoyed would have become the norm—which is what is reflected in the archaeological record. This is where archaeology has provided an incomplete record of our past. If the cataclysm virtually destroyed almost all remnants of previous high civilization, then the available archaeological record, which indicates fairly primitive lifestyles in many areas of the world after 9500 BC, would be a false indication that all peoples shared that lifestyle prior to that time period.

The cataclysm would have had definite effects on the ancient Khemitians and their culture of 9500 BC. If indeed the cataclysm triggered a series of devastating explosions to the pyramids on the gridline of the Land of Osiris, the power plant that was the Great Pyramid and the energy producing machines of the Khemitians would have suddenly, and violently, stopped. Although the geophysical record does not indicate the severe devastation in northern Africa for 9500 BC as it does in other areas of the world, there were definite changes.

With the tilt in the earth's axis and shifting of magnetic fields, climate changed drastically. The once abundant rainfall in ancient Khemit virtually ceased, the great Ur Nil and other tributaries in northern Africa began to disappear and the Libyan and Saharan Deserts began to develop. Andrew Collins has stated in his reading of the Building Texts at the Temple of Horus at Edfu that massive migrations of the ancient Khemitians began at this time. Collins also states the Khemitians later returned to Khemit thousands of years later to begin the so-called dynastic civilization.[1]

As I mentioned in *The Land of Osiris*, Hakim and I had engaged in many discussions of the Building Texts at Edfu. We returned to these discussions in 2003 and 2004. At first, Hakim totally disagreed with previous discussions and translations of these texts by previous authors, including most Egyptologists. Hakim has always been adamant that it was not an "outside" people, whether extraterrestrials or "Atlanteans," who erected the ancient Khemitian civilization, carved the Sphinx and constructed the great pyramids and ancient temples. However, Hakim has agreed there were many migrations of the ancient Khemitians after the great cataclysm, the Deluge. He also concurred that they may have gone to other tribal lands that were connected to Khemit in the Middle East, Central Asia, the Far East and lands around the Mediterranean.

This does agree with some of Collins' conclusions. This will be an important point I will return to later concerning the origins of and identity of the Hebrew and later Jewish people and their connection to the king titled Akhenaten.

But Hakim was also adamant that only a small portion of the people left Khemit proper, and the civilization, although greatly impacted and changed, remained in Africa. Again, the known archaeological record for this timeframe, from 8000-4000 BC in northern Africa, ancient Khemit, is too confusing and incomplete to reflect the level of consciousness and awareness of the people. After all, although in twilight-transition, it was still the Age of Aten, the stage of highest consciousness. Therein lies a paradox—can people in an almost universal state of high consciousness, virtually everyone enlightened, enter into a state of "shock" and collective fear and panic? Or would they maintain the high awareness, just "roll with the punches," and continue to flow in harmony and adjust to the changes?

In my discussions with Hakim on this subject, I now believe the answer is all of the above. It is quite possible, as Clow states, a collective fear and panic did pervade much of human awareness after the cataclysm, and the results were the Neolithic Mother Goddess civilizations, some showing advanced knowledge behind them. The new emphasis on astronomical awareness, detailed observations of the heavens, and development of astrology and precessional knowledge, an obsession with precise predictions of equinoxes and solstices, the creation of accurate calendars and dating, all indicate an intelligent response with a high awareness not credited or realized by the linear paradigms of academia.

But according to Hakim's oral traditions, high civilization continued in Khemit, although apparently different than before 9500 BC. The power grid of the Land of Osiris had been disturbed by the cataclysm and the energy production of the pyramids ceased. But megalithic construction of temples continued and many of these are still under the sands of Egypt waiting to be found. There seemed a greater need to record observations during this time, not only astronomical and astrological, but to preserve knowledge itself. This led to the direct advent and use of symbols and eventually writing.

The accepted paradigms state that the advent of writing started around 4000 BC in Sumer, present day Iraq. But evidence of the use of symbols to record phases of the moon have been shown to go back to around 12-14,000 years ago in a period known as the Magdalenian of the Upper Paleolithic in Europe. Rock paintings and cave art in Africa may also prove to be as old. But, according to the present state of knowledge in archaeology, there seem to be no actual writing scripts before 4000 BC. According to Hakim's tradition, however, writing did begin in Khemit before the supposedly separate Sumerian culture, which was in fact a part of Khemit known as *Sa-Mer-Ra*, and may eventually be traced as far back as 6000 BC. Hakim has always maintained to me that writing began in Khemit thousands of years earlier than anthropologists and Egyptologists are currently aware of. Interestingly, the date of 6000 BC would be in or near the range of the astrological Age of Gemini. Gemini, a mutable air sign, is the sign of communication and has been considered the sign that rules writing in astrology. Is it a coincidence that writing would have begun in this time period?

The reasons for the advent of writing that Hakim teaches are in alignment with our paradigm of cycles. As we were in the twilight period, the Age of Aten waning into the coming Age of Amen, there were those who knew that consciousness was "falling" and the senses would be waning. As I have stated in the last chapter, we believe much communication at the height of the Age of Aten was telepathic, mind-to-mind—awareness and the senses so highly developed that telepathy was the norm. Not only was there not a written but neither a spoken language—sound was sacred and was only utilized in chanting and singing to maintain high levels of consciousness and optimum health, and to cut, shape and lift stone, but as the twilight period moved in, these abilities began to fail. It was realized symbols would need to be created and utilized to convey complex understanding and preserve knowledge other than the oral tradition.

The Neter responsible for all this was considered to be *Djehuti*, known by the Greek name Thoth, later identified with Hermes, and as the Roman Mercury, the patron and ruling planet of Gemini. Djehuti was considered a masculine lunar Neter of wisdom, the creator principle of sacred sounds, called *Heka* (plural *Hekau*) by the ancient Khemitians (see Figure 16). Djehuti was considered a lunar principle of wisdom in masculine form. The Khemitians saw all created principles as the Neters, as masculine-feminine polarities, the "compliment" or feminine consort of Djehuti was Seshat. I will discuss these concepts such as the Neters in greater detail when I delve into the creation of religion in dynastic Khemit, but it is necessary here to discuss the Neter of writing. Djehuti was depicted as a man with the head of an Ibis, the animal considered to be representative of the divine or cosmic principles Djehuti exhibits. Seshat was depicted as a woman with a seven petaled flower on her head, seven being an important number for the principles she represents (see Figure 17). Seven is an important number of sacred geometry; the triangle (3) plus the square (4)—the number of sides and the base of a pyramid.

Seshat literally meant "women" to the ancient Khemitians. I discussed the term Sesh in my first book as referring to "the people," meaning all members of the forty-two tribes that made up the civilization of Khemit, and not being gender specific. However, with the creation of writing began the concept of gender specific realities, masculine and feminine nouns, and Seshat was one of the first concepts to incorporate this thinking, where the "t" ending denotes a feminine polarity. This clearly represents the change in consciousness as Aten was waning and sliding inexorably towards Amen. People were considered more holistically and collectively in Aten, but with the beginnings of writing, consciousness began to differentiate more into polarities, viewing the world in gender specific realities, which has culminated in the patriarchal sexist value

Figure 16: Abydos. Temple of Osiris. Djehuti (Thoth), masculine lunar Neter of wisdom. Djehuti was the principle of the sacred sounds that led to writing. Photo by author 1998.

Figure 17: Dendara. Temple of Hathor. Seshat, the Neter of sacred geometry and writing. Seshat provided the forms for the sacred sounds to produce the symbols for the first written scripts. Photo by author 2004.

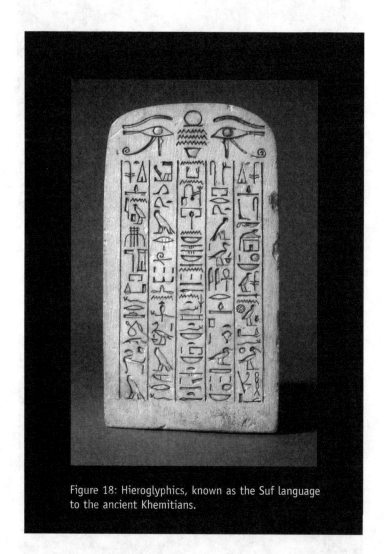

Figure 18: Hieroglyphics, known as the Suf language to the ancient Khemitians.

systems of the Age of Amen.

But to return to Seshat, even though it could be said she represents the first inklings of the rampant sexism characteristic of the Age of Amen/Patriarchy, by just adding the "t" ending to the concept of the people (Sesh) to produce the female, the Khemitian matriarchal/matrilineal consciousness still affords her the key role in the advent of writing. As I mentioned, Djehuti is considered to be the "inventor" of writing to Egyptologists, and Seshat's role is typically understated, dismissed or not fully understood.

According to the indigenous oral traditions as taught by Abd'El Hakim, Seshat's role in the process is at least as important, or more so, than Djehuti. Djehuti created the sacred sounds, Hekau, which were used for chanting to raise vibrations and consciousness, for healing, and for cutting and lifting the stones and producing anti-gravity. But Seshat is the one who created forms. She gives the sacred sounds form, creating sacred geometry and the symbols of the sounds, which became writing. An obvious analogy is that though the male provides the "seed" for life to begin, it is the female that creates the form, the body, within her and gives birth to the form. The written language of Khemit has been known as the *Suf* language (see Figure 18), the origin of the term "Sufi"—the man of "wool."

In all of the history of dynastic Khemit, Seshat was the first Neter invoked whenever there was to be a construction or building created, as she ruled over all forms in the physical—the process of bringing the concepts of sacred geometry into material forms and structures.

So writing as originally conceived around 6000 BC was considered to be also sacred as the symbols represented the physical manifestation of the sacred sounds. In order to preserve and facilitate the understanding of the oral wisdom teachings, the symbols were considered the divine gifts of Djehuti and Seshat to maintain and transmit the understanding of the Neters. A select group of adepts and sages, later to become the inner group of priests, took on the task of creating the symbols and their meanings. The earliest Khemitian writings (which may still wait to be discovered) were the "original" sacred texts, as they would have discussed the Neters and their meanings.

Interestingly enough, even though I have postulated that the earliest symbols leading to all written scripts were considered sacred and "from" the Neters, and were created to attempt to maintain high consciousness and preserve the knowledge of the Golden Age of Aten, Abd'El Hakim has always been skeptical of written texts. As a staunch defender of the purity of his oral tradition, Hakim has always maintained that "if it had to be written down, it was not the whole Truth"—a true Taoist stance akin to Lao Zi. This will be elaborated upon in the next few chapters as I explain that writing, although sacred and with lofty meaning and goals in its inception, increasingly became a tool of the Age of Amen to control knowledge and keep true understanding hidden.

One of the great mysteries in Egyptology is how the "sacred signs" the Greeks labeled *Hieroglyphica*—the Suf language—seem to appear suddenly and full-blown in ancient Khemit. The earliest known examples of the glyphs, ca. 2700 BC to as early as 3300 BC, appear to be an already well developed system presupposing many years of evolution. If the oral tradition is correct, then there were indeed thousands of years of refinement and development before the supposed unification period, the rise of dynastic Khemit, ca. 3100 BC. I believe more archaeological evidence of earlier examples of writing will be found (if it hasn't already) that will push the dates prior to 4000 BC.

Before ending this chapter and moving on to the creation of religion in the dynastic period, I would like to return to the cataclysm. The theory of the cataclysm and its ramifications also presents great evidence to cast doubt on other major paradigms of academia. The idea of primal events, like global catastrophes, being major causes of earth changes and the present geophysical topography clashes with the accepted paradigm in geology, that of Uniformatism. This theory, first postulated by Charles Lyell about 1830, states that geological changes occur gradually over millions of years.[2] The opposing viewpoint, called Catastrophism, declares that sudden, violent geophysical events, like the one proposed in 9500 BC, are the major factors for earth changes. Geologists D.B. Delair and Robert M. Schoch are two of the strongest modern supporters of Catastrophism.

The theory of Uniformatism also gave rise to the concept of ice ages. In an interesting article, "The Case for the Flood" by Peter Bros, the author speculates that Swiss naturalist Louis Agassiz created the theory of ice ages as a reaction to the general popularity of the flood myth from the Bible. The empirical evidence supports the flood/ cataclysm theory, but Agassiz chose to create an alternative because of the great trend in the nineteenth century of "rationalism," using science to oppose religious theories derived from the Bible. Totally not understanding or ignoring how the Bible was constructed based on the longstanding oral traditions, Agassiz chose to ignore the data of catastrophism and formulate a theory more aligned with the academic paradigm of gradual, uniform geophysical changes becoming popular in his day in geology.[3] This long, slow process of change also fits well with Darwinian theories of evolution, a linear process.

I have never been content with the ice age theory and recognize now the overwhelming evidence against it. In my own observations over the last thirty or so years, especially in areas of the U.S. such as Colorado, Utah, Arizona and California, it became obvious to me much of the geophysical evidence of earth changes was the result of massive flooding involving tremendous amounts of water. Ice age theorists would have us believe that huge sheets of ice slowly moving across the landscapes, up and down mountains and across valleys and canyons—and their subsequent retreat during warming periods—caused all the observable scarring and damage, and the form and shape of the present earth terrains. It now seems highly improbable that slow moving ice sheets (how did they go up and down mountains or even form mountains to begin with?) could have caused any of these changes. Only water flowing rapidly and in tremendous quantities could have lifted thousands of megaton boulders and left them in the multitude of precarious positions one can find these rocks in all over the landscape of North America.

The evidence presented by Allan, Delair, and Clow for the cataclysm of 9500 BC is overwhelming. This cataclysm not only left scars all over the earth, but also, according to Clow, in the collective human psyche. The matriarchal civilizations that arose around 8000 BC, showing distinct evidence of advanced knowledge such as using megalithic architecture and the knowledge of which wild cereal grains to domesticate, became obsessed with calendars, zodiacs and the need to consistently predict equinoxes and solstices, in their desire to respect and fear The Great Mother/ Nature.

Even if there were ice ages—and I believe if there were, they were "mini ice ages" lasting only hundreds of years, not hundreds of thousands of years—they had little or no effect on northern Africa. As I mentioned in my first book, the Paleoclimatic and geological record indicates periods of thousands of years of lush rainfall and idyllic conditions for the rise of the ancient Khemitian civilization ca. 30,000 years ago, while most of Europe and North America were in the supposed grip of ice ages. At the time, the ice age theorists suggest the climate radically changed and the ice sheets retreated, rainfall dramatically ceased, the present desert conditions of northern Africa started and the Khemitians had to alter their lifestyle. A much better explanation for me is the sudden catastrophe, the global cataclysm of 9500 BC, causing massive flooding and tsunamis, a radical tilt in the earth's axis dramatically altering global climates and causing a violent effect to the pyramids aligned on the grid line of the Land of Osiris. This radical shift actually caused a minor ice age in certain areas of the world, as in the mammoths found in Siberia flash frozen, and this minor ice age was the only one there was.

The ancient Khemitians, in response to the great cataclysm, definitely changed their lifestyles. With the ending of the power grid of the Land of Osiris, there were some great migrations to other lands, such as the

Middle East, the Mediterranean area, Central Asia and even the Far East. Many remained in Khemit, continued to build temples (yet to be found) and developed writing and settled agriculture. Egyptologists have always assumed, based on the scant archaeological record, that the Khemitians of the period 8000-4000 BC were a fairly primitive people, living quite simple lifestyles. Archaeologists have found artifacts and cultural remains from this period throughout Egypt and have given these cultures names such as Badarian (5500 BC), Amratian (4000 BC), and Gerzean (3500-3300 BC).[4] Egyptologists see these cultures in their linear paradigm as being developmental phases leading to the great dynastic culture to follow. Hoffman states, "It is a period that witnessed the introduction and formative development of the mainstays of later historic ancient Egyptian society: effective farming and herding, metallurgy, pottery making, the shaping of hard stone by grinding, ceremonial architecture, elaborate burials, effective river-going sailing craft, long-distance trade, and stratified political and social systems."[5]

However, instead of viewing the systems that Hoffman states as being a linear development, some of these systems can be seen in the light of cyclical changes, and some as a definite degeneration, not progression, from previous cycles and time periods. Only writing (not mentioned by Hoffman) and possibly the domestication of plants and animals could be considered innovations of this period, and practices such as using megalithic stones such as granite, alabaster and limestone in architecture can be effectively argued to have degenerated during this period and throughout dynastic history. Spiritual practices also degenerated in the creation of formal religion, the subject of the next few chapters. The apparent primitiveness of the lifestyle of this period was a reaction to the great cataclysmic changes of 9500 BC, not a progression. With the almost total destruction of previous high civilization, humanity resorted to simpler, subsistence lifestyles as witnessed throughout Africa, Asia, Europe and the Americas. It should also be mentioned, and I do so as a trained archaeologist, that the archaeological record is vastly incomplete and does not present a complete or coherent record of the last 100,000 years of human existence. But as Hakim has consistently stated, "Nothing is completely lost. Things will always be uncovered as we move into the Awakening."

A good example of how linear thinking can reach the wrong conclusions, albeit with the best of intentions, can be applied to the great British Egyptologist and archaeologist, Sir William Matthew Flinders Petrie. In the late nineteenth century as a result of his excavations of sites of predynastic Egypt, Petrie attempted to formulate a coherent system of dating for the pottery and potsherds he was finding in significant quantities. Before the advent of radiocarbon dating and other modern methods, Petrie proposed a system called "Sequence Dating." Using logical deductions based on the accepted paradigm of linear cultural evolution, Petrie decided that pottery could be dated stylistically by the complexity of patterns used, the oldest being the most simple patterns, the more recent utilizing more complex patterns. Again, the thinking that prevailed in his time period was linear progression, from the simple to the complex. When carbon-14 dating "proved" the situation to be the opposite—complex stylistic patterns were older and simpler patters more recent—Egyptologists discarded his system almost completely.

But what the modern dating apparently showed was that pottery making had not developed in a linear pattern, but regressed stylistically, which is in alignment with the proposed cycles we have been presented with by indigenous wisdom keepers. I propose we "resurrect" Petrie's theory of Sequence Dating based on style, but not in a linear pattern. Huge megalithic constructions devoid of inscriptions such as the Sphinx and her related structures, the Great Pyramid and the other stone masonry pyramids, the Osireion at Abydos constructed of large granite blocks, represent an earlier time period than dynastic sandstone constructions. Hakim assures us the ancient Khemitians still continued to produce megalithic structures during the period 8000-4000 BC, but decidedly inferior in engineering prowess and style. Two examples are the Step

Pyramid at Sakkara and the Temple of Osiris at Abydos. The Step Pyramid, dated by Hakim to around 4000 BC (about 1300 years earlier than accepted by Egyptologists), is constructed with small limestone blocks and was originally faced with mudbrick which has all but eroded away, obviously inferior to the pyramids of Giza (see Figure 19). Instead of seeing the Step Pyramid as a developmental phase leading in a few hundred years of a quantum leap to the utter brilliance of the Great Pyramid, it was a regression, built by people whose consciousness was falling from its once lofty heights of 20,000 years earlier. The Temple at Abydos, not built by or for any king with the title Seti, was originally

Figure 19: Sakkara. Step Pyramid. Dated by Egyptologists to 2700 BC, Third Dynasty of Old Kingdom Period. The structure was built in several stages and may actually have been started ca. 4000 BC, is predynastic, and is not a true pyramid but a symbolic tomb. Photo by author 1999.

Figure 20: Abydos. Temple of Osiris. Dated by Egyptologists to 1200 BC, 19th Dynasty of the New Kingdom Period. The temple may be as old as ca. 4000 BC and was dedicated to the Neter Wizzer (Osiris), and not constructed for any king. Photo by author 1992.

dedicated to Wizzer (Osiris) and is also dated by Hakim as being originally constructed around 4000 BC (see Figure 20). We would have to discover and excavate some of the "original" Khemitian temples still existing under the present temples to be able to compare them with the dynastic temples still standing.

So the ancient Khemitan civilization continued from 9500-4000 BC, but following the cyclical transition from Aten to Amen, in a much less highly developed way. Barbara Hand Clow has labeled this period "The Blank" because of the lack of archaeological evidence and artifacts to document the ancient Khemitian civilization at that point.[6] But "Sequence Dating" of the Step Pyramid and the Temple of Osiris at Abydos fill in some of this gap, and as I have predicted, more archaeological evidence will be uncovered from this time frame—if archaeologists dig in the right places by following the pattern set out by indigenous oral traditions. This would mean following the path of the ancient river, the Ur Nil, and digging in the Western Desert and under the present temples. It is now the evolution of temples and the dynastic religion that I will address in the next few chapters.

CHAPTER SIX

EARLY RELIGION IN KHEMIT

In the beginning those who knew the Tao
Did not try to enlighten others,
But kept them in the dark.

—Lao Zi, *Dao De Jing*

LMOST EVERYONE who gets a Ph.D. in Egyptology has either written a book or an article on some facet of ancient Egyptian religion. But none of these written works presents a coherent explanation of the evolution of the religion. It is assumed, following the dominant paradigm of linear evolutionary theory, that primitive animism and shamanic practices led to the vast complexity of dynastic rituals. It is also universally assumed that ancient Egyptian religion was polytheistic—that hundreds of various gods and goddesses were recognized and worshipped. Even alternative theorists who write about the complexity of the metaphysical practices in ancient Egypt speak of the many deities worshipped—and here is a major paradox: they are all both right and wrong.

As I mentioned in *The Land of Osiris*, the confusion lies in the translation of the term Neter. Only R.A. Schwaller de Lubicz, writing in the 1950s, challenged the accepted definition of Neter as Deity, either god or goddess. Schwaller defined Neter as divine principle, force of nature. Abd'El Hakim has further defined Neter as an aspect of consciousness, a sense like seeing or hearing. So if the ancient Khemitians over 10,000 years ago, during the Age of Aten, were aware of the interconnectiveness of all things, that the **All** was **One** and **Many** at the same time, then it can be said that monotheism preceded polytheism, and that is indeed a paradox.

Actually, the ancient Khemitians of the Age of Aten, and all previous ages, were not really monotheistic either, but that is another paradox that can only be explained in the last chapters of this book. It is enough here to follow our progression from the spiritual practices of the ancient Khemitians to the early phases of dynastic religion to state that the orthodox academic translations and understandings of Neter are incorrect.

But since all books written about religion in ancient Egypt usually start with the Neters, so shall we. It is interesting to note that some of the early Egyptologists' explanations of the Neters were actually closer to the truth than they ever could realize. James H. Breasted, recognized as the first great American Egyptologist, wrote, "Nature thus makes the earliest impression upon the religious faculty; the visible world is first explained in terms of religious **forces** (emphasis mine), and the earliest gods are the controlling focus of the material world."[1] An interesting statement in that Breasted does recognize that the Neters are forces, a realization that is not understood by modern Egyptologists, but his bias is also clearly evident.

First of all, Breasted mentions the "religious faculty" again presupposing that religion is hard-wired into the human psyche. I maintain it is not. Also saying "religious forces" for the Neters instead of aspects of creation or divine principles implies the same bias. But the key to me is how he spells gods with a small "g," a clear Judeo-Christian bias that the gods or Neters of the ancient Egyptians were "only" forces of nature, not the "true" God who only first revealed himself to Abraham and thus began the "progression" to Judaism. Although Breasted does not state this directly, it is definitely implied. I will discuss in detail in a later chapter that the concept of God that is supposedly distinctly Judaic was borrowed wholesale from dynastic Khemitian religion.

Other Egyptologists exhibit much more confusion than Breasted. German Egyptologist Siegfried Morenz stated, "I realized that one has to have experienced oneself the meaning of religion and of God if one is to interpret from the sources the relationships between God and Man in an age remote from their own."[2] I consider this statement to be totally ludicrous—that one has to be a religious person in order to understand the spirituality and/or religion of ancient peoples. Actually, I believe it is quite the opposite; a person who is an atheist or agnostic would be better able to comment objectively on ancient religions without the burdens of personal religious bias.

I could go on with more equally absurd quotes from other Egyptologists, but that is not the aim here. The point is that religion in dynastic Egypt began with the Neters; their description, definition and elucidation became a separation from the totality of existence, which became the basis for religion.

Hakim has shared a simple teaching to explain the origins of religion in predynastic Egypt. After the state of total consciousness of Aten began to wane in the period after the great cataclysm of 9500 BC, people became concerned with what happens after the body ceases to function. A group of people, the early shamans, by the use of various practices such as consumption of psychotropic or psychoactive plants, chanting and breathing rituals, alchemical activities producing substances that raised consciousness and increased longevity (the original philosopher's stone), were able to continue to realize that consciousness was more than the body, that there was no death and there were invisible worlds beyond the physical. These people became the *Hanut* (plural *Hanuti*), the Khemitian words for priest. Hakim's teaching then is that one day these early Hanuti went to the farmers, or the food-producing people, and said to them, "You people produce more food than you need to feed yourselves. Why not give half of your harvest to us (and later the temple) each year and we (the Hanuti) will take care of your body when you die and see that you have an afterlife." The farmers, noticing that predators attacked the bodies of the dead, decided that they did indeed grow more food than they needed, agreed and that was the beginning of religion in ancient Khemit.

There are several key concepts that arise from this simple little story. First, the understanding is that people had become aware of physical death being attached to the body—that destruction of the body by predators, in Africa mainly the jackal, was a factor in reincarnation. The fact that there was already a concept of an afterlife and reincarnation shows a descent, not an ascent, in thinking from the Age of Aten, the Golden Age, where there was no concept of death, just continual energy flows and changing of form. Hakim points out that this idea of the jackal as the body-eater, the preventor of reincarnation, resulted in the creation of a very important sign or glyph, the *Mesu*, which meant rebirth (see Figure 21). The sign is actually three jackal skins. Hakim teaches that, in essence, the sign is saying, "The jackal is dead, the jackal is dead, the jackal is dead!"—three times to insure the power of the sign. Therefore, the body

Figure 21: Luxor. Karnak Temple. Glyph of *Mesu,* which means rebirth. The sign is composed of three jackal skins. Photo by author 2004.

Figure 22: Deir el Bahri. Temple of Hatshepsut. The Neter Ra depicted with falcon head of Horus with solar disc on top to symbolize the sun at noon. Photo by author 2004.

is protected and the jackal cannot get at it, which guarantees rebirth.

Most people who study Egyptology are familiar with Mesu as *mose* or *mosis* as in the kingly title *Ramses* or Ramose, which should be correctly pronounced *Ra-Mesu*, The Rebirth of the Second Stage of the Sun, Ra (see Figure 22). There are several things also implied here. The Hanuti (priests) created the beliefs that there was an individual soul, an essence that did not die with the body and could return, and that there was an essence to the body that was also important for reincarnation, the Ba (spirit or soul) and Ka (physical projection of the soul that was attached to the body). I will elaborate on this idea later, but it is important to state here that the concepts of Ba and Ka were not a part of ancient Khemitian wisdom teachings and were essentially formulated during the creation of dynastic religion.

It is also implied in Hakim's story that temples were in existence before religion fully evolved in dynastic times. This is a radical understanding, that temples were a part of earlier spiritual practices long before writing and formal religion were established. The word "temple" is said to be derived from the Greek word *temenos*, which meant "sacred enclosure."[3] This is another example of how the Greek word does reflect an accurate understanding of the Khemitian concept. In *The Land of Osiris*, I mentioned how the Greek word *pyramidos*, meaning "fire in the middle," became a basis for "pyramid," accurately reflecting the Khemitian term for pyramid, *Per-Neter* (House of Nature) which functioned as a machine, not a tomb.

Hakim has related another story to illustrate the origin of temples. In early antiquity, people would go to an area considered sacred for meditation because of subtle energy fields found there—to become "energized." This area consisted of a few stones, usually igneous rock with high crystalline content—placed on a stone altar (also igneous rock—granite or alabaster) near or on top of an underground or above ground active flow of water. There were no priests or intermediaries for spiritual connections to be made—everyone had access. Later, as the early shamans or individuals who would become the Hanuti maintained higher levels of consciousness while the general populace's senses declined, these priests built an enclosure around the sacred area which became the first "Holy of Holies." Only the early shamans or Hanuti then had access to the Holy of Holies; everyone else stood outside the small enclosure.

As time moved on, there were courtyards, pylons and gates created and the temple was born. As dynastic religion was created, only the Hanuti had access to the inner temples and the "common people" were only allowed to be outside the temple walls. Therefore, temenos, meaning sacred enclosure, is a very accurate understanding of the early Khemitian temples which no doubt the early Greeks learned about from the dynastic Khemitians. The Khemitian term for temple was *Per-Ba*, the House of the Spirit, later to be known as the House of the Soul.

In more recent discussions on this subject with Hakim in Egypt in November 2004, he further elaborated on the concept of Hanuti. Although we refer to the priesthood (including priestesses of course) with the general term Hanuti, Hakim was careful to emphasize to me that the original meaning of Hanuti referred to the individuals who maintained the care of the dead body and provided the magical incantations and rituals they promulgated were necessary for protection of the dead and for rebirth into that body—those who have been called mortuary or funerary priests by Egyptologists—but that we use the term Hanuti in the present to refer to all the priesthood. The emphasis that Hakim wanted to convey was that Hanuti refers to those who **originally** created the practices of caring for the dead and providing for reincarnation, creating the original religion as a means to profit on the concepts of death, soul, and rebirth—those who created religion as an ongoing business for the last five thousand years.

So to return to our discussion of the Neters, agreed upon by all researchers as the basis of dynastic religion, Hakim has taught there were 360 main Neters, although Egyptology lists hundreds more. Hakim would state the others are just variations on the main 360. The number 360 for the basic principles of creation makes it obvious where the concept of the 360 degrees in a circle came from—the circle being the most ancient symbol of existence, reality, "God," and the complete human sensory faculties. Enlightenment to the ancient Khemitians would entail "circular consciousness," to "walk with the Neters" or to be "one with the Neters." So how did the Neters become gods and goddesses?

The great myths and stories that were created by the survivors of the cataclysm of 9500 BC became the basis of all spiritual systems and later religions that evolved from 8000-3000 BC. The Neters, once understood as divine principles, aspects of consciousness, took on a more outer than inner role in these myths as awareness decreased. Many people have written books discussing the creation myths of the early dynastic Khemitians—again, essential for any discussion of ancient Egyptian religion. There are many different creation myths, so many in fact as to cause much confusion among Egyptologists as to which one came first and if there were different groups of peoples migrating into Khemit with different creation mythologies.

In these different creation myths, various Neters appear as the dominant one in stories of the creation of cycles or the physical manifestations. In one myth it is *Atum*, translated by Egyptologists as the "Great-He-She," but actually meaning "That which arises from the Void (Tum)"—essentially saying the principle of creation arose from the uncreated, the "nothing." Theoretical physicist Dr. Volodymyr Krasnoholovets of Ukraine calls this "nothing," the supposed "vacuum" of space, the *Space-Substrate*, the nineteenth century concept of aether returning in modern guise.[4] Ra, the second stage of the Sun, replaces Atum in other myths. In fact, all five Neters of the stages of the sun have mythologies as being the prime creator—Kheper, Ra, Oon, Amen and Aten. Djehuti (Thoth) also appears as prime creator in another set of mythologies. The explanation for all this can be reactions to the cataclysm and the decline in awareness that caused polarities in thinking where different aspects of the whole were promoted to be prime factors in themselves, parts of the whole becoming as important as the whole.

The myth of *Wizzer* (Osiris) always played a key factor, especially at this beginning period. I mentioned in *The Land of Osiris* how the people of prehistoric Khemit were comprised of 42 tribes. One of the oldest myths describes Wizzer being torn into 42 pieces by his brother *Set*, also known as *Sutekh*. Since Set represented the principle of duality and separation, the myth is actually describing the conflict between wholeness (Wizzer) and separation that existed in the transitional period after the Age of Aten. Hakim often pointed out to me that all who see Set as the principle of evil—the foreshadowing of Satan in Judeo-Christian-Islamic mythology—were missing the point. The ancient Khemitians did not view Set as evil, but as the necessary principle of duality, which becomes vital after the fall from wholeness—reductionist thinking as opposed to holistic thinking. In the Second Dynasty of historical Khemit, Set was actually the dominant Neter, as many of the titles of kings had Set in them. Even 19th Dynasty kings had Set in their titles (Seti I & II) to show that the importance of the principle of Set was maintained throughout dynastic history. A major element in the myth of Wizzer and Set is the descent from circular consciousness, the wisdom of the whole-ness of Wizzer known as *Sahu*, into fragmented thinking. Each of the 42 tribes of the Sesh was given a piece of Wizzer to be rejoined when humanity was ready to be whole again. That time is now, the Dawn, the Awakening, when all people will recognize their unique part in creation and become whole—Wizzer will truly be "resurrected" and true wisdom will reign again.

In discussing the Neters, mention should be made as to why they were often depicted as humans with animal heads. This is defined as zoomorphism, depicting God or the gods with the forms and attributes of lower animals. The definition would be more accurate if God or gods was dropped and just simply defined as principles personified by the attributes of certain animals. Early Egyptologists actually believed that the ancients worshipped animals as deities; some orthodox theorists still do. The ancient Khemitians realized that everything in nature is a reflec-tion of the divine, that there is no separation of the divine and nature, that certain animals exemplified the principles of the Neters. When the early Hanuti formulated the symbols for the Neters, they chose animals that were living examples of the aspect that each Neter was. I will not discuss all the Neters here. Hakim and I agreed in November 2004 on the poten-tial of a future work to discuss all the Neters in detail, that in a third book with me he will list and elaborate on all 360 Neters, but I will here speak of some key examples.

Djehuti (Thoth) is depicted with the head of a particular bird, the red Ibis (see Figure 16). Djehuti is a masculine lunar principle of wisdom and brought forth the sacred sounds of creation which led to writing. The Ibis is seen as a very mystical bird to the Khemitians. The red Ibis in Egypt sleeps in the shallow waters of the Nile River with one leg tucked under it—appearing to levitate above the water in the shimmering light, the act of levitation considered the realm of the wise sage or adept and the high wisdom that Djehuti represents.

Heru or *Hor* (Horus) is depicted as a man with the head of a falcon (see Figure 23). Heru is the origin of the Greek word "hero," the subject of many great myths. Hakim fully translates Heru as "The Face of the Falcon"and states it was originally conceived as the principle of the boy, the undeveloped young male who becomes the realized man, the initiate who has passed and survived the major trials and tests of obtaining a

Figure 23: Abydos. Temple of Osiris. The Neter Hor/Heru (Horus) depicted with falcon head and "double crown" to represent kingship. Photo by author 2004.

degree of self-awareness—thus becoming one with Wizzer. Heru later became the symbol of the king in dynastic Khemit. The falcon is seen as the most realized bird, a champion of the skies, the swiftest of aviary flight. The falcon, hawk, eagle and all other raptors are considered the lords of the sky and have been the symbols of kingship for thousands of years.

Sekhmet is depicted with the body of a woman and the head of a lioness—one of a series of so-called "Lioness Goddesses." Her name literally means "The Power" and she is a venerated principle from the earliest stages of Khemitian symbology (see Figure 24). That a lioness could be a symbol of power is obvious, but also depicted as a female symbol demonstrates the matriarchal nature of the ancient Khemitian social system—that true power descended through the female line. She also represents the power of maternal love, the unconditional love of mother—

Figure 24: Luxor. Karnak Temple. The Neter Sekhmet depicted with lioness head with solar disc symbolizing maternal power. Photo by author 1999.

tough love, but unrelenting toward her progeny. Later Sekhmet was considered the symbol of warfare to the dynastic Khemitians, a corruption of power in a corrupted age, the Age of Amen.

The most important point I want to make in this chapter is how dynastic religion came to be. The priesthood, the Hanuti, rose to power as a result of the people falling from awareness. In the Age of Aten there was no need for priests, rabbis, Popes, Imans, etc., for everyone knew the Neters both within and without. At the beginning of the dynastic time period of Khemit, ca. 4000 – 3000 BC, the Hanuti fully created religion, created the necessity of their newfound vocation—to be the intermediaries between the people and the Neters. The Hanuti convinced the people that they could no longer access the Neters themselves, that only priests could speak to them. The Hanuti strongly invoked the principle of Set—that they had to be separate, spiritually superior and above the "ordinary" Khemitians because of their special abilities to access the Neters.

Different groups of Hanuti arose, each advocating a specific Neter. Some became the spokespeople for Kheper, some for Ra, some for Ptah, some for Djehuti, etc. A state religion was created around the myth of Wizzer (Osiris)—that Wizzer was the perfected state of being, the wise, benevolent ruler who had sacrificed himself for the benefit of all, the first resurrection mythology. But the real understanding is that the Hanuti promoted Set, duality and separation, and not the holistic state of awareness that was the wisdom of Wizzer.

After the time of the cataclysm of 9500 BC, many people left Khemit when climate patterns severely changed in northern Africa. Some of these groups prospered in other lands as far off as Central Asia and the Far East. In the time periods of 5000-3000 BC, some of these groups returned with their own Hanuti favoring their own Neters. It is believed by Egyptologists and some alternative researchers that these outside groups introduced the concepts of kingship and royalty to Khemit. The existing Hanuti embraced the "invaders" because of their wealth and power, and a coalition was formed to bring about what is known as dynastic Egypt. The Hanuti would be protected and materially supported in their now elevated status by these wealthy and powerful rulers, and in return the Hanuti would create mythologies of the special place and role the Neters imbued on these rulers to keep the people subservient to both the ruling families and their clergy.

The most important group of these "invaders," the to-be ruling families that entered Khemit from approximately 5000–3000 BC, was the Falcon Tribe. This Falcon Tribe was under the aegis of the Neter Heru, known to students of ancient Egyptian religion as Horus the Elder, to differentiate him from Horus the Son of Osiris and Isis in later mythology. The original Heru had nothing to do with Wizzer. In *The Land of Osiris* I discussed these people, mentioned by many authors as the *Shemsu Hor*. Both Hakim and I believe the title is wrong and should be correctly rendered as the *Seshu Hor*, the people or followers of Heru (Horus). The Falcon was the symbol of this tribe and became the symbol of kingship throughout all of Khemitian history.

But since the Neter Wizzer had already been established as the basis of the "state" religion, the dominant mythology, a compromise was created. The myth of the supposed conflict between Wizzer and Set was created (Hakim has always maintained that there was no real "conflict" to the Hanuti; both Wizzer and Set were respected Neters) and Horus was added as the son of Osiris who "avenges" his father's death and becomes the resurrected Osiris. Egyptologists know this Heru as Horus the Younger, but both concepts were merged. Thus truly began dynastic religion—the king would be identified with both Wizzer-Osiris as the benevolent, wise ruler and his son, Heru-Horus as the resurrected, living embodiment of his now divine father.

Hakim further elaborated to me in 2004 that in the indigenous tradition there were no separate concepts of Horus The Elder or Horus the son of Isis and Osiris—that the term Heru was the Face of the Falcon, the symbol of the realized male.[5]

Although this myth became the basis of the outward religion, centers arose in Khemit promoting different Neters. This has led to the belief of Egyptologists and those in the fields of cultural anthropology and comparative religion that this was a system of polytheism—but the inner teachings of the Hanuti, kept in the oral traditions and not written down in the newly created "sacred texts," was that the Neters were not Gods and Goddesses in the same understanding of Deity later established in Judaism. It was the great Hermetic scholar R.A. Schwaller de Lubicz who first realized this in the midst of the twentieth century when he wrote of there being an outer and inner temple, an outer and inner distinction of Hanuti, and that only a select few had access to the true meaning of the Neters, the Inner or Greater Mysteries. This aspect of an inner order of adepts who were rigorously initiated into maintaining secrecy of the Great Mysteries will be explored in more detail in a later chapter discussing the origin of the Mystery Schools.

It was in this timeframe of 5000-3000 BC that many of the rituals, practices and outward trappings of the system arose that we now call dynastic religion. As the Neters were known as being aspects of consciousness, the 360 senses, the senses themselves played a key role in the development of these religious parameters. Hakim emphasized to me in 2004 how this development proceeded. We know today how all religions utilize feast days and fasting as major parts of their practices. Hakim stated that the nose, as per the sense of smell, was utilized by the early Hanuti to bring the people to the temple. As a "reward" for donating their harvest to the temples, the priests initiated the concept of special "feast days" to celebrate the Neters' bestowal of grace to the Hanuti for their prayers and loyalty. The smell of cooked food would draw people to the temples and make them aware through the use of their primordial sense of smell that the time for the feasts had arisen. Hakim was clear that the use of the sense of smell preceded the use of the sense of hearing, that the nose was before the ear—that it was later that the "call to prayer" was used to draw people to the temple for prayer, and it was originally five times per day for the call to prayer to correspond to the five stages of the sun of the ancient Khemitian wisdom teachings, which is still utilized today in Judaism and Islam.

Another different facet of Hakim's tradition deals with the beginnings of the dynastic period. It is assumed by Egyptologists that there always was this clear distinction of Upper (south) and Lower (north) Egypt. This is assumed because it has been determined that different groups like the Falcon Tribe entered the south, then conquered the people of the north to establish a unified kingship and "one country." This is reflected in one of the titles given to dynastic kings, *Nb Twy*, written as *Neb Tawy*, and translated by Egyptologists as "Lord of the Two Lands," signifying a clear distinction between the north and south. But Hakim maintains the translation is incorrect—that Neb Tawy means "Precious of All Lands," and that there was no demarcation or separation in prehistoric times. It was all Khemit.

It remains clear though that the new found coalition between the priesthood (the Hanuti) and the ruling families resulted in an outer religion that served the needs of both to maintain control and power over the people. This template has remained in place for the last five thousand years, and the clergy and ruling families have supported each other throughout recorded history. This system began in predynastic Khemit much earlier than Egyptologists believe as the Hanuti began their rise around 5000 BC. When the supposed "union" of the north and south (ca. 3100 BC) unfolded, religion in Khemit was firmly established. The final solidification of the system would arise in the next one thousand years and it is this period we will next draw our attention to.

CHAPTER SEVEN

THE RISE
OF
AMEN

If men are not afraid to die,
It is of no avail to threaten them with death.
If men live in constant fear of dying,
And if breaking the law means that a man will be killed,
Who will dare to break the law?
There is always an official executioner.

—Lao Zi, *Dao de Jing*

A S I HAVE MENTIONED SEVERAL TIMES, as an indigenous wisdom keeper Hakim does not concern himself with exact dates and numbers, preferring the essence of quality over quantity. But he has always maintained to me that the Age of Amen was in full force around 2000 BC. Since the major symbol of Amen in the New Kingdom Period (ca. 1550-1100 BC) was the ram, this date corresponds to the astrological Age of Aries, the Ram. It is obvious that astrology was a well-established practice in ancient Khemit by studying the famous zodiac on the ceiling of the Temple of Hathor at Dendara. Again, it was the brilliance of Schwaller who noted that the zodiac there, carved around 200 BC, was based on a much older zodiac in use in prehistoric times. Schwaller came to this conclusion by noting the special importance of the position of the crab, the symbol for the sign of Cancer, and the twins, the symbol for the sign of Gemini—this led him to believe the zodiac was formulated sometime between 8000-4000 BC.[1]

Two other examples stand out; around 6000 BC was the Age of Gemini ruled by the planet Mercury. Mercury was the Roman title for Hermes, the Greek Thoth and Khemitian Djehuti, and Hakim dates writing beginning in Khemit during the Age of Gemini when Djehuti was the dominant Neter.

Around 4000 BC we entered the Age of Taurus, the Bull, and the bull appears in Khemitian symbology at this time. It could be stated that the concept of Two Lands, Upper and Lower Egypt, arose between 6000-4000 BC in the Age of Gemini, the Twins, represented by two lands. In Taurus, a fixed earth sign of materialism, the two lands are united in the First Dynasty ca. 3100BC under the king the Greeks called Menes, whose symbol was the bull. I wrote an article in 1995 in which I stated "Menes" was actually the king with the title *Men-Aha*, also known as *Hor-Aha*, not his father *Nar-Mer* whom Egyptologists identify as Menes. I also argued in this article that the unification was a result of a compromise between powerful ruling tribes that was symbolized by a union with the heiress of the north, *Neith-Hotep*, and Nar-Mer, and was not the result of a purely military victory—true to the matriarchal/matrilineal nature of ancient Khemit as taught by Abd'El Hakim.[2]

Around 2000 BC we entered into the Age of Aries, the Ram. This also coincided with the full enfoldment of the Age of Amen, the Hidden, whose symbol in the Age of Aries was the ram. An important point here is that Amen, as the Hidden, was originally understood to have no image. During the Age of Aries Amen assumes the symbol of the ram, originally used to represent Ra, The Stubborn (see Figure 25). The ram became the symbol although there was to be no image of the Hidden. Obscured and veiled—only the Hanuti had access to his domain.

When religion was first formulated in predynastic Khemit, Amen was just one of the 360 Neters, one-fifth of the understanding of the five stages of the sun. But around 1800 BC, Amen was elevated to the primary Neter, the state "God," especially in the period Egyptologists label

Figure 25: Luxor. Temple of Amen. Avenue of sphinxes, originally having rams heads to represent Amen. Photo by author 1998.

the Middle Kingdom. Families began to appear as the dominant tribe with Amen as a title, such as *Amen-en-het*, the "Place of the Hidden." The myth of Wizzer-Set-Hor (Osiris-Isis-Horus) was still maintained as the foundation of kingship, but Amen now became the primary Neter and the Hanuti created texts to show that the kings are "chosen" by Amen to rule over the people. Because the vowels were considered sacred and only pronounced but not written, and anyone who has ever chanted vowel sounds (especially in large groups) knows the power of the sounds produced, the title has been spelled many ways: Amun, Amon, Ammon, Amen. The pronunciation, according to Hakim, should be Imen (Imn), but we adopt Amen for consistency.

As Amen became the "State God," the primary Neter, the Hanuti decided to expand his influence, not only as the protector and creator of kings, but as the Neter of the people, too. To satisfy the common people of Khemit, Amen is now given an image, that of a man, not with an animal head, but with a particular crown of two feathers (see Figures 26 and 27). The feathers are said to be those of a goose, another early symbol of Amen before the ram.[3] Hakim said to me in November 2004 that the feathers of Amen's crown were that of a heron, not goose as believed by Egyptologists. Statues of Amen were cast in pure gold and taken out of their recessed, hidden chambers—the now Holy of Holies—and paraded about by the Hanuti in front of the people on special feast days. These feasts would be sacrificial meals of rams and/or lambs, the sacred animal of Amen.

By the period known as the New Kingdom, Amen was fully entrenched as the Supreme Neter. But the priests of Ra, who traced their beginnings to the earliest founding of religion in predynastic and Old Kingdom times, were still very important and influential. To overcome any loss of influence of their "God," the Hanuti now bestow another title on Amen as *Amen-Ra*—King of the Neters. As mentioned, the original symbol of Ra was the ram, the stubborn animal to the ancient Khemitians. To placate the followers of Ra, the falcon, the symbol of Hor

Figure 26: Deir el Bahri. Temple of Hatshepsut. The Neter Amen depicted as a man with feather crown. Photo by author 2004.

Figure 27: Luxor. Karnak Temple. The Neter Amen depicted with feather crown. Also shown are Neters Ptah and Sekhmet with king. Photo by author 1999.

(Horus) was given to Ra in this period. To differentiate between the two, the Hanuti portray Ra as a human with the head of the falcon with the solar disc on top of his head as the Sun at noon. Horus was then depicted with the falcon-head having the so-called two crowns on his head, to still represent kingship. So the symbol of kingship, the falcon, was utilized in the new title of Amen-Ra, the King of the Neters. The Ra temples and cult still remained active, but all Hanuti of all Neters now had to pay deference and homage to Amen as the Supreme Neter, as the Age of Amen went into full expression.

Amen was to remain the Supreme Neter for the rest of dynastic Khemitian history. All groups of people who entered Khemit, including invaders, adopted Amen as their "God." The Greeks identified Amen with Zeus, the Romans with Jupiter, etc. I will explain in a later chapter that the Israelites who formed the religion which would eventually be known as Judaism even identified Amen with Yahweh and adopted many of his ritualistic practices, although this statement will be vehemently denied by almost all Judaic scholars.

Amen ruled supreme until the end of Khemitan history and the Arab invasions of ca. 200 AD. With the rise of Islam ca. 600 AD, Amen is fully replaced by Allah—who in actuality is a variation of El or Eloh, a Semitic God, Yahweh of the Jews, and Jehovah of the Christians. I will maintain that since we have still been in the Age of Amen for the last five thousand years that El/Eloh, Yahweh, Jehovah and Allah are just Amen in different disguises. But how did El/Eloh, Yahweh, Jehovah and Allah come to be? This will be addressed in the next few chapters.

It is in the so-called New Kingdom Period of dynastic Khemitian history that the prevalent concept of judgment, so familiar in the religions of Judaism, Christianity and Islam, appears in full expression. Many scenes on tomb walls and funerary papyrus from this period reflect the concept of being judged "on the other side" after physical death (see Figure 28). I will address this subject again in the next chapters, but here I state that the idea of leading "a righteous life" and following the dictates

Figure 28: Modern papyrus depicting judgment scene from New Kingdom Period (ca. 1400 BC).

of the supreme Neter, Amen, came into full existence at this time. Although Amen was now the supreme Neter, the role of the "judge" in the netherworld (Neter-world) was given to Wizzer-Osiris, so that he still played an important part in the overall religious practices. Instead of just being the symbol of the benevolent, wise ruler, the sacrificing king who guides resurrection, Wizzer was now the supreme judge of the dead. In these judgment scenes, Wizzer/Osiris was accompanied by 42 judges, one to represent each ancient Khemitian tribe who held one of the pieces of the whole of the sacrificed Wizzer.

In a previous paragraph I stated that Amen reigned supreme from 2000 BC to the end of the historical Khemitian civilization. I now amend that statement. A brief interlude of some twenty years in the middle of the New Kingdom period, around 1350 BC, interrupted the supremacy of Amen. This brief period, only a blip in the history of Khemitian religion, did little to affect the course of Khemit at the time, but was a major factor in the future of a great portion of humanity for the next 3300 years. The events of this period were to affect the course of religion in inexorable ways. This period, known in Egyptology as the Amarna Period, has also been a major factor in the course of my own life—the primary reason I became so drawn to Egyptology in the last thirty odd years.

CHAPTER EIGHT

AKHENATEN AND MOSES

Therefore the sage takes care of all men
And abandons no one.
He takes care of all things
And abandons nothing.
This is called "following the light."

—Lao Zi, *Dao de Jing*

I N MY FIRST BOOK, *The Land of Osiris*, I discussed how I came to this profound interest in the civilization I now call ancient Khemit. I will now go into more detail on the one event that has determined the course of my life for more than thirty-five years. In January of 1968, facing the possibility of being drafted into the army during the Vietnam War, I joined the U.S. Air Force. In the late spring of that year, having completed basic training, soon to be assigned to a base for permanent duty, and facing the bleak prospect of four long years of service during a war I did not agree with, I decided I would use that time of servitude to expand myself into areas of study I had not had time for before.

This meant going deeper into the academic subjects I had to study in college and going beyond—which led me to metaphysics, "beyond physics." I started to study Eastern mysticism and aspects of Western mysticism, such as the Kabala. Perhaps it was the war or some other reasons that made me decide to look at written works I would never have embraced in my undergraduate days. One day in June of 1968, I was in a bookstore in New York City and came across a used paperback with the title *Moses and Monotheism*. I was surprised to see the author was Sigmund Freud. I had studied Freud's psychoanalytical theories and knew he had a dim view of religion, but had not known he had written about the history of Judaism. Freud had started his research into this subject in 1934, but because of the rising anti-Semitism in Nazi Germany, not wanting to lend fuel to that fire by "exposing" Judaism, he abandoned the project for several years. He published his first two essays on the subject in the psychoanalytic journal *Imago* in Vienna, Austria in 1937. The third and last essay was written six months before his death in London, England in 1939 and the three were published together in book form right before his death.

It was through reading this little paperback that I first became aware of a king of ancient Egypt who had titled himself *Akhenaten*. In these essays, Freud postulated that the Hebrew lawgiver Moses had been a priest of this king and that it was this king's unique teachings that became the basis of Mosaic Judaism.

I still treasure my little copy of this work with its now yellowed pages. I consider this little known part of the whole of Freud's writings as his greatest contribution to our collective thought, far more important than any of his psychological or psychoanalytic theories. This book launched my career, as I have spent the last thirty-six plus years reading dozens of books and hundreds of articles about the king Akhenaten and his time, labeled by Egyptologists as the Amarna Period. This chapter could have been a book in itself as more books have been written about this king and his brief period than any other figure in all of ancient Egyptian history—and many books have been written about Moses. I will cite many of these references in the bibliography section for those who want to study these books on their own, but I will state here categorically that, based on the indigenous oral traditions of Abd'El Hakim and my own research, almost all what had been previously written about Akhenaten, with a few exceptions, is blatantly incorrect.[1] This view is taken because the teachings of the wisdom keepers of ancient Khemit are devoid of any Judeo-Christian-Islamic biases about this king. Even the many metaphysical treatments of Akhenaten written in the last fifty years or so, although some being somewhat more objective and accurate than the purely academic treatments, still suffer from a lack of basic understanding of Akhenaten, his teachings, and the basics of Khemitology as introduced in my first book.

So I wish to present here a fresh treatment instead of just regurgitating all that has been stated before. There are several key errors of understanding that all authors have made previously, and that is where I will offer an alternative explanation. This is only possible because of the rich oral tradition about Akhenaten and his time that is presented by Abd'El Hakim.

Those who have written about Akhenaten have fallen into two distinct camps. There are those, mainly academic Egyptologists, who denounce him as a religious fanatic, a despot, a homosexual and a pacifist (as if these were undesirable and unacceptable traits) and a madman. On the other side are those who see him as an enlightened master, the creator of monotheism, a Christ figure, and the founder of all western mystery schools. On the basis of over thirty-six years of research about him and his teachings, covering the academic, metaphysical and now oral traditions, I would tend to fall into the second camp. I will elaborate on this position in this and the next few chapters, but even those who revere and exalt him have been guilty of ascribing way too much to him and are not aware of the full story.

Perhaps it would be best to first provide the known details of his brief period in dynastic Khemitian history for those who may not be aware of Akhenaten and the Amarna period. Most people do not realize that before the early nineteenth century, this king was virtually unknown in Egyptian history—at least outside of the indigenous oral tradition. As early as 1714, Jesuit priest Claude Sicard had copied some inscriptions relating to Akhenaten, without any knowledge of who he was or being able to read the glyphs. Napoleon's savants visited the area of Amarna in 1798 but could not understand what was there. Champollion, the so-called "father" of modern Egyptology, also visited the area in 1828 but it was the Prussian (German) Egyptologist Karl Richard Lepsius who conducted the first serious excavation of the Amarna site in 1843.[2] Since then, other Egyptologists such as Sir William Flinders Petrie, Auguste Marriette, Gaston Maspero, Heinrich Brugsch, James Henry Breasted, Arthur Weigall, Cryril Aldred, Donald Redford, Jan Assmann and Erik Hornung have written about or discovered information concerning this period.

Akhenaten was king of ancient Egypt towards the end of the 18th Dynasty of the New Kingdom period (ca. 1350 BC). His father was the previous king, titled Amenhotep III, and his mother was titled *Tiye*, about whom I will have much more to say in this and succeeding chapters. His title at birth, following the tradition of the 18th Dynasty in

which most kings had titles dedicated to Amen, was also Amenhotep
(The Offering to the Hidden One) and he is first designated Amenhotep
IV by Egyptologists. There is evidence that he co-ruled with his father,
but argument as to how many years.[3] Somewhere between the fifth and
seventh year of his reign, perhaps after his father developed a debilitating
illness, he changed his royal title to Akhenaten (see Figure 29).

Egyptologists differ on the spelling and pronunciation of the title,
but I prefer the translation and interpretation of Abd'El Hakim. Hakim
translates *Akh* as "shade" or "shadow," also as "reflection," not "spirit" as
most Egyptologists translate the term. Therefore, Hakim has translated

Figure 29: Cairo Museum. Statue of King Akhenaten
in exaggerated style of Amarnan art, ca.1350 BC.

Akhenaten as "The Shade or Shadow of the Wiser." I would further add the term "The Reflection of the Enlightened State." Obviously then, Akhenaten perceived himself as somewhat enlightened or in the highest state of awareness—even if most Egyptologists do not. With this change of title, Akhenaten brought forth Aten as the supreme principle and, at first, tried to coexist with the wealthy and powerful Hanuti of Amen at Thebes, the new capitol of the so-called Middle and New Kingdom periods of Khemitian history. But soon after, Akhenaten wearied of this coexistence and moved his court to a new capitol in Middle Egypt, in an area now known as Amarna, thus the term Amarna Period. He called his capitol *Akhetaten* (The Horizon of the Wiser) to signify the dawn of a new beginning of Aten. He then began a vigorous and rigorous campaign to eliminate the corrupt worship of Amen and the dependence on the other Neters as deities, only advocating his Aten teachings and the wholeness of all existence. This has led many to believe that Akhenaten was the founder of monotheism, as he disdained all other Neters but Aten. His revolution failed and after his death or fall from power, the Hanuti of Amen rose back to power and returned the supremacy of Amen.

Before his decline, Akhenaten attempted to maintain his influence by co-ruling with a prince who had the title *Smenkhare*. Again, Egyptologists present varied theories on this king, of whom there is little actual evidence—that he was Akhenaten's younger brother, his son, or even his consort in disguise, *Nefertiti* (see Figure 30). The famous Nefertiti played a large role in Akhenaten's attempted reformation (see Figure 31). Her title has been translated as "The Arrival of Beauty," but I prefer Hakim's translation, which is "She Walks in Harmony"—a much more profound understanding. Nefertiti's parentage and relationship to Akhenaten has also been the subject of debate and I will discuss this also in this chapter. After Akhenaten's disappearance—and there is debate about how long he ruled; most Egyptologists stand with the time of 17 years, although independent Egyptologist Ahmed Osman argues there is

Figure 30: Berlin Museum. Portrait bust of Nefertiti. Found at Amarna 1912, ca.1350 BC.

Figure 31: Luxor Museum. Relief depicting Akhenaten and Nefertiti making offering to the Neter Aten. Limestone fragment ca.1350 BC. Photo by author 1998.

evidence of a rule of 21 years—the person we all know as Tutankhamen is made king around the age of 8-10 years.[4] The city of Akhetaten is abandoned, the court returns to Thebes and Amen returns to supremacy.

There is even debate on the exact parentage of King Tut. Many consider him to be Akhenaten's son, his younger brother or even the son of another of Akhenaten's consorts named Kiya. He actually had the title Tutankhaten at birth, which does clearly indicate a familial relationship to Akhenaten. When the court returns to Thebes, the Hanuti force the change of his royal title to Tutankhamen. After Tut's short reign—he most likely was murdered—a king titled Aye, who may have been Nefertiti's father and Akhenaten's maternal uncle, rules for a few short years and then a non-royal general of the army, titled Horemheb, is the last king of the 18th Dynasty and the Amarna Period is over.

This was a necessarily brief account of this period (I will return to add more details later in this chapter), but I wanted to lay groundwork so as to be able to add the oral traditions as presented by Hakim, which have never appeared in print before.

Two important points that need to be made clear are that Akhenaten did not invent a religious tradition around the concept of Aten nor introduce the idea of monotheism. He is credited with both feats by many authors and they are quite incorrect in these assertions. Even Egyptologists such as Erik Hornung recognize that the Aten is mentioned before Akhenaten—in reliefs of his great-great grandfather titled Tuthmose III, by his grandfather titled Tuthmose IV, and often in reliefs of his father, Amenhotep III. Hakim has pointed out that the Aten is mentioned in reliefs of the Third Dynasty of the Old Kingdom Period (ca. 2700 BC) and even earlier—at least 1500 years before Akhenaten's time. Where Hornung and others go astray is by not understanding Aten as an ancient principle, the fourth stage of the Sun, equal in importance with Kheper, Ra, Oon and Amen, and this was understood in ancient predynastic Khemit.

Even whether Akhenaten was promoting "true" monotheism is a

subject of confusion for many authors. Hornung seems particularly confused as he mentions that Akhenaten still recognized the Neters of Ra, Ma'at and Ptah, particularly early in his reign—so that he cannot be considered as promoting "pure" monotheism, as he still recognized other "Gods." This confusion I addressed in *The Land of Osiris*, as the term Neter did not mean Deity, but a divine principle, attribute of creation, an aspect of consciousness, a sense.

I have already argued that monotheism was understood in ancient Khemit **before** the descent into polytheism, and Akhenaten was **not** worshipping the disc of the sun, the symbol of the Aten for him, but light, as the illumination and elimination of darkness that the sun provides, and the elimination of ignorance that the light of enlightenment brings. Hornung is thus closer to the metaphysical understanding of Akhenaten's teachings than any other Egyptologist by titling his book, *Akhenaten and the Religion of Light*, but is unaware of how or why he is closer to the truth of the whole situation.

Hakim and I have engaged in many lengthy discussions about Akhenaten and the Amarna Period. The indigenous wisdom keepers of Egypt revere Akhenaten as a great master and part of the ancient oral tradition. Even Hornung seems to recognize this as he states, "Akhenaten left no holy scripture, so what he founded does not belong to the religions of the book. The inscriptions frequently mention a 'teaching' or 'instruction' of Akhenaten's, which he placed in the hearts of his subjects . . . . In the Amarna Period it seems in fact to be exclusively a matter of a teaching and instruction imparted **orally** (emphasis mine) by the king; no where is there a trace of religious tracts."[5]

This very interesting realization by an academic who does not recognize the oral tradition existing today provides insight as to why Akhenaten is so revered by the indigenous wisdom keepers. Akhenaten did not try to create a new religion, not even a new teaching, or to introduce monotheism that was already understood in the inner temple teachings. What he was trying to do was breech the darkness of the Age of

Amen, to break the power and corruption of the Hanuti/Priests of Amen, and try to return to the high consciousness and pure spirituality of the Age of Aten. Using himself and Nefertiti as living examples of higher consciousness, as being "God Intoxicated" according to Breasted, he attempted to impart this understanding to all people, not just the clergy and royal families. If he is to be criticized, it could be that he was naïve to think he could end the Age of Amen by himself, that just by his "presence" he could raise the consciousness of all people and that he could teach a universal understanding that was holistic in its presentation, that all people, not just Khemitians, could grasp and embrace.

He also has been roundly criticized about the means he utilized to promote these ideas. He has been called "ruthless" and a "fanatic," because of the supposed fervor with which he challenged the supremacy of Amen. Hornung calls him "perhaps the first fundamentalist in history" because he sees extremism in his practices.[6] It is too easy to judge someone 3300 years after the fact, but that seems to be the fashion among Egyptologists. All this based on the fact that Akhenaten banned the worship of Amen, and that he hacked out his father's titles with Amen in them and the image of Amen on temple inscriptions. But I have often pointed out that way too much is ascribed to the actions of kings by Egyptologists. They often say, "Ramses II had this temple built," or this king ordered this built, and so forth. Most kings (not Akhenaten) were figureheads and it was the Hanuti who determined what was built, where and when, and who dictated the inscriptions to be put on temples, tombs and all monuments—all in the king's "name."

All the histories of reigns, kings' supposed accomplishments, and the majority of declarations attributed to kings were actually dictated by High Priests to lesser priests, the scribes, to be inscribed and engraved. Akhenaten set up a loyal and dedicated Aten priesthood, and it may have been them, in an effort to please their master and king and to promote his teachings, who were "ruthless" in their zeal to lessen the influence of Amen, to eliminate the degradation of polytheism, and spread "the gospel." Has not the Roman Catholic Church done the same thing in attempting to spread Christianity and the supposed teachings of Jesus, and in his name?

And it must be stated, with the label applied to him as a "fanatic" or "fundamentalist," that there is no evidence of any person being tortured or imprisoned for not following his teaching, nor any priest of Amen being killed for still worshipping Amen or any harm done to anyone by Akhenaten or the Aten priests—quite different from the known history of Jewish, Christian or Islamic fundamentalists. I see Akhenaten as quite similar to Jesus, Buddha, Lao Zi, Guru Nanak and even Moses and Mohammed. I use the symbol of the Tao, the yin-yang symbol, to state that even in the age of darkness, there is the spot of light, just as in the age of light there may be a spot of darkness—and this may explain the cataclysm of 9500 BC being in the Age of Aten.

Akhenaten did **not** create a new religion, but wanted to return to "the good old days" before there **was** religion. A return to basic spirituality, that all people could access "God," and using himself and Nefertiti as the prime living examples, reach levels of higher consciousness and awareness. I would argue these concepts are basically the same teachings as those of the Master Jesus, and Akhenaten was the pioneer and forerunner of all who followed and attempted to bring Light into this age of darkness: Moses, Buddha, Jesus, Mohammed, Guru Nanak, etc. In my opinion, people who have not attained any spiritual insight or awareness, have not been initiated into any path or Mystery School tradition, or who conceive of spirituality and religion as essentially the same thing cannot understand the meanings here and are not properly equipped to judge any spiritual teacher or master.

As with any teacher, Akhenaten did not reach his level of awareness totally by himself. He had his own teachers and masters, and since he was part of the oral tradition, was initiated and trained in the Khemitian wisdom teachings. Most of them have not been mentioned or their importance not realized by other authors. The most important early influence upon

Figure 32: Cairo
Museum. Portrait
bust believed to
be of Tiye, mother
of Akhenaten,
ca.1350 BC.

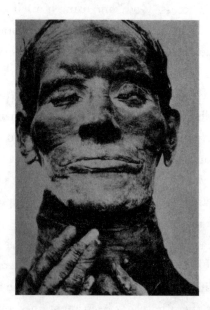

Figure 33: Cairo
Museum. Mummy
of Yuya, father
of Tiye and grandfa-
ther of Akhenaten.
Yuya may have
been the Jewish
Patriarch Joseph.

Akhenaten was, naturally, his mother Tiye. Her title has been pronounced many ways, but once again I prefer the pronunciation of Abd'El Hakim, that of "Ty-ee." Hakim stated to me in November 2004 that Tiye literally means "She Is The One," a powerful title that provides a deeper understanding of how much she was venerated in her lifetime (see Figure 32). Her origins are also disputed, but are clearly known in the oral tradition. She is said to have originated outside Khemit—some say the Kingdom of Mitanni in Northern Syria. Hornung states she was from Akhmin, but never indicates where this was.[7] According to Hakim's tradition, Tiye was an "Asiatic," which could mean anywhere from the Middle East to Central Asia or even the Far East.

Tiye's lineage is very important to this work, and the oral tradition speaks of her reverently. As an Asiatic, she is considered to be of Semitic origin, but related to some of the original indigenous 42 tribes of Khemit that had earlier migrated to parts of Asia. Ahmed Osman, an Egyptian born alternative Egyptologist, has written several interesting books on the Amarna Period. His first book, *Stranger in the Valley of the Kings*, presents the hypothesis that Tiye's father, known as *Yuya*, was actually the biblical Joseph, one of the important patriarchs of the Old Testament Judaic tradition (see Figure 33). The evidence he presents to amplify this argument is very persuasive—all the same titles accorded to Joseph in the Old Testament can be verified as the same titles given to Yuya by his "father-in-law" King Amenhotep III, Akhenaten's father. I had extensive discussions with Hakim on this subject on several occasions and he agreed the Judaic myth of Joseph may have indeed been based on the real person of Tiye's father, Yuya. If this was indeed so, then we have another paradox. If Tiye's father was the Jewish Patriarch Joseph, then her son Akhenaten could have been **both** Semitic Hebrew and Khemitian Hebrew. I realize this statement may be confusing and I will return to this point later in this chapter in the discussion of Moses.

The important thing here is that the oral tradition of Abd'El Hakim agrees with many authors who have stated that the first and foremost teacher of Akhenaten was his mother Tiye. Hakim would state that this is true about all creatures. Who is the first to teach a person to behave as a human being but our mothers? Who teaches a cat to be a cat, a dog to be a dog, etc? In Hakim's tradition of the primacy of matriarchy and matrilineal descent as the main model of ancient cultures, this could be described as a bias, but it's obviously true of most species as many times the father/male is absent and mother is the first and only teacher. But for our case here, it is even more important a point because Tiye was the first spiritual and intellectual influence upon Akhenaten. Some authors, like Osman and Devi, see evidence that Tiye was the major influence on Akhenaten to both adopt the "religion" of Aten and monotheism. As Osman sees the Hebrew lineage going back through Tiye's parents, as her father Yuya was the Jewish Patriarch Joseph, Osman feels the idea of monotheism was borrowed from Asiatic/Semitic sources. Again according to Hakim's tradition, the emphasis is wrong. The concept of Aten as the fourth stage of the sun and the "Golden Age" of prehistory was still well known in the Khemitian inner temples, as was a monotheistic understanding in Akhenaten's time.

Tiye's influence was to give her son a complete spiritual education with the inner teachings of the five stages of the sun and the cycles of human development. Because of his rigorous training and initiations, it was his decision to try to bring an understanding of Aten back to the people and vigorously oppose the concept of Amen and his powerful and corrupt priesthood. Tiye completely supported her son's "revolution" and was an important influence upon him even after her physical death. She also provided for him another very important teacher.

A figure who first appears in the court of Akhenaten's paternal grandfather Tuthmose IV, as well as that of his father Amenhotep III, has always been of great interest to me. He was also known with the title "Amenhotep," but was differentiated by the title *Amenhotep, Son of Hapi* (also written *Hapu* or *Habu*). Hapi, the Neter of the River Nile, was depicted as a hermaphrodite, a male with female breasts (see Figure 34).

Figure 34: Luxor. Karnak Temple. The Neter Hapi, the principle of the river Nile depicted as a hermaphrodite. Also shown is the symbol for Nefer, harmony. Photo by author 1999.

This returns to a concept that Hakim introduced to me and I wrote about in my first book: *Asgat Nefer*, The Harmony of Water. The Nile, although known to the Arabs by the colloquial expression "The Mother of Rivers," was seen by the ancient Khemitians as a perfect balance of masculine and feminine energies in total harmony. So this was a very important title given to this man.

Amenhotep, Son of Hapi, first appears at the court of Tuthmose IV (ca 1400 BC) and is an important figure in the court of Amenhotep III. By the time Amenhotep IV (Akhenaten) is a young man, the son of Hapi is an old respected, venerable sage. In later generations, later dynasties, Amenhotep, Son of Hapi, is almost deified and remembered as one of the great, wise teachers—the Khemitian term is *Wir-Wir* (WR. WR.)—of all dynastic history. There is no doubt that he played an important role in the

101

education of the young prince. Two statues have been found of Amenhotep, Son of Hapi, and they both are very interesting. The first shows him as a young man in typical Khemitian style (see Figure 35). The second shows him as an old man and this one has always fascinated me. This statue shows Amenhotep, Son of Hapi, with a distinctively Asian appearance, in my opinion almost Tibetan looking (see Figure 36). I believe this is to show that he was an "Asiatic" and some of his teachings may have had an Asian origin. Hakim has pointed out to me that the statues are in the style called "block" or "cube" by Egyptologists. Hakim has further stated that this style was utilized by the Khemitian priests to denote a "special" or highly evolved individual. The seating style depicted in the cube statues was distinctively Asiatic.

Was Amenhotep, Son of Hapi, a pre-Tibetan master and sage living in dynastic Khemit over 3300 years ago? The oral tradition of Tibet certainly speaks of a pre-Buddhist culture known as *Bon*, or *Bon-Po*, existing in prehistoric time periods, but this early culture has been classified as primitive shamanism, not a source for the development of great sages and enlightened masters. This negative assessment of the Bon culture may suffer from the same prejudice that is given to all ancient shamanic practices, that they were crude, primitive, tending towards "Black Magic" and so forth. Many of the current practices and rituals of Tibetan Buddhism are directly derived from the ancient Bon tradition.

I believe the possible Tibetan, or at least Asian, lineage of Amenhotep, Son of Hapi, and his role as a major influence on Akhenaten greatly strengthens the links that Akhenaten has with the teachers already mentioned: Moses, Buddha, Jesus and Mohammed. Although Akhenaten's influence upon his own people, the dynastic Khemitians, was minor, his influence upon the history of modern religions was major— and this is because of the person/myth to be discussed next, Moses.

Before leaving a discussion of Akhenaten, however, some mention should be made of his physical appearance in the known statues that have been discovered. Akhenaten is shown in statues of his period, especially

Figure 35: Cairo Museum. Statue of Amenhotep, son of Hapi as a young man depicted as a scribe. Ca.1380 BC. Photo by author 1997.

Figure 36: Cairo Museum. Statue of Amenhotep, son of Hapi as an old man depicted in typical "Asiatic" style. Ca.1350 BC. Features appear definitely Asiatic. Photo by author 1997.

Figure 37: Cairo Museum. Full figure statue of
Akhenaten in typically exaggerated Amarnan style.
Ca.1350 BC. Photo by author 1997.

the early part of his reign, with an almost grotesque or cartoonish appearance. He is shown with a long, hatchet-like face, a swelling belly, exaggerated hips and spindly legs (see Figure 37). However, I believe it clearly can be shown that this was an intentional exaggeration by the Aten priests who directed the sculptors of the time to portray him that way. Akhenaten always used an appellation for himself, *Ankh-en-Ma'at*, which has been translated as "Living in Truth." The actual translation should be "Living According to Divine Law." I believe Akhenaten used this expression to indicate that he was much more concerned with living a true spiritual life and realizing the illusory and transitory nature of the physical world. In this he was predating the teachings of Siddartha of the Sakyamuni tribe, known as Gautam Buddha, by about four hundred years. In the book *Son of the Sun*, Savitri Devi discusses the many similarities between Akhenaten's teachings and the teachings of the Far East, Vedantism and Buddhism. Again, I believe Amenhotep, Son of Hapi, may be the key link here.

But to return to the portrayed physical appearance of Akhenaten. Many Egyptologists and other authors have gone to insipid extremes in attempting to interpret the physicality shown in many of his statues, from stating that he was a woman disguised as a man, that he suffered from genetic or endocrine disorders, was "grotesque" in appearance, was impotent (but still fathered six daughters!), etc.—all concentrating on trivial matters from very limited mundane perspectives.[8] Akhenaten directed his priests not to portray him as a "superman" as kings had been previously depicted, but to show him as a man with whatever physical limitations he might have had. In their zeal for realism, a facet of Amarnan art that is highly praised by art historians and many people, the sculptors went quite overboard and exaggerated Akhenaten's physical appearance. In the portrait bust found of him at the ruins of Akhetaten in the workshop of the artist titled Tuthmose, who also executed the famous portrait bust of Nefertiti, both currently in the Berlin Museum, Akhenaten is shown very much as he really was, not at all ugly, but with a sensitive face that appears

Figure 38: Berlin Museum. Portrait bust of Akhenaten ca.1350 BC. Realistic style depicted Akhenaten as he actually appeared. Executed by sculptor Tuthmose who also did bust of Nefertiti. Found at ruins of Akhetaten in 1912. Photo by AMORC.

very Semitic or "Jewish"—clearly indicating his mother's Hebrew/Asiatic roots (see Figure 38). His body is not shown in this portrait bust, but one can logically assume it was not as distorted as was portrayed in the statues.

Sigmund Freud established the linkage of Akhenaten to Moses in his series of essays published as *Moses and Monotheism* in 1939. German Egyptologist Jan Assmann is the only one in the field of Egyptology who has at least addressed the conclusions made by Freud and treated them seriously in his book *Moses, The Egyptian*. Almost all other Egyptologists who have written about Akhenaten have either ignored or dismissed Freud's claims and deny any connection between Akhenaten and Moses or Judaism. Even German Egyptologist Erik Hornung, who has a seemingly better understanding of Akhenaten's teachings than his colleagues, also dismisses any connection between Akhenaten and Moses.

Only a few other authors, such as Gary Greenberg and Ahmed Osman, have taken Freud's claims seriously enough to realize a connection between the two. Osman, an Egyptian born independent Egyptologist, has written two meaningful books that pertain to this chapter and the next. I already discussed his first book, *Stranger in the Valley of the Kings*, in relation to identifying Akhenaten's maternal grandfather, Yuya, as the Biblical Jewish Patriarch Joseph. This, I contended, made Akhenaten both Semitic/Hebrew and Khemitian, and linked an Asiatic tradition with an indigenous Khemitian Hebrew ancestry. I will return to this in more detail in the next chapter in discussing The Exodus and the rise of Judaism. Osman's second book has been even more controversial. First published as *Moses: Pharaoh of Egypt* in 1990, it has been reissued as *Moses and Akhenaten*. Osman makes the startling revelation that Moses and Akhenaten were the same person. One other book that I will discuss here and in the next chapter is Gary Greenberg's *The Moses Mystery*, in which he essentially supports Freud's claim that Moses was a priest of the Aten under Akhenaten. What I will do here is briefly discuss these works and add the indigenous view as presented by Abd'El

Hakim, never before put down in print.

Jan Assmann refers to Akhenaten as a "figure of history" and Moses as a "figure of memory" to attempt to make a clear distinction between the two.[9] This is to indicate that since archaeological finds in the nineteenth and twentieth centuries have given us physical evidence of Akhenaten's existence, which had almost been virtually wiped out by the Amen priests of the 19th Dynasty of New Kingdom Khemit, he has historical standing, but that the only evidence of Moses is in the Old Testament of the Bible or in the Koran of Islam as memory or pure mythology. I will argue that there is archaeological evidence of Moses and I will present who I think Moses was.

All authors who have attempted to discover the identity of Moses first have to deal with the derivation of the name. The common belief, that which is presented in the Torah account of Exodus, is that Moses was raised by a daughter of the king of Egypt after his Hebrew mother set him adrift in a reed basket to prevent his murder at the hands of the Egyptians. It is then said the Egyptian princess called him "Moses" based on the Hebrew word *Mosheh*—to "draw out"—because she drew him out of the water. But Freud was the first to challenge this standard interpretation and argue that Moses was a derivation of a Khemitian term.[10] I am amazed that any Egyptologist or religious scholar could even consider that an Egyptian royal woman, a daughter of the king, could possibly have given a child a Hebrew name—mainly because there was no known Hebrew language separate from Khemitian in the period of New Kingdom Khemit ca. 1350 BC. Since I have argued and will continue to state in this and the next chapter that the original Hebrews were part of ancient Khemit, and were indigenous African people—and that Freud was right that Moses was a native Khemitian—there cannot possibly have been a separate Hebrew language from Khemitian at the time of Moses' birth. Hakim has stated that modern written Hebrew is about 70 to 80 percent ancient Khemitian with just local dialects and differentiation based on ancient Semitic spoken tongues. As I mentioned in *The*

Land Of Osiris, French scholar Fabre D'Olivet wrote a book in 1815, *The Hebraic Tongue Restored*, arguing that modern Hebrew was derived from ancient Egyptian.

Both Osman and Greenberg agree with Freud that the term "Moses" must have been derived from the Khemitian ending "Mose" found in titles such as Tuthmose, Kamose, or Ramose. Since the Greeks changed the ending to "Mosis" as in Tuthmosis, they argue that is where Moses comes from. The actual Khemitian term was not "Mose," which Egyptologists and Osman and Greenberg believe is translated as "son," "daughter" or "child," but Mesu, which meant **rebirth** as I have stated earlier in this book. The title of the kings Ramses was actually *Ra-Mesu*, the Rebirth of Ra, The Stubborn. Moses is also said to mean "child" which would be close to the indigenous definition of rebirth, but not exact. So it would indeed seem to be fact that "Moses" was derived from "Mosis," the Greek variation of Mesu, the ending appearing in many Khemitian titles.

Ahmed Osman does make a compelling case that many of the aspects of the life of Akhenaten were incorporated into the myth of Moses. I believe he is correct in many of his assertions which I will discuss in the next chapter, but I also believe there was a "Moses" separate from Akhenaten. Freud had originally postulated that Moses was a priest of the Aten under Akhenaten and I will now present the evidence that has not been discussed before. The only link of Moses in the Torah to this connection appears in Exodus 11:3, "The man Moses was exceedingly important in the land of Egypt."[11] In the New Testament there is another reference to Moses in Acts 2:22, "Moses was brought up in all the wisdom and sciences of the Egyptians."[12] Greenberg presents what he believes to be the Egyptian version of the Exodus, citing as his examples excerpts from the history of Egypt presented by a priest titled Manetho during the third century BC. Manetho's writings have only survived in excerpts—those quoted by Greenberg are from the Jewish historian Josephus who wrote his history of the Jewish people in the first century AD.

I will not go into the details of these accounts here; one can refer to Greenberg's book for the full rendering, but I will comment on these two historians.[13] I mentioned in *The Land of Osiris* that it is not clear whether Manetho was an indigenous Khemitian or a Greek born in Egypt. At any rate, he wrote in Greek for a Greek audience and presented a purely patriarchal history of Khemit as dynasties of kings and their sons—completely antithetical to actual Khemitian matriarchal/matrilineal descent patterns that were the norm. Flavius Josephus, although a Jew, wrote in Latin for a Roman audience. I am highly suspect of the historical accuracies of both men who wrote slanted versions for specifically non-Khemitian and non-Jewish audiences. I, therefore, reject the images and histories of Moses that both presented.[14]

Otto Rank, a follower of Sigmund Freud, created a concept that he called "The Myth of The Great Man."[15] Essentially what Rank was postulating is that the myths of certain important individuals in history, particularly people whose lives and teachings that religions are based upon such as Moses, Jesus and Mohammed, are actually the lives of more than one historical person fused together. I believe that to be exactly the case with Moses. Osman is correct that aspects of and events in the life of Akhenaten were fused into the myth of Moses, and, I believe, there were two other individuals who were also fused into the myth. Greenberg actually came the closest to the correct identity for the priest of the Aten that Freud speculated was the true identity of Moses. In attempting to find the "Mose" who was the Egyptian source of the name Moses, Greenberg mentions there was an important official in Akhenaten's court titled Ramose.[16] Indeed there was such a man.

In November of 1998, I had the great fortune to go to Amarna with Abd'El Hakim, the site of Akhenaten's city of Akhetaten. The site is mostly deserted, but excavations conducted over the last thirty years or so have uncovered some of the ruins (see Figures 39 and 40). Hakim took me to the tombs cut into the east cliffs of the site. Knowing my interest in the connections between Akhenaten and Moses and the indigenous

Figure 39: Amarna. Ruins of Akhetaten, The Horizon of The Wiser.
Photo by author 1998.

Figure 40: Amarna. Ruins of Akhetaten. Photo by author 1998.

Figure 41: Amarna. Tomb of Ramose, the Vizier of Akhenaten depicted in Amarnan style, ca.1350 BC. Author believes Ramose was a "Moses." Photo by author 1998.

traditions concerning the true history of the Hebrews and Judaism, Hakim took me into one specific tomb. Because Akhenaten disdained the "common" religion of Osiris and the afterlife promoted by the early priesthoods, none of the tombs at Amarna were occupied and there is no evidence of mummification practiced during Akhenaten's reign— although tombs were cut for Akhenaten, Nefertiti and the close members of his court.

The tomb we went into was indeed that of Ramose (Ra-Mesu), whom Greenberg had mentioned and who was one of two viziers of Akhenaten (see Figure 41). *Vizier* is a term used by Egyptologists, from the Turkish word *Wazzer*, meaning one who was second in importance to the king and handled all administrative duties, like a Prime Minister today. I believe the Turkish word "Wazzer" is derived from *Wizzer*, the Khemitian form of Osiris, the Wise Ruler. Hakim was deliberate in

Figure 42: Amarna. Tomb of Ramose. Statue of Ramose/"Moses,"
ca.1350 BC. Priests of Amen probably damaged statue.
Photo by author 1998.

intent when he informed me that not only was this Ramose Vizier, but he was also known as the "Fan Bearer" of the king. Hakim told me this also meant that Ramose "had the ear of the king," which meant he was a close advisor to and confidante of Akhenaten (see Figure 42). I believe it is quite possible, since no body or mummy or evidence of burial has ever been found, that this Ramose may have left Khemit with the Aten followers of Akhenaten and was the main historical person who was later incorporated by Jewish scribes into the myth of Moses. So, I believe Assmann was wrong when he stated Akhenaten was a man of history and Moses a man of memory—there is historical archaeological evidence that Ramose, the Vizier of Akhenaten, was "a" Moses.

Hakim showed me another piece of evidence in the tomb of Ramose. On the walls were reliefs showing Ramose serving his king Akhenaten, but also showing several scenes that Hakim said portrayed "The Twelve

Tribes." He intimated to me that the twelve tribes depicted were part of the original 42 tribes of Khemit known as the Sesh (see Figure 43). These twelve tribes depicted were Hebrews, original Khemitians who became Atenists under Akhenaten and would later be known as "The Twelve Tribes of Israel." I will return to this point and elaborate upon it in the next chapter.

Sigmund Freud made many claims in his three essays that were published as *Moses and Monotheism*. The most salient point he made for me, that launched my over thirty-six years of research in this area, was that Moses had been an Egyptian priest under the king Akhenaten, and it was Akhenaten's teachings that became the foundation for Mosaic Judaism. The indigenous oral tradition as presented by Abd'El Hakim essentially supports these views. To further illuminate this understanding, I will now present the indigenous teaching about the single, most pivotal event in the history of Judaism, The Exodus.

Figure 43: Amarna. Tomb of Ramose. Relief depicting twelve tribes of Hebrews who later became known as the twelve tribes of Israel. Ca.1350 BC. Photo by author 1998.

CHAPTER NINE

THE EXODUS AND JUDAISM

If the sage would guide the people, he must serve with humility.
If he would lead them, he must follow behind.
In this way when the sage rules, the people will not feel oppressed;
When he stands before them, they will not be harmed.
The whole world will support him and will not tire of him.

—Lao Zi, *Dao de Jing*

IT SEEMS THAT EVERY YEAR in the past decade or so, several new books come out concerning The Exodus. Egyptologists and other authors writing about Egypt all have their own theories and ideas when the great event in Jewish history occurred—often differing by hundreds of years with their dates. This is because the main source of information about the event, the Book of Exodus of the Old Testament, The Torah, does not give specific data with which one can formulate a solid timeline of actual events. The account of The Exodus in the Torah never mentions which specific Egyptian kings were involved. The story of the Patriarch Joseph forms the beginning phase of the so-called "sojourn" in Egypt, but the king who appointed Joseph to his important position is never mentioned by name or title. After all of Joseph's kin are settled in Egypt, in an area called Goshen in the Bible, there is a reference to an Egyptian king "who knew Joseph not," but he also is not given a title or name. The same is also true of the "Pharaoh of the Oppression," and the "Pharaoh of the Exodus"—no names or titles are given.

It is interesting to note that the majority of Egyptologists place The Exodus far away from the reign of Akhenaten—their distaste for him and his "movement" has resulted in a general consensus that he had no connection to Moses, The Exodus or Judaism. Even German Egyptologist Jan Assmann, the only one of his colleagues to at least treat Freud's contentions and theories seriously enough to discuss, arrives at a conclusion that Akhenaten's teachings did not lead to Judaism nor had any connection with The Exodus, mainly because he does not see the Aten teachings relating to Judaism. Many Egyptologists now place The Exodus at the end of the rule of a group of supposedly Asiatic or Semitic people labeled "invaders" who have become known as the Hyksos—about three hundred years before the time of Akhenaten. The main reason for this view is the evidence presented that some of these Hyksos rulers may have had Semitic names or titles, and the Jewish historian Flavius Josephus, who wrote for a Roman audience, names them as being involved in the Exodus scenario.[1] The oral tradition presented to me by Abd'El Hakim totally disagrees with this view by stating that the original Hebrews were indigenous Khemitians, not Semites, and The Exodus was not in any way connected to the Hyksos and their timeframe.

Hakim engaged in further discussions on this subject with me in November of 2004. According to his tradition, Hakim states that the Hyksos were not "invaders," did not conquer any part of ancient Khemit, but were native Khemitians and some of them may have adopted seemingly Semitic titles. They were known as "geologists," experts in the extraction of precious metals. Egyptologists speak of "revolts" by the native Khemitians against the "rule" of the Hyksos that resulted in the formation of the 18th Dynasty of the New Kingdom Period, ca.1600 BC. Hakim maintains there were no "revolts" to remove the Hyksos—that the Hyksos (correct Khemitian term *Hekau-Khoswet*) were northern tribes who did not engage in the power struggles that took place in the south of Khemit for control of the whole country. Later, in the 18th Dynasty period, priests condemned them as "invaders" because they had not supported the families that came to dominance in that time period.[2] This is a radical interpretation and very different than all the previous discussions in print by Egyptologists and alternative researchers discussing the Hyksos period.

Only alternative researchers Ahmed Osman and Gary Greenberg have come very close to the indigenous oral tradition of the wisdom keepers of ancient Khemit that I will present. Both men correctly link Akhenaten and Moses, and see The Exodus in the timeframe that Hakim has shared with me. The major difference between them is that Osman sees Akhenaten and Moses as the same person, while Greenberg agrees with Freud (as I do) that Moses was an official/priest serving under Akhenaten. Amazingly, neither Osman nor Greenberg cite each other as references—especially Greenberg whose work was written after Osman—but neither does Osman cite Greenberg in the revised version of his book published in 2002.

The story of The Exodus presented to me by Abd'El Hakim becomes an assimilation of both the works of Osman and Greenberg, but with significant differences from both of them also. Greenberg attempts a meticulous cross-referencing of known Egyptian kings and the approximate timeframes for the Jewish Patriarchs Abraham, Isaac, Jacob and Joseph with the intent of formulating a date for The Exodus. While I believe his timeframe for The Exodus is essentially correct, his attempt to correlate Joseph with a particular Egyptian king is wrong and I will explain why. Greenberg has not considered or shown he is aware of Osman's book *Stranger In The Valley Of The Kings*, which presents an excellent argument that Akhenaten's maternal grandfather who had the title *Yuya* was the Jewish Patriarch Joseph.

Since Yuya's tomb was found in the Valley of the Kings near Luxor in the south of Egypt in 1905, he is a historical figure (see Figure 44). All the titles attributed to Yuya that were found in inscriptions or in papyrus scrolls in his tomb match the same titles given to Joseph as mentioned in

Figure 44: Luxor. Valley of the Kings. KV 47, the tomb of Yuya.
Photo by author 2004.

the last parts of the Book of Genesis.[3] Osman also, I believe, correctly matches the king who would have made Joseph his Vizier as the king with the title Tuthmose IV. Greenberg postulates that Joseph came to power much earlier under the king Tuthmose I, but I believe he is wrong for the reasons Osman gives for his connection. According to The Torah, Joseph rose to prominence in Egypt because of his ability to interpret the king's dreams when all the wise men of his court could not. The only king that we have evidence of who was interested in dreams was Tuthmose IV.

A stele erected between the paws of the Sphinx tells how Tuthmose IV, as a young prince who was not in line for kingship, fell asleep by the Sphinx after a day of hunting (see Figure 45). The story then relates that the Sphinx, in the masculine guise of *Har-Em-Akhet* or *Har-Herakte* (Horus of the Horizon), an obvious masculinization of the Sphinx which occurred during the patriarchal tendencies of the Age of Amen in the

Figure 45: Giza. Stele in front of Sphinx attributed to King Tuthmose IV, ca.1450 BC. Photo by author 2003.

New Kingdom period of dynastic Egypt, appears to the prince in his dream and promises to make him king if he will clear away the sand from around the statue and enclosure. The stele declares that because he did remove the sand he was made the king Tuthmose IV.[4] Hakim further added to me in 2004 that the stele is actually describing a "repair" made to the Sphinx, what Hakim calls "mendenation"—that the Sphinx was "mended" to masculinize her from Tefnut to Har-em-Akhet with the addition of a false beard that has since fallen off and can be found in a corner in the Cairo Museum. I believe Osman is correct in aligning the dreamer Tuthmose IV with the famous interpreter of king's dreams, Joseph/Yuya.

Osman also points out that the name Joseph, in Hebrew and Arabic *Yu-sef*, and Yuya both contain one of the Hebrew names for God, Yahweh, and seem to be related. When I first mentioned Osman's theory that Yuya was Joseph to Hakim in 1992, he was cool to the idea, being not much concerned with the historical veracity of the Bible. But in 1997, we engaged in protracted discussions on this theme and Hakim agreed that Osman's theories have merit because Yuya was Tiye's father and that Akhenaten had both Khemitian/Hebrew (through his father Amenhotep III) and Semitic/Hebrew (through his mother Tiye) lineage. Osman points out that the mummy of Yuya shows him to have been a very Semitic looking man and not typically Khemitian (see Figure 46).

Hakim has always consistently said to me that his tradition states that The Exodus was essentially the Amen Priests chasing the Aten followers of Akhenaten out of Khemit, agreeing with Freud, Osman and Greenberg. Of these authors, I believe Osman is the closest to the oral tradition of Hakim when he states Tuthmose IV was the king who Joseph/Yuya served as vizier ca. 1400 BC, and then Yuya's daughter, Tiye, became the main consort to Tuthmose IV's son, Amenhotep III. The title attributed to both Yuya and Joseph as "Father to the King" would fit his status as father-in-law of Amenhotep III. It was Amenhotep III who would have afforded Tiye's parents, Yuya and Thuya, the special

Figure 46: Cairo Museum. Profile of mummy of Yuya, possibly the Biblical Joseph. Note distinctive Semitic features.

Figure 47: Sakkara. Tomb of Horemheb. Relief depicting Amen Priest and subservient "captives," ca.1310 BC. Scene may show oppression of Hebrew/Atenites, the followers of Akhenaten. Photo by author 2004.

Figure 48: Sakkara. Tomb of Horemheb. Close-up of scene possibly depicting oppression of Hebrew/Atenites before The Exodus. Ca.1310 BC. Photo by author 2004.

privilege of being buried in the Valley of the Kings amongst royalty after they had died.

The general Horemheb became king of Egypt after the last of the Amarna family of kings, Aye, who ruled for a short four years after the death of Tutankhamen, and who was possibly Nefertiti's father and the brother of Tiye (making Akhenaten and Nefertiti first cousins). It was Horemheb who was both "the King who knew Joseph not" and "the Pharaoh of the Oppression." Under the rulership of Horemheb the Hanuti/Priesthood of Amen totally regained their power and elite status, and took revenge against the reforms of Akhenaten and the Aten priests (see Figures 47 and 48). Akhenaten's titles and reliefs were hacked out and defaced in an attempt to remove him from history. This did indeed almost succeed because Akhenaten was unknown in Egyptology until the beginning of the nineteenth century—but **not** in the oral tradition. After the death of Horemheb, one of his generals with the title Ramose became king and is known today with the title Ramses I, the supposed founder of the 19th Dynasty of Egyptian kings. He ruled for only two years or so and very little is known of his time as king. Osman identifies him as the "Pharaoh of the Exodus," and I believe he is right. The Exodus probably began ca. 1304 BC towards the end of the reign of Horemheb and concluded in earnest during the brief reign of Ramses I.[5]

The mythology created in the Book of Exodus of the Old Testament which declared the Hebrews had a 400 year "sojourn," were made slaves and had to endure hard labor was created by later Jewish scribes under the guidance of a series of redactors/editors with the title *Ezra* in order to remove any direct connection to ancient Khemit except as captives, but the oral tradition of Abd'El Hakim tells a very different story. The Hebrews were an original indigenous Khemitian people, part of the overall Sesh, and already had a concept of "monotheism" ingrained in their conscious, or at least subconscious, minds from their own prehistorical past. Added to this was the Asiatic tradition of long established monotheism brought in by Akhenaten's grandfather, Tuthmose IV, who had taken a Semitic consort from the Middle East, had promoted Yuya/Joseph as his vizier, and the entire family of Yuya through his daughter Tiye who became the main consort of Tuthmose IV's son, Amenhotep III. All this was the background for the "revolution" of Akhenaten. The Exodus, therefore, was a "religio-spiritual" struggle, not a revolution of slaves nor a Khemitian imposition of monotheistic values upon an ignorant, Semitic ragtag group of shepherds and goat herders.

Again, Akhenaten did not "invent" monotheism or the concept of Aten, but what he did do was try to eliminate the polytheistic degeneration that had become Khemitian religion, attempt to destroy the corrupt power of the Amen priesthood, and bring Light into the darkness of the supremacy of Amen. His loyal Vizier, Ramose, who had the "ear of the king," may have led the Aten followers out of Khemit, and he became the main basis for the myth of Moses. Ahmed Osman is correct in proposing many of the characteristics of and events in the life of Akhenaten were incorporated into the myth of Moses, but I believe the Vizier Ramose was the source of the Greek, not Hebrew, name and the one who led the Hebrew/Atenists out of Khemit.

German Egyptologist Jan Assmann is the only one of his colleagues to even reference Ahmed Osman and give serious consideration to the theories of Sigmund Freud on this subject. But even he cannot accept the evidence that Akhenaten's teachings became the major basis of Mosaic Judaism. The majority of Egyptologists date The Exodus either before or after the time of Akhenaten. The most popular theory amongst many academic Egyptologists and alternative researchers is that The Exodus occurred with the "expulsion" of the Hyksos kings and their followers. Again, this is mainly because of the supposed Semitic titles attributed to Hyksos kings and the belief that the Book of Exodus is essentially true in the story of the Hebrews having been Semitic tribes from Canaan and other Middle Eastern areas. The oral tradition of Khemit is quite clear that the Hebrews were indigenous African people and The Exodus was not connected to the Hyksos time period.

THE EXODUS AND JUDAISM

An older group of academic Egyptologists still adhere to a date and time period for The Exodus in the early 19th Dynasty of New Kingdom ancient Egypt, about 100 years after Akhenaten, again to distance the event from him based on scant evidence. A reference in the Book of Exodus that states that the Hebrews were put at hard labor to build store cities called *Pithom* and *Ramsees* has led to the general consensus that the king titled Ramses II was the "Pharaoh of the Oppression" and the king that followed him, his thirteenth son, with the title *Merneptah* was the "Pharaoh of the Exodus." This belief is further enhanced by a stele erected during the reign of Merneptah that has become known as the "Victory Stele" or the "Israel Stele." The reason for these appellations is that the stele—which can be seen in the Cairo Museum and was created by Amen Priests—lists the cities of the Middle East that were conquered by Egyptian armies and has the only inscription ever found in Egypt referring to Israel (see Figure 49, on following page). But as pointed out by both Osman and Greenberg, the fact that Israel is referred to as both a place/land and a people would indicate that The Exodus occurred many years before the date of the stele (see Figure 50, on following page). In order for Israel to become a known land and people, a significant amount of time would have had to pass. This stele could not have referred to the time of The Exodus.

In 1997 while in the Cairo Museum with Hakim, we stopped at the Victory/Israel Stele and engaged in discussions about it. Hakim stated that the stele, although erected by priests during the reign of Merneptah, was in fact describing events that had occurred during the reigns of the earlier kings of his direct lineage, namely Rameses II, Seti I and Ramses I. The stele records and celebrates the "victories" of the armies of Amen over the Atenists fleeing Egypt and the conquests of the lands they had settled in. The mention of "Israel" instead of Hebrews or Atenites is significant and will be discussed in greater detail, but it is enough to state here this indicates that perhaps as much as a hundred years had passed from the event of The Exodus, as Israel was already established as both a

Figure 49: Cairo Museum. Israel Stele, ca.1210 BC. Attributed to reign of King Merneptah. Photo by author 1997.

Figure 50: Cairo Museum. Close-up of Israel Stele of Merneptah. Glyphs in second register from bottom mentions "Israel" as both a people and a place, ca. 1210 BC. Photo by author 1997.

place and the Israelites as a known people.

The Israel Stele is not the only piece of historical evidence that can be cited as relating to The Exodus. Greenberg has stated that the Egyptian versions or evidence of an Exodus are the writings of Manetho as preserved in the works of Josephus. But, as I have mentioned, I do not consider either Manetho or Josephus to be objective historians and I would not consider either to be accurate sources. I have mentioned the reliefs in the tomb of Ramose, one of the viziers of Akhenaten and the possible historical Moses, that show twelve tribes of Hebrew Atenists which I believe relates to The Exodus as the later known twelve tribes of Israel. Another piece of archaeological evidence can be added here.

In the south of Egypt in an area known as Medinet Habu is a temple referred to by Egyptologists as "The Ramasseum." It is called this because it is believed the temple was constructed during the reign of Ramses II and is dedicated to him. Hakim has said the temple was actually begun during the brief reign of Ramses I and continued during the reigns of Seti I and Ramses II. The temple is located on the west bank of the Nile across the river from Luxor in the area known as Medinet Habu. The Khemitians themselves referred to it as the *Temple of Time and Timelessness*. It was called this because in the daytime the passage of the Sun over the temple was marked by the priests to record the time of day, but at night nothing could be observed but stars, indicating an overall understanding of no time or timelessness. The important point to mention here is that the priests of Amen during the time period right after the reign of Seti I had reliefs placed on some of the inner temple walls depicting some scenes of The Exodus. The reliefs are only partially intact today, but they do show the armies of Amen defeating the Aten followers in a sea battle, a sort of reversal of the Red Sea incident in the Book of Exodus where the king and the pursuing armies of Egypt are said to have drowned when the sea closed in on them after the Hebrews had safely passed through. This propagandist series of reliefs shows the

Figure 51: Luxor. Medinet Habu. The Ramasseum, the Temple of Time and Timelessness. Relief depicting a sea battle ca.1200 BC. Scene depicted is victory of armies of Amen over the "Shasu," the Hebrew/Atenite followers of Akhenaten, The Exodus. Photo by author 1998.

Figure 52: Luxor. Medinet Habu. Temple of Time and Timelessness. Another relief depicting armies of Amen in victory over their enemies, The Exodus from "the Egyptian side," according to Abd'El Hakim. Ca.1200 BC. Photo by Theresa L. Crater 1999.

Egyptian armies of Amen being the ones who are victorious, and Hakim points out that the losers are shown as the twelve tribes of Hebrews/Atenites (see Figures 51 and 52). Hakim refers to these reliefs as "The Exodus from the Egyptian side."

It is in the 19th Dynasty that the Amen priests, during the reigns of Seti I, Ramses II and Seti II, refer to Akhenaten as the "Heretic" or the "Criminal of Akhetaten" in an effort to eliminate his teachings and distance themselves from the Amarna Period.[6] As I have mentioned, the Amen priests carefully removed Akhenaten's images and titles from reliefs, dismantled the city of Akhetaten and attempted to remove him from history (see Figures 53 and 54, on following page). In this they almost succeeded, as Akhenaten almost had disappeared from history until the ruins of Akhetaten were found in the early nineteenth century— but his teachings survived in the mythology of Moses and the creation of the religion of Judaism.

It would be beyond the scope of this work to fully cover the complete history of Judaism—that might entail several books in itself—but I do want to continue this thread to the time period right after the historical, not mythological, event of The Exodus from Khemit. In essence, I believe Judaism to be an assimilation of several earlier religions and traditions that were finally fused together from the fourth to the second century BC. In the modern religion of Judaism can be found elements from Hellenistic traditions of Greece, Persian traditions relating to the religion of Zoroaster, and distinctly Egyptian/Khemitian and Middle Eastern Semitic elements. For our purposes here, I will concentrate on the Khemitian and Semitic elements already discussed and the timeframe right after the migration out of Khemit that was The Exodus.

For many years in my lectures I have told people that there are distinct differences in the terms "Hebrew," "Israelite" and "Jew," and that they were not the same people. The word *Hebrew*, according to the wisdom teachings of Abd'El Hakim, was derived from the Khemitian word *Kheperu*, the plural of Kheper, the scarab beetle that signified the

Figure 53: Amarna. Tomb of Ramose. Scene showing images of
Akhenaten and Nefertiti defaced by Amen priests, ca.1350 BC.
Photo by author 1998.

Figure 54: Amarna. Tomb of Ramose. Another scene with images of
Akhenaten and Nefertiti defaced by Amen priests, ca.1350 BC.
Photo by author 1998.

first stage of the Sun, the Dawn. The Hebrews were considered to be indigenous Khemitian people, twelve tribes of the original 42 tribes of Khemit known as the Sesh, The People. Therefore, the word *Hebrew* could not have been derived from the Egyptian terms "Habiru" or "Apiru," as the overwhelming majority of Egyptologists and alternative researchers believe, as these terms are popularly translated as "strangers" or "foreigners," and the Hebrews were indigenous Africans. The Hyksos kings were considered invaders and usurpers—the believed correct translation of Hyksos being "Chieftains of a foreign-hill country"—but, as mentioned, Hakim does not accept this translation. He sees the Hyksos—Hekau-Khoswet—as native Khemitians who specialized in the use of sacred sounds, Hekau, to extract precious metals. They were early geologists. As such they may have been related to, but were not the Hebrews of Khemit.[7] Gary Greenberg has subtitled his book, *The Moses Mystery, as The African Origins Of The Jewish People*—he is essentially correct, but it should read "The African Origins Of The Hebrews" with the knowledge of the indigenous oral traditions presented in this book.

The next area to cover is the origin and meaning of the terms *Israel* and *Israelite*. The term Israel first appears in the Old Testament in the Book of Genesis in relation to the Jewish Patriarch Jacob, the father of Joseph. Greenberg presents the two versions of the story—the most famous one being that Jacob either had a wrestling match with an angel or with God Himself.[8] As it does seem quite absurd that a man could wrestle with God (or an angel), Greenberg interprets the story to indicate Jacob really had a conflict with his brother Esau. I believe Greenberg does present an effective argument in his book that the stories of the Jewish Patriarchs presented in the Old Testament are based on Egyptian mythology (see Appendix C)—stories that were brought out of Khemit by the followers of Akhenaten. In this regard Jacob would represent Osiris/Wizzer and Esau his brother Set.

At any rate, after Jacob's wrestling match, he is told by a supposedly divine source that his name would be changed to *Israel*, "The One who struggles with God." He is also told he would have twelve sons and each one of them would be the head of a tribe. Greenberg believes that there were no actual twelve tribes of Israel and the stories were created to give a Semitic lineage for the Hebrew/Jewish people.[9] But Greenberg is not aware of the Khemitian oral tradition that states the twelve tribes of Hebrews were part of ancient Khemit. There may be truth in his contention that Khemitian myths were a background for the myths of the Patriarchs, but there may also be historical evidence for a Semitic-Babylonian lineage of ancestors that was fused into the mythology also.

The oral tradition that Hakim has presented to me adds much more depth to the overall picture. Hakim translates the term Israel as *Isra-El*, "The Slaves or Servants of El." *El* or *Eloh* was a Semitic name for God and is still found in Judaism in the masculine plural form, *Elohim*. El or Eloh is essentially the same Deity as *Allah* of Islam as the Semitic El became Al in Aramaic, which is the earliest form of Arabic.

So the question arises—how did the Aten followers of Akhenaten, led by Ramose (Moses), become the Israelites? A significant clue is the aforementioned "Israel Stele" attributed to the reign of Merneptah, ca. 1210 BC. This is the first and only reference ever found in Egypt that pertains to Israel, and the glyphs denote not only a place but also a **people**. So if we put the date of The Exodus at approximately 1304 BC and Israel was noted as a place and people ca. 1210 BC, it was during this almost one hundred year span that the Israelites came into being. The Atenite/Hebrews who left Khemit during The Exodus would have called themselves the *Seshu Aten*, "The People/Followers of The Wiser"—so how did they become "The Servants of El?" There are some interesting clues to follow.

I believe the Semitic religion and tradition of El/Eloh was already known and established among the Atenite/Hebrews of Khemit before The Exodus. The Asiatic families who established themselves in the Khemitian royal groups during the 18th Dynasty would have introduced this tradition. Tuthmose IV, the dreamer prince who was not in line to become king but who did, by clearing the sands around the Sphinx, aligned himself with an Asiatic family by taking as his consort a woman titled *Mutemwiya* from the kingdom of Mittani, believed to be in ancient Northern Syria. Tuthmose IV appointed Yuya/Joseph as his Vizier and a further Asiatic lineage was secured when his son Amenhotep III chose Yuya's daughter, Tiye, as his main consort. The Semitic tradition of El/Eloh would have been introduced at this time, possibly by Yuya himself. El would have been equated with *Yahweh*, whom Freud called a "Volcano Storm-God"—Yahweh possibly introduced by the Midianites, a Semitic tribe located near Ethiopia, related to the families of Yuya.[10] I have mentioned in the last chapter how the title Yuya is related to Yu-Sef (Joseph) and was derived from Yahweh.

There is another archaeological clue recently discovered. In 1986, French Egyptologist Alain Zivie discovered a tomb in Sakkara of a second vizier of Akhenaten, a man of Asiatic origin. Zivie translated the man's name or title as *Aper-El*.[11] Hakim stated to me in 1997 and reiterated in 2004 that the translation of Zivie is incorrect; the proper title should be *Ib-Ra-El*. This title is therefore "The Heart of Ra/El"—clearly linking the two traditions I am discussing. In November 2004, Hakim further added that the original title would have been *Ib-Ra-Ir*, but Asiatic peoples could not pronounce the "r" sound, so it was changed to "l" to relate to the Semitic Deity, El. Years ago Hakim taught me that the ancient Khemitian term for the river Nile was *Nir*, but was changed to "Nil" by Asiatic peoples because of their inability to pronounce "r." Ibra-El must have entered Khemit with the Yuya/Joseph families, maybe even a relative, perhaps even a Midianite again linking El with Yahweh.

Therefore, the almost one hundred year gap from The Exodus to the known existence of Israel and the Israelites must have been one of a compromise among and assimilation of several traditions and peoples. The Book of Exodus maintains the forty-year wanderings of the Hebrews in the desert was because of the inequities of the people in returning to

Figure 55: Aswan. Elephantine Island. The Neter Hathor depicted with cow ears. The worship of the golden calf mentioned in the Book of Exodus of the Old Testament by the Hebrew followers of Moses was an image of the sacred cow, a symbol of Hathor. Photo by author 1999.

worship of the golden calf (sacred cow = the Neter Hathor, see Figure 55). But I believe the time spent was to affect a compromise between the people leaving Khemit and the tribes they encountered in Canaan and the Middle East. The Hebrew/Atenite followers of Akhenaten led by Ramose would have wanted to strictly adhere to the Aten teachings, but Ibra-El would have been able to strike the following compromise. Connecting and aligning with other tribes that they were related to like the Midianites who followed El/Yahweh, the Seshu-Aten became Isra-El—the Slaves or Servants of El. But the compromise allowed Aten to still be prominent in this early Hebrew/Israelite religion as I will now explain.

The most sacred prayer of Judaism, and in my opinion one of the oldest, is called the *Shema*. In Hebrew it is recited as *Shema Yisroal, Adonoy Elohaynu, Adonoy Echad*, translated in English as "Hear O'Israel, the Lord Our God, The Lord is One." This is Judaism's most outspoken declaration of monotheism, that the Jewish God is the one true God. But Greenberg accurately points out that the prayer is not original and is based on earlier and similar prayers that are found in ancient Khemit.[12]

Freud was the first researcher to point out that the Hebrew name for God, *Adonoy*, also written in English as *Adonai*, was a derivation based on Akhenaten's Aten. Most Judaic scholars, as well as any Egyptologist who would comment on this idea, vehemently deny any such connection. Jan Assman, the only one of his colleagues to comment on Freud's theories, also denies this connection, but never explains why.[13] Ahmed Osman has provided us the best analysis and explanation. Born in Egypt, therefore having Arabic as his native language, Osman moved to London as a young man and studied Hebrew and the Khemitian Suf language known as Hieroglyphics. He understands that Hebrew was directly derived from Khemitian with only some local and slight linguistic changes. Osman tells us that "t" in Khemitian became a "d" in modern Hebrew.[14] The name of God, Adonoy or Adonai, can be reduced to Adon as the oy or ai are only alliterative endings for chanting or singing. So the Hebrew Adon is, in reality, the Khemitian Aton or Aten. The other name of God in the prayer, *Elohaynu*, is the Semitic Eloh with another alliterative ending, aynu, for chanting. So the Jewish prayer is, in essence, *Shema Israel Adon Eloh Adon Echad*. But the name of God is written as the famous tetragrammaton, with the Hebrew letters *Yod-He-Vod-He*, in English Yahweh. Without ever explaining why, we are told in Judaism that the "true" name of God is never to be pronounced and Yahweh is recited as Adon. But other names of God in Judaism, both in formal Orthodox Judaism and in the Kabalistic tradition, are pronounced as written, so this prohibition does not make sense.

The only explanation I can see for this paradox is the compromise struck by the survivors of The Exodus and the Semitic tribes they chose to live with in ancient Canaan. To keep the teachings of Akhenaten, Ramose/Moses, and Ibra-El in harmony, the name Aten was substituted for Yahweh and sung in its stead. The correct translation of the most sacred Jewish prayer should then be: "Hear O Servants of El, Aten, Yahweh and El are One." As pointed out by Greenberg, the supposed exalted monotheism of Judaism, Christianity and Islam is actually the same disguised polytheism found in dynastic Khemitian religious texts.[15] The compromise concluded with the Atenite/Hebrews allowing themselves to be known as Israel or Israelites as we now refer to them, The Servants of El. Their identity also as Hebrews was maintained by using Aten as the name of their God to be pronounced, but Yahweh was to be "hidden" in the tradition of Amen.

In November of 2004, I further discussed these ideas with Abd'El Hakim. He agreed with me that the followers of Akhenaten, upon leaving Khemit in The Exodus, could have called themselves the Seshu-Aten before striking a compromise and becoming the Israelites. Ahmed Osman discusses in *Moses And Akhenaten* what Egyptologists have called "The Shasu Wars."[16] A series of reliefs believed to be from the time of Seti I and Ramses II, found at Karnak and Luxor Temples, discuss battles fought against certain tribes, known by Egyptologists as the "Shasu." Osman identifies the "Shasu" as nomadic Bedouin tribes and equates them with the Israelites. The Shasu are mentioned during the reigns of Seti I and Ramses II, but are not mentioned on the Israel/Victory Stele of the time of Merneptah. Osman states, "On the evidence the inescapable conclusions are that *Merenptah* never fought Israel, but his father and grandfather did, and the terms Israelites and the Shasu are, in this particular case, one and the same people."[17] I would further add that the term "Shasu" is a misreading of the term Seshu-Aten, and they were the people of The Exodus who became the Israelites.

Hakim and I also further discussed the Jewish prayer, *The Shema*, in 2004. I mentioned earlier how the Hanuti/Priesthood had used the concepts of the Neters as senses to bring people to the temples. Hakim maintained the sense of smell, through the use of the nose, was the first and primordial way to call people to the temples by using cooked food to appeal to the sense of smell. He cited the Khemitian term *Nesu*, which has the symbol of a stalk of wheat, to represent the sense of smell and where the word "nose" comes from (see Figure 56). Hakim told me the term *Hotep-d-nesu* meant "the offering to the sense of smell, or nose" which we would translate today as "Harvest Feast"—the origin of the feast days prevalent in Judaism and Islam today. Hakim then stated the Shema would represent the shift from the sense of smell, the nose, to the sense of hearing, the ear. He further translated the beginning of the ancient Jewish prayer, from the Khemitian perspective, as "The Listener to El" (Shema Israel) as the first "call" to prayer, chanted by the Hanuti to bring the people to the temple without having to offer a feast as incentive.

The whole concept of Judaism being so different from earlier religious traditions, such as the dynastic Khemitian religion of Amen, can be exposed as utter nonsense. One major reason presented as to why Judaism is so different than Egyptian religion is given in the Book of Exodus. The Egyptians are condemned by the Jewish God in the Old Testament as

Figure 56: Relief with the glyph *Nesu*, a stalk of wheat. The term also indicated cooked food utilizing the sense of smell and may be where the word nose originated.

idolaters, worshipping idols and graven images. Therefore, the Jewish God has no image, no idols, and no physical images. But this practice is totally borrowed from the teachings of Akhenaten. Contrary to the erroneous beliefs of Egyptologists and others, Akhenaten was neither worshipping the sun nor the sun disc, the symbol of Aten. He used the disc of the sun to represent Light and the life-giving power behind the sun and he condemned the practices of the Amen priests in parading gold statues around representing their concept of God. But here is the irony and paradox. Amen is "The Hidden" and originally there were to be no images of Amen. This idea was finally adopted into Judaism and presented as an original concept, a reaction against the idolatry of dynastic Khemitian religion. But Yahweh is fully equated with the original meaning of Amen, no images or idols. He (Yahweh) becomes The Hidden as his name is written as Yahweh but pronounced as Adon, who is Aten, the invisible "God" of Akhenaten.

The real tragedy of Judaism is that although the ethical teachings of Akhenaten of a loving, forgiving, universal, holistic concept of divinity was incorporated into the Mosaic tradition, it is the Semitic Yahweh/El Volcano God, a jealous, vengeful, sexist, militaristic, judgmental Deity, who came to dominate the religion. Thus Judaism has become essentially the same as the Amen religion of dynastic Khemit. Many researchers point out that the early Israelite religion was a reaction against their Egyptian "task masters" and was contrary to Egyptian religion. Besides the above idea of no image or idol of God, they point to certain rituals. It is pointed out that in the Passover feast, the celebration of The Exodus practiced by Jews all over the world every spring, there is the sacrifice of the Paschal Lamb. The Paschal Lamb is said to represent the hated religion of the oppressors, the Egyptians, by sacrificing the animal sacred to Amen, the lamb or ram. But the real reaction against the practices of the Amen priests was by Akhenaten who banned all such "burnt offerings" or sacrifices to any "God." It has not been clearly demonstrated that the Amen priests forbade the sacrifice of rams, the animal sacred to Amen.

There are plenty of reliefs showing meals of geese on tomb walls of New Kingdom dynastic Egypt, and the goose was also sacred to Amen. Hakim confirmed this idea to me in 2004, stating that the Amen Hanuti did indeed sacrifice lambs and rams in offerings to Amen during the New Kingdom Period.

In fact, rituals of sacrificial meals, "burnt offerings," were quite prevalent throughout Khemitian history and this custom was fully adopted in the early Israelite religion in what is known as Temple Judaism. This custom of sacrifices to God, clearly "pagan" in origin, was a part of Judaism until the first or second century AD, when so-called Rabbinical Judaism banned all such "burnt offerings."

Even the Ten Commandments, the beginnings of the Law of God given to Moses on the mountain, and Yahweh as a Volcano God have Khemitian origins. Greenberg presents an excellent analysis of a series of ethical pronouncements that appeared in tombs of the early 18th Dynasty kings and nobles known as "The Negative Confessions."[18] These confessions, 42 of them based on the original number of prehistoric Khemitian tribes, declare the deceased to be free of sin by stating, "I have not done this or that" and these became incorporated into the Ten Commandments. In fact, the Ten Commandments replace the statues of Amen, for in Temple Judaism the inner chamber of the temple, the Holy of Holies, would contain the Ark of the Covenant supposedly containing the stone tablets of the commandments. Only the Levite Priests, the high priests of Temple Judaism, could access the Ark and the Commandments, as only the High Priests of Amen could access the Holy of Holies where the golden statues of Amen resided.

There are so many aspects of Judaism that owe their origins to ancient Khemit that it would take a whole book in itself to enumerate them all. Besides those already mentioned, there are a few others I would like to discuss. Just as Ahmed Osman brought a unique perspective to this research being a native-born Egyptian with knowledge of Arabic and then studying Hebrew and Khemitian Hieroglyphs, I have my own particular background in this area. I come from a long tradition of Orthodox Jews, there being a Rabbi or Cantor in my family for many successive generations, and a long family tradition of Talmudic scholars. Although I rejected a path into Orthodox Judaism at a young age, there is one aspect of the practice that I have always deeply loved. The group practice of praying together in synagogue, particularly singing and chanting the prayers, has always resonated deeply within me. I feel the same listening to Gregorian chants of Christianity and hearing Muslims chant verses from the Koran. In fact, I have always felt the link is closer in Islam and Judaism, because of the similarities between Hebrew and Arabic, and the similar style of chanting as opposed to the English and Latin prayers of Christianity. I know now it is **sound** that is the link, the sounds that resonate to the very core of our beings. There is an expression in the Jewish Kabala that has always remained with me. In describing the sacred name of God, the tetragrammaton Yod-He-Vod-He, the Kabala states, "It is the **sound** that rusheth through the universe."

I have often mentioned in lectures and interviews that there were two main aspects of research that Hakim emphasized to me—that he wanted me to concentrate upon water and sound, and the special interplay of both as utilized by the ancient Khemitians. I wrote extensively in *The Land of Osiris* about the ancient Khemitian's knowledge and use of water, not only for sustenance, but also energy. I also discussed that sound was used in conjunction with water, not only to overcome gravity and lift stone, but to cut and shape stone also.

But there was also a primordial use of sound by the ancients that needs to be discussed here in terms of spirituality, that of raising consciousness. I did discuss the use of sound for healing in my first book, but now I will address why this came to be so. Hakim has spoken often to me of the sacredness of sound—that the glyph *Nefer*, which we translate as Harmony, relates to that area of the human body that produces sound, the larynx, pharynx, trachea and lungs (see Figure 34 on page 101). This is the area of the body that Hakim would identify as the "soul." Although the physical organs may disintegrate and seemingly disappear, the primordial vibrations of sound are ever present—the energy is never created and never destroyed as the universe is forever "vibrating."

Hakim and I have discussed that there was a time in the Age of Aten when not only was there no written language, but there was not a spoken language either. In the Age of Aten, consciousness was at the maximum for humanity and communication was mind-to-mind, telepathic. Sound was only used in a sacred way, chanting and singing to maintain high states of being and wellness. I have been fortunate in the last few years to become friends with Jonathan Goldman, who along with Tom Kenyon and Don Campbell and many others, are pioneers in the use of sound for healing. They are all in a line of musicians and healers that go back to the deified Khemitian master Imhotep who taught and utilized sound for healing and raising consciousness at the ancient Khemitian site now known as Sakkara.

It is the sound of prayer in Judaism and Islam and chanting in Christianity that hearkens us back to the primal days of ancient Khemitian spirituality. There was not a separation between the sacred and profane use of sound or music to the ancient Khemitians; **all** sound was sacred. I have always found it interesting that the fundamentalist or orthodox aspects of the major religions have condemned "pop" or secular music and have only allowed "religious" music or prayer to be utilized. I remember as a boy that on the very holy Jewish holiday of Yom Kippur, The Day of Atonement, one was supposed to spend the whole day singing and praying to God and no secular things such as watching television or listening to music were allowed. My father was not strict in this, him being more a Conservative Jew than an Orthodox one, but his father, a very Orthodox Jew, would never have allowed anyone in his family to deviate from this practice in his home. I had a very close African-American friend when I lived in California in the 1970s who had been raised in the "Holiness Church," Pentecostal Evangelical Christianity. This church is so strict that it states that listening to Jazz or Rock music,

141

virtually invented by African and Jewish Americans, is considered a sin of major proportions.

The same is true of Islam—in Saudi Arabia, Iran and Afghanistan under the Taliban, all secular music is/was banned. But the situation in present-day Egypt is interesting. Although Islam is the predominant religion, fundamentalism is in the minority and Egypt is considered to be the most moderate Islamic nation. It is a joy to walk the streets in Egypt as music, singing and dancing are everywhere. I believe this is because of the heritage of ancient Khemit where all sound was sacred. It is even a fact that some oral traditions are sung instead of just being recited. The great mystic George Gurdjieff used to relate that his father was part of the Greek oral tradition of bards—that his father could relate the ancient Sumerian epic myth of Gilgamesh in song, that such histories were put in verse to be sung.

Since I have covered the origins and differences in the terms Hebrew and Israelite, the only remaining concept to discuss is that of *Jew*. A complete history of the Israelites and their kings, wars and conquests of Canaan and Palestine are again beyond the scope of this work, but I will provide a brief history of the time from 1000 BC to the Roman occupation of Palestine in the First and Second Century AD. The Biblical figures of Saul, David and Solomon are considered the kings who led the Israelites in victory and established the first Jewish kingdoms. It is after Solomon that the kingdom is split in two, under the rival kingship of Solomon's two sons, Rehoboam and Jeroboam. The kingdoms were split into Israel in the north and Judah in the south.[19]

There are conflicting stories about the reasons for the split. Some say Solomon was unpopular in the north and ten of the twelve tribes split away and formed the Kingdom of Israel there. Others say it was the rivalry of Solomon's sons that created dual loyalties. Whatever the reason, it is a matter of historical fact that the northern kingdom was invaded by the Assyrians, a group from the north of present day Iraq, and the Kingdom of Israel ceased to be. According to tradition, the Assyrians

THE EXODUS AND JUDAISM

scattered the ten tribes of the north to different lands, which supposedly led to the term "Wandering Jew," a misnomer as the term should be "Wandering Israelite." According to Jewish tradition, that left only two of the twelve tribes, Benjamin and Judah, in the Kingdom of Judah in the south and in control of the ancient sacred city of Jerusalem.

The next event is well known from Biblical sources. Another foreign powerful kingdom arose after the Assyrians in the south of ancient Iraq centered in the city of Babylon. The Babylonians conquered Judah (and almost all of the Middle East), sacked and burned the Temple built by Solomon in Jerusalem, and took the two tribes of Benjamin and Judah to Babylon, the famous "Babylonian Captivity" in 586 BC. The sojourn in Babylon is interesting for several reasons. Although there is some evidence that attempts were made to codify Israelite tradition into a written form before the Babylonian Captivity, it is after this time that the Torah or Old Testament was actually created. The Israelites were exposed to Babylonian/Sumerian traditions while in captivity and these elements were later fused into Judaism—it may be that older "flood" myths recorded in Sumerian and Babylonian records were completely absorbed into the familiar flood myth of the Old Testament.

There is another interesting piece of this great puzzle of the Israelites to relate here. Most academicians and researchers speak of a part of Babylon called *Chaldea* and often equate the two, calling Babylonians Chaldeans as well. But Chaldean, according to French scholar Fabre D'Olivet, comes from two Hebrew words, *Chasdain* and *Chaldain*, and meant "The Sages, Venerable Ones, Those Who Knew the Secrets."[20] D'Olivet indicates that the Chaldeans were a group of adepts who were separate from the ordinary Babylonians. As in the Israel Stele of Khemitian King Merneptah, Chaldea may have referred to both a place and a people, but they were separate from the general term Babylonians. Hakim has further stated that the Chaldeans were the Hanuti of Babylon, and the term should be translated as "Those who **kept** the Secrets."

The captivity provided the tribes of Judah and Benjamin much contact with the Chaldeans, who may have been relatives and shared the
written and oral Babylonian and Sumerian traditions with the
Hebrew/Khemitian and Semitic traditions already established. After the
return to Palestine, all these traditions merged, adding Greek and Persian
elements, and the Old Testament was created. There are differing dates
given for this compilation into written form. Many argue different versions of the early texts were recorded prior to the Assyrian invasion of 722
BC, but the fact remains that no complete written versions of the Old
Testament have been found that date prior to the sixth century BC.
Others argue that the Old Testament was not fully compiled into the
"Five Books of Moses," the Torah, until the fourth to second century BC
under a school of scribes headed by a redactor named Ezra.[21] It may also
be that "Ezra" was a title applied to the head of this scribal school for sev-
eral centuries, and it may be that this title "Ezra" was a corruption of the
Khemitian term Ib-Ra (see Appendix C).

Whatever the case may be, by the time of the Roman conquest and
occupation in the first century BC, there is a written holy book known as
the Torah and the tribe of Judah is known to the Romans as "Jews," and
their religion as Judaism. Therefore, "Jew" only referred to one of the
twelve tribes. Although the spoken language of almost all peoples at this
time is called Aramaic, the Torah was written in a sacred language called
Hebrew, still preserving the connection to ancient Khemit. D'Olivet stated in 1815 that Hebrew letters were given to the Israelites by the
Chaldeans, but the language was essentially ancient Khemitian. I have
studied Hebrew characters and found some interesting things. In Hebrew
there are several letters known as "Mother Letters," some being vowel
sounds which are sacred. The first letter in Hebrew, *Aleph*, which corresponds to "A" in English, is given the numerical value of one, which is
sacred because it relates to "One God." The letter Aleph contains the
Khemitian glyph for Neter, erroneously translated as God or Goddess,
but being an attribute or aspect of the divine, a principle of creation or

aspect of consciousness (see Figure 57). The Hebrew letter *Shin* is even more interesting, usually pronounced as "s." The Shin is another divine character and relates to God (see Figure 58). Every morning, before they begin to pray, Orthodox Jews put on Tephillim, leather wrappings on the hand and forehead. The wrappings on the fingers represent the Shin, which is said to indicate one of the sacred names of God, known in Kabala as *El Shaddai*—the El or Eloh of the Semitic name for God. The letter Shin can be seen to contain or be clearly derived from the Khemitian glyph *Neter-Neteru*, the Triple Neter, "The Neter of Neters," the only Khemitian term that could actually mean "God" as a universal primal concept (see Figure 59). I believe all Hebrew letters can be seen as cursive forms of the Suf language, the written language of Khemit the Greeks called Hieroglyphics, sacred signs.

One last connecting piece of Judaism to ancient Khemit I would like to mention. I just spoke of the "Mother Letters" of Hebrew—interesting to note even in the patriarchal religion of Judaism where a wife takes her husband's last name, descent is from father to son, status and careers are usually from father to son, where an Orthodox male Jew prays every day thanking God for not making him a woman, etc., the sacred letters are called "Mother Letters." In Orthodox

Figure 57: The Hebrew letter Aleph, "A" in English. The Khemitian sign for Neter can be seen in the Hebrew letter. Photo by author 2005.

Figure 58: The Hebrew letter Shin, "S" in English. The Khemitian sign for Neter can be seen used three times in the Hebrew letter. Photo by author 2005.

Figure 59: Aswan. The Temple of Isis at Philae. The Khemitian glyph Neter-Neteru, the "triple Neter," The Neter of Neters. The triple Neter was utilized in the Hebrew letter Shin, a letter representing El Shaddai, a Kabalistic name of the Jewish God. Photo by author 2004.

Judaism, one is considered to be a Jew, whether one practices the religion or not, by virtue of one's **mother** being Jewish, not one's father. This fact and the reality of mother letters being sacred has to be a direct remnant of the matriarchal/matrilineal patterns prevalent in pre and dynastic Khemit for many thousands of years. No matter how much the stories have been changed and traditions altered to remove all Egyptian elements from Judaism, as Hakim has often said, nothing is ever completely hidden and the Khemitian origins of Judaism are revealed (see Appendix A and B) (see Figure 60).

Figure 60: Abydos. Abd'El Hakim pointing to glyph of Mesu, the three jackal skins meaning rebirth. Photo by author 1998.

CHAPTER TEN

THE ROSICRUCIAN ORDER AND WESTERN MYSTERY SCHOOLS

Look, it cannot be seen—it is beyond form.
Listen, it cannot be heard—it is beyond sound.
Grasp, it cannot be held—it is intangible.
These three are indefinable;
Therefore they are joined in one.

—Lao Zi, *Dao de Jing*

I F THIS WORK HAD BEEN a "standard" or "normal" treatment of the evolution of spirituality and religion in ancient Egypt and a discussion of the King Akhenaten and his influence on other spiritual or religious traditions, it would have ended with the last chapter. A few authors, writing in the spiritual or metaphysical vein, have gone further in discussing Akhenaten's influence on other traditions, but because of restrictions on fully disclosing the extent of those traditions, these discussions have been limited in scope.[1] The other traditions that have been linked to Akhenaten and his teachings are the so-called Western Mystery Schools, sometimes referred to by the falsely comprehensive appellation "secret societies."

The major mystery school or "secret society" most linked to Akhenaten has been the Rosicrucian Order. Known in the West in the past one hundred years or so with several different titles, the Rosicrucian tradition that I want to discuss has been known as *The Ancient Mystical Order Rosae Crucis*, abbreviated as AMORC. The Rosicrucian Order, or Order of The Rose Cross, has been the subject of many books and articles detailing its history. The majority of historians of Western Mystery Schools, most of whom have not been members of the Order, document that the Rosicrucian Order first appeared in Europe in the seventeenth century and have made the assertion that claims of the greater antiquity of the organization are purely mythological.[2] But these historians, not being members, have not had access to the archives and documents of the Order itself, as I have.

The name or title "Rosicrucian" had very little meaning for me before the late 1970s. As a young man I would see adds in various magazines for this shadowy organization called "The Rosicrucians," but upon learning it was a group whose symbol was the "Rosy Cross," I incorrectly assumed it was just another Christian organization, and neither being a Christian nor into Christianity, I just ignored these adds and did not inquire any further. Besides, in my immediate family I did not know or hear about any Rosicrucians or Masons, and if there was any metaphysical or mystical bent amongst any one, it was towards the study of the Kabala, the mystical area of Judaism. The only message that I received about the Kabala was from my father, who had attended a rabbinical high school in Brooklyn, NY and had at one time considered a career in the clergy, which he rejected for a secular life. He said to me once when I was a teenager that anyone who had studied the Kabala had "either gone insane or committed suicide"—a standard warning he had been given by Orthodox Jewish rabbis to discourage anyone from studying the mystical path. In later years I found another tradition that stated one did not attempt to study the Kabala until the age of at least 45, when the early years of marriage, children and career were behind and there was the time to devote to the study of mysticism.[3]

It was not until I was a grown man and had decided to study Eastern and Western Mysticism in the 1960s and 70s that I returned to the subject of the Kabala—not being married, nor having any children nor a "normal" career, I was able to devote extensive time to the pursuit of mysticism. In the 1980s, a cousin of mine who had become a rabbi engaged in a conversation with me about the Kabala. Although he had become a very orthodox religious person himself, he was a natural mystic and had some interest in Jewish mysticism. He defined the term Kabala for me as "The Hidden Transmission From God," and said it was considered to be the oral teachings of Moses that were not written into the Torah. Today we notice that the Khemitian words *Ka-Ba-La* make up the term. Ka is the personality, the etheric double, the physical projection of spirit; Ba is the spirit or soul; and La, which means "no" in Arabic today, was a term of affirmation to the ancient Khemitians. So Ka-ba-la were teachings that presented a positive affirmation of the spirit and personality.

Hakim has further discussed with me his belief that the word Kabala is derived from the Khemitian term *Kabila*, which means "heel," like the heel of our foot. I believe this is to indicate that the Kabala was a "heel" or foundation teaching, and does refer to the secret oral tradition that was not to be written down. Therefore, I also believe that the Kabala was part

149

Figure 61: Rosicrucian Park, San Jose, California. The author and Shawn Levin standing in front of AMORC Administration building constructed in the style of the Temple of Horus at Edfu in Egypt. Photo by Diane Hardy 1997.

Figure 62: Rosicrucian Park, San Jose, California. One of the many depictions of Akhenaten found at Rosicrucian Park. Photo by author 1997.

of the oral tradition of ancient Khemit, part of the inner tradition of the Greater Mysteries that was not written into texts but only transmitted by the use of symbols.

I came to live in San Jose, California in 1972 after having spent four years in the U.S. Air Force during the Vietnam War. I came to San Jose in order to do graduate work at San Jose State University. After living in San Jose for a while, I learned that one of the most popular tourist attractions in that city was Rosicrucian Park, a fairly large complex that included a museum, planetarium, temple, library, auditorium and office facilities. But what most amazed me was the Egyptian style of the architecture—I had never heard or read about any connection between the Rosicrucians and ancient Egypt (see Figure 61).

What even piqued my curiosity more was not only did Rosicrucian Park feature the architectural styles of ancient Egypt, but a preponderance of one style of Egyptian architecture, that of Amarna and King Akhenaten (see Figure 62). In fact, reliefs and drawings of Akhenaten are to be found all over Rosicrucian Park and there is a small chapel completely done in the Amarnan style. The early and mid 1970s was a time when I was obsessed with all I could find out about this king and his period, and I was amazed to see this Egyptian-Amarna oasis in the midst of present day San Jose, California. But I did little to follow up on this for a few years.

I mentioned earlier that I had a close African-American friend in San Jose whose mother and family had been deeply involved in the Pentecostal Holiness Church. This man, named Porkey Lewis, lived next door to me and became a very close friend. Porkey was and still is a very talented actor and director. When I first met him in 1972, he was trying to break into acting and theatre. In the course of our friendship, we formed a professional theatre group and produced many successful plays in the San Jose area in the 1970s.

Porkey got a job doing maintenance at Rosicrucian Park in the late 1970s and convinced the officers of the Order to allow us to stage a play in their theatre, the Francis Bacon Auditorium, in 1977. The play was Arthur Miller's *The Crucible* and I served as assistant director and even played a bit part. In the course of doing this play, I met many Rosicrucians—many of whom acted in our play, were excellent actors and actresses, and still to this day remain close and dear friends. Because of these outstanding individuals, I became interested in the Order. I went to work at Rosicrucian Park myself in 1978, first in shipping and receiving, then serving as a Staff Research Scientist from 1978-1980. What had really impressed me and eventually convinced me to join the Order was working at an International Rosicrucian Order conference/conclave and gathering held in San Jose in the summer of 1978. I was very impressed to meet people from all over the world, from all over the U.S., Canada, Mexico, South America, Europe, Africa and all parts of Asia. All were Rosicrucians, from many different religions, races and socio-economic backgrounds—all had come for the common cause of sharing and experiencing metaphysical beliefs and Rosicrucian teachings. I came to work for AMORC and joined the Order—and, although I am no longer a dues paying member, I still consider myself a Rosicrucian.

It was in my time as a Staff Research Scientist that I had access to the library and the archives of the Order. In the course of this, I found out the "true" history of the Order and why reliefs and images of Akhenaten were to be found all over Rosicrucian Park and the Order's literature. Again, the accepted view of many historians is that the Rosicrucian Order was first established in the early seventeenth century. In 1610, two documents appeared in Germany, France and England known as *The Fama Fraternitatis* and *The Chymical Wedding of Christian Rosenkreuz.* Actually, research has shown that other documents appeared in Europe even earlier than this date that mentioned either the Rosicrucian Order or similar organizations, so 1610 is not a hard date for the beginning of the modern Rosicrucian Order, even in conventional historical analysis.

The Fama, as it became known, and *The Chymical Wedding* basically were an announcement that the Rosicrucian Order was in physical form and soliciting like minds all over Europe to join. The documents announced that the traditional founder of the organization was a "Christian Rosenkreuz" who had lived in the fifteenth century. But the name means "Christian of the Rosy Cross" in German and is just a mythological, not an actual name. Traditionally, it has been assumed a Johann Valentin Andrea of Germany wrote the two documents.

However, all the Egyptian style architecture and reliefs of Akhenaten seemed to me to indicate there was an Egyptian connection to the Rosicrucian Order and I was determined to find this information. I learned that the modern cycle of the Rosicrucian Order, AMORC, was started by a man named Harvey Spencer Lewis in 1914 in New York City. H. Spencer Lewis, as he preferred to be known, was born in 1883 in New Jersey and grew up in New York City.[4] Developing an interest at a young age in philosophy and metaphysics, Lewis was told by a psychic reader that he had been involved with "the Rosicrucians of Egypt" in a past life. He began an investigation into the Rosicrucian Order, but could find no references to them having been in Egypt. After getting married and having two children, Lewis developed a fledgling career in photography and printing. Harvey Spencer Lewis would never forget these skills and became a pioneer in both the fields of photography and radio. But in the early years of the twentieth century, he maintained his interests in metaphysics and his search for any information on the Rosicrucians.

He discovered information that the Rosicrucians had been in France and sent some inquiries to some French professors in Paris. He received a reply advising him to come to Paris to find out more about the Rosicrucians. In the summer of 1909, H. Spencer Lewis accompanied his father on a business trip to Paris and was able to make his connections with a French professor who questioned him intently on his motives and interests in the "Order Rosae Crucis." Lewis was then directed to travel to the south of France for more information. He was finally directed to the town of Toulouse and then to the ancient city of Tolosa. There he passed all the "tests" and was initiated into the Ancient Mystical Order

Figure 63: Dr. H. Spencer Lewis, Imperator of AMORC
1909-1939. Photo by AMORC.

Rosae Crucis by the head of the Order in Europe, a man with the mystical title *Sar Hieronymus*.

But Harvey Spencer Lewis received much more than just membership into the Rosicrucian Order. The French officers and elders of the Order told him they had been expecting him, that his coming to France had fulfilled a prophecy. He was further initiated as an *Imperator*, a Latin

Figure 64: Rosicrucian Park, San Jose, California. The author pointing to one of the many sphinxes found in RC Park with the face of H. Spencer Lewis. Photo by Diane Hardy 1997.

word based on emperor, and given the task and jurisdiction to reestablish the Rosicrucian Order in North and South America. Lewis was then shown and given secret documents that had been kept in France for many centuries, presenting a detailed history of the Order. According to these documents, Johann Valentin Andrea was a pseudonym for Sir Francis Bacon who was the secret head of the Rosicrucian Order, that Bacon was "Christian Rosenkreutz," and also was the primary author of the Shakespeare plays.

It is this detailed history that concerns us the most here. Lewis received the information that he had been seeking—that the Rosicrucian Order, according to its own tradition, had begun in ancient Egypt. Lewis began the modern cycle of the Rosicrucian Order, AMORC, in New York City in 1914-1915 (see Figures 63 and 64). Many influential and wealthy individuals responded and helped Lewis make the Order a success. The Order greatly expanded under Lewis' direction in the next few years. Because of his background in printing, Lewis was able to publish a magazine of the Order in 1916, called *The American Rosae Crucis*, which later became *The Rosicrucian Digest*, still published today. After a few years in Tampa, Florida, Harvey Spencer Lewis established a permanent

Figure 65: Rosicrucian Park, San Jose, California. Rare photo of the first administrative staff of AMORC in 1927. H. Spencer Lewis is seventh from the right in the third row. Photo by AMORC.

center for the Rosicrucian Order in San Jose, California in 1927 (see Figure 65).

Lewis began to write articles about the history of the Order going back to Egypt starting in 1916 and continuing through to the 1920s. Harvey Spencer Lewis first wrote of a secret, inner organization begun in ancient Egypt, which had become known as The Great White Brotherhood or The White Lodge. These terms had been popularized by Madame Helena Blavatsky who helped start the Theosophical Society in Europe in 1875, and had written about a group of ascended masters and adepts who aided the formation of secret societies many centuries before. Today it is not politically correct to refer to a "White Brotherhood," the terms seemingly racist and sexist, although the white did not refer to race or brotherhood to any male-only membership.

I believe the terms "Great White Brotherhood" or "White Lodge" refers to what Hermetic philosopher and alternative Egyptologist R.A. Schwaller de Lubicz had termed the Inner Temple—those sages, masters and adepts in ancient Khemit who maintained the oral tradition and were responsible for knowing and transmitting the true histories and meta-physical truths known as The Greater Mysteries. Harvey Spencer Lewis wrote that it was the royal families and high priests who emphasized these inner temple traditions in the 18th Dynasty of the New Kingdom Period, ca. 1500 BC. The documents that Lewis received in France indicated that one particular king of this dynasty started the modern tradition of mystery schools and he held the title known in Egyptology as Tuthmose III (see Figure 66, see following page).

When I first became aware of this information in the late 1970s, it was a complete revelation. Nowhere in any part of the literature of Egyptology was this facet of the life of Tuthmose III ever mentioned. The standard history of this king is that he was the son of Tuthmose II and a woman who was not in the royal family as the official heiress to the throne or Per-Aa, so Tuthmose III was not considered to be in line for

Figure 66: Cairo Museum. King Tuthmose III.
Considered to be the traditional founder of the
mystery school that became the Rosicrucian Order.
Photo by author 1997.

kingship. Tuthmose I had been a strong king and had chosen his favorite daughter, Hatshepsut, herself heiress to the throne, to co-rule with him. When Tuthmose I died, the priests of Amen wanted his weak and sickly son, Tuthmose II, to become king and co-rule with Hatshepsut. When Tuthmose II died after only a few years of rulership, the priests then decided that his young son of eight, titled Tuthmose III, should continue to co-rule with his aunt, Hatshepsut.

Hatshepsut, one of the great and powerful women of all Khemitian history, refused to co-rule with her young nephew, and having co-ruled with her father and brother, declared herself king, breaking the pattern of traditional male domain of kingship. Many Egyptologists have written how unusual this was, how unique that Hatshepsut was the only woman to declare herself king of Egypt. In this statement they are quite wrong for in 1978 for my second master's degree project for the Social Sciences Department of San Jose State University, under the aegis of the now defunct Women's Studies Department, I presented information that many women had been kings of Egypt, with titles such as Neith-Hotep, Mer-Neith, Neith-Akert, Tausert, Sobek-Neferu and Cleopatra VII. Besides Hatshepsut, many women had either co-ruled or served alone as king of Egypt.

Upon Hatshepsut's death, Tuthmose III ascended the throne as king of Egypt. Whether due to being suppressed during his youth by his aunt or for whatever reason, Tuthmose III became one of the great "warrior-kings" of all Khemitian history. Tuthmose III became a great military king, and continuing into the reign of his son, Amenhotep II, extended Egypt's border and empire further than it had ever been before—and this is how he is known in Egyptology, as a great military, conqueror king.

H. Spencer Lewis presented a more detailed history of this king according to Rosicrucian Order records. In his later years, after a life of military conquests, Tuthmose III underwent a spiritual reformation. Disdaining further conquests, he turned for the rest of his life into the Greater Mysteries and the actualities of the Inner Temple or White

Lodge. According to Lewis, Tuthmose III organized the activities of the Inner Temple into a series of initiations and rituals, which became the foundation for the modern practice of Rosicrucianism. This is why the cartouche with one of the kingly titles of Tuthmose III, *Men-Kheper-Ra*, was placed on all the literature of AMORC by Lewis, to recognize this Egyptian king as the traditional founder of the Order (see Figure 67).[5]

But it has been Tuthmose III's great-great grandson, Akhenaten, who has most concerned us in this work. Following up on the system established by his great-great-grandfather, Akhenaten chose the symbol of the rose-cross for the Order and established the different degrees and initiations used today by the Rosicrucian Order. There is not one Egyptologist (that I know of) and very few alternative researchers who have been aware of this tradition about Akhenaten. The Rosicrucian Order, AMORC, recognizes Akhenaten as its first Grand Master and this tradition adds a much deeper understanding of the "revolution" of this king. Being recognized as a great spiritual master and mystic by the Rosicrucians, and having instituted the forms and teachings of all modern mystery schools creates a much more profound awareness and appreciation of Akhenaten and the reformation he attempted in the Khemit of his

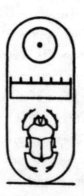

Figure 67: Men-Kheper-Ra, one of the titles of King Tuthmose III. The title was used by AMORC in the *Rosicrucian Digest* to indicate the tradition of this king being the founder of the RC Order.

day.[6] Instead of viewing him as a failure and fanatic as the overwhelming majority of Egyptologists do, the indigenous wisdom keepers of Khemit such as Abd'El Hakim portray Akhenaten as a great master, spiritual leader and teacher, an important part of their oral tradition. Far from being a failure, Akhenaten's legacy remains in the oral tradition of the wisdom keepers of Khemit, in the true ethical basis of Mosaic Judaism, and in the vast mystery school traditions of the West.

Another esoteric piece of information about Akhenaten's legacy was revealed by H. Spencer Lewis in other secret Rosicrucian documents. When Lewis was initiated into the Order in Tolosa, France in 1909, he was given several ancient prophesies of the Order. One specific one mentioned that it would be "a reincarnation of Amenhotep IV (Akhenaten) who would reestablish the Order in the land where the eagle spreads its wings" in the modern era. Lewis was given the jurisdiction for North and South America, and the eagle has been the traditional symbol of these continents. Harvey Spencer Lewis fulfilled that ancient prophecy

Figure 68: Giza. First modern pilgrimage to Egypt of Rosicrucians led by H. Spencer Lewis in 1929. Photo by AMORC.

Figure 69: Rosicrucian Egyptian Museum, San Jose, California. Painting by H. Spencer Lewis depicting Nefertiti sitting for her portrait bust for the sculptor, Tuthmose. 1935. Photo by AMORC.

and that is why Rosicrucian Park in San Jose, California has so many images of Akhenaten, and chapels and examples of the Amarna style of Egyptian art and architecture. Lewis never made a big display or brought attention to himself as a "reincarnation of Akhenaten," but did accept that he had fulfilled the prophecy and the "spirit" of Akhenaten had moved through him (see Figures 68 and 69). It was the images of Akhenaten at Rosicrucian Park that led me to the Rosicrucian Order and to Harvey Spencer Lewis. This book is a fulfillment of a promise I made some twenty-five years ago, to write about both Akhenaten and H. Spencer Lewis.

I have met or heard about other people who have claimed to be a reincarnation of Akhenaten. Mark Prophet, first husband of Elizabeth Clare Prophet, claimed to be so and there are currently two people living in Sedona, Arizona who have felt the spirit of Akhenaten overshadow them. One of these two, a friend of mine who uses the title *Ehrton*, has written a historical novel about Akhenaten called *Born of the Sun*. At the end of his book, Ehrton claims that as many as sixty people may be present on the earth at this time who carry an aspect of the spirit of

Akhenaten—this concerning someone who was "lost" to history and a complete failure to most Egyptologists.[7]

Harvey Spencer Lewis mentioned some very famous people of world history in his list of past Rosicrucians. Besides Tuthmose III and Akhenaten, a short list would include the Greeks Solon, Anaximander, Parmenides, Empedocles, Socrates, Pythagoras, Euclid, Epicurus, Plato, Philo; the Romans Cicero, Seneca and Plotinus; Europeans and Americans such as Charles Magnus (Charlemagne), Raymond VI (Count of Toulouse, France who defended the Cathars), Albertus Magnus, Roger Bacon, Thomas Aquinas, Arnold of Villanova, Raymond Lully, Dante Alighieri, Nicholas Flamel, Cornelius Agrippa, Alphratus Bombastus Hohenheim (Paracelsus), Dr. John Dee, Giordano Bruno, Sir Francis Bacon, Robert Fludd, Jacob Boehme, Dr. William Harvey, Rene Descartes, Sir Robert Moray, Thomas Vaughan, Robert Boyle, Baruch Spinoza, Sir Christopher Wren, Sir Isaac Newton, Gottfried von Leibnitz, Johannes Kelpius, Benjamin Franklin, Thomas Jefferson, Johann Wolfgang von Goethe, William Blake, Dr. John Dalton, Michael Faraday, Honore de Balzac, Anton Rubinstein, Claude Debussy, Nicholas Roerich and Francois Jollivet Castelot—and this is just a partial list![8]

As can been seen, many of the great scientists of the past few hundred years and before were Rosicrucians.[9] This is because the Order stresses the importance of science and applies the principles of science to metaphysics. Harvey Spencer Lewis created a system of at-home study, providing lessons in monographs that were sent to members a few at a time. This was criticized as "mail-order mysticism" but was a very effective system in the 1920s, 30s and 40s. Many, including myself, feel the system is outdated and antiquated today with our present access to information with computers and the Internet, television, radio, magazines and easy access to all books in print. The original monographs typewritten by Lewis are the most powerful for me, but many monographs and teachings have been rewritten, altered and changed today, and I have found this to be to the detriment of the pure vision of Dr. H. Spencer Lewis.

The monographs and lessons provided metaphysical and mystical teachings, and also experiments and exercises to experience these teachings in a simple but scientific method. When I worked as a Staff Research Scientist for AMORC, although we were poorly funded, we conducted many rigorous scientific experiments to test the Order's principles. I also personally tested members' so-called psychic abilities—whom we preferred to call sensitives.   Many people demonstrated unique and extraordinary abilities in areas such as clairvoyance, clairaudience, precognition, psychometry, telekinesis, remote viewing and PSI or extrasensory perception. Rosicrucians tend to be more open minded and aware than non-members—one of the major reasons they seek out the Order in the first place. H. Spencer Lewis constantly impressed audiences and scientists in the 1930s with his extraordinary precognitive and sensitive abilities. He would hold lectures and provide demonstrations of Rosicrucian principles every Sunday night to packed houses in Francis Bacon Auditorium in San Jose, California during the 1930s (see Figures 70 and 71). H. Spencer Lewis passed away in August 1939 and was succeeded as Imperator by his son, Ralph M. Lewis.

When I came to work for AMORC in 1978, Ralph Lewis was still the Imperator. Because of the Second World War, the Supreme Grand Lodge of AMORC based in San Jose had to financially bail out many lodges and chapters of the Order in Europe, Africa and Asia. As a result in the late 1940s, San Jose became the International See (headquarters) of AMORC for the entire world—this was not the original jurisdiction given to H. Spencer Lewis in 1909. Although not the mystic, orator or teacher his father was, Ralph Lewis was supremely loyal to AMORC and his father's dreams, and was a good administrator and leader of AMORC for 48 years. Ralph Lewis passed away in 1987.

As can be seen by the partial list provided, several key people of the Founding Fathers of the U.S. were Rosicrucians, such as Benjamin Franklin and Thomas Jefferson. There were more and other key people such as George Washington, John Hancock, Benjamin Rush and John

Figure 70: (right) Dr. H. Spencer Lewis at Rosicrucian Park, San Jose, California 1934. Photo by AMORC.

Figure 71: (bottom) Dr. H. Spencer Lewis in his office at Rosicrucian Park 1936. Photo by AMORC.

Adams were Free Masons, a group very closely connected to the Rosicrucians. The Masonic Order or Order of Freemasons has made various claims to its antiquity, but was established in its present form in the sixteenth and seventeenth centuries in Europe.

The Masons have claimed their traditions grew out of the craft guilds that arose in the Middle Ages, but that their teachings and tradition extend back to the builders of the First Jewish Temple under Solomon, ca. 1000-900 BC. This involved the use of sacred geometry and metaphysical principles of architecture and engineering. I have not been a member of the Masons, but have studied them and their connections to the Rosicrucians extensively. Freemasonry was very connected to the Rosicrucian tradition throughout the last few hundred years and both groups were very closely linked in Europe, but not so in the U.S. In Europe of the eighteenth and nineteenth centuries, one could not become a Rosicrucian unless one first joined the Masons. In the Scottish rites of Masonry, the 18th degree is known as the Rose-Croix Degree. In other words, one had to go through 18 degrees of Masonry in order to become a Rosicrucian. The two systems are related, but no longer connected in the present day U.S.

I would like to mention other groups, such as the Knights Templar, briefly. The Poor Knights of the Temple of Solomon, or Knights Templar, was formed in France in 1118 AD. The Knights Templar was ostensibly formed to protect Christian travelers to the Holy Land and Middle East, but that was not the real reason. The Knights also took an oath to the Pope and the Catholic Church, but their true loyalty was not to them either. There are many excellent books written about the Knights Templar, especially in the last twenty years, and I would urge readers to consult them for a more detailed exposition of these unique and amazing warrior monks.[10]

Many authors have written that the Masons and Rosicrucians were offshoots of the Knights Templar, but this is quite wrong, especially concerning the Rosicrucian Order. As mentioned, the Rosicrucians can claim antiquity back to dynastic Khemit and there were definitely artifacts and documents presented to H. Spencer Lewis in France in 1909 and in later years to establish that connection. The Knights Templar were formed as a spiritual-military order to protect ancient wisdom and reconnect the traditions of the East with those of the West. The traditional enemies of the Knights Templar were the Jesuits and the Catholic Church, the same enemies of the Rosicrucian Order. The Jesuits formed rival groups such as the Knights of Malta as well as the Inquisition to persecute and undermine the Templars and Rosicrucians, as well as all alternative mystical traditions to Roman Catholicism in the past eight hundred years or so.

I must mention here the group known as the Illuminati. Founded in Bavaria in 1775 by Adam Weishaupt, this group has been much written about in recent years. I will not dwell in detail about this group here, but some comment is necessary. Many people who write or talk about such "secret societies" tend to lump them all under the rubric of "The Illuminati." Many popular works in the last few years have put the Rosicrucians, Masons, and Knights Templar all under the umbrella of the Illuminati—and this is quite wrong. Most of the people who have written these works have been neither Rosicrucians, Masons, nor known anything about the true Knights Templar. While there have been definite attempts by the Knights of Malta, or the modern "Illuminati," to undermine, infiltrate and transform the Masons, Rosicrucians and Knights Templar in recent years, only those who know the truths of the founding intentions of these groups and have been initiated into the mysteries know the true intent of these orders and schools: to attempt to illuminate humanity and free people from the ignorance and mind control of those groups that serve darkness and only themselves.

There are other groups that can be briefly mentioned. The Theosophical Society founded by Madame Helena Petrovna Blavatsky and others in London in 1875, and the Anthroposophical Society founded by Rudolph Steiner, are two other groups that attempted to merge metaphysical and mystical traditions of the East with those of the West.

I have also been a member of the Theosophical Society and have found the writings of HPB, as Madame Blavatsky was known to friends and followers, to be one of the true, pure traditions that came to the West. But a warning to all—Blavatsky's writings are very erudite and difficult for many to undertake as she tended to take hundreds of pages to state what could have been succinctly written in a few chapters.

The main purpose in mentioning these groups, albeit briefly, is my contention that all Western Mystery Schools had many of their origins in ancient Khemit. The Rosicrucian Order as the template was originally formed in the middle of the 18th Dynasty of the New Kingdom Period of ancient Egypt ca. 1450 BC, as a reaction to the excesses of the religion of Amen-Ra. All modern Western Mystery Schools and the Sufis in the Middle East and Central Asia were created in response to the excesses of Orthodox Judaism, the Catholic Church and Fundamentalist Christianity, and Fundamentalist Islam.

All practices and facets of the so-called "New Age," which is really the Old Age become the Now Age, such as alchemy, the Tarot, the Kabala, astrology, numerology, sacred geometry, use of crystals, runes, dowsing, vibrational healing, reflexology, sound healing—all aspects of metaphysics and mysticism can be traced to dynastic and predynastic Khemit. All of these techniques and practices were attempts to preserve the ancient wisdom presented by the oral tradition of the great wisdom keepers of Africa, Asia and all indigenous peoples. The irony is that all these traditions and practices, and the Mystery Schools have had to go "underground" and keep their membership and techniques **hidden** in the last few thousand years to avoid persecution from the established religious orthodoxy—who themselves kept the wisdom hidden in the spirit of the Age of Amen.

The information presented in this and previous chapters of this book have been in preparation for the next chapter—that of the pure wisdom teachings of the indigenous oral tradition of Khemit as presented to me by Abd'El Hakim.

CHAPTER ELEVEN

THE SOURCE: ANCIENT KHEMITIAN WISDOM TEACHINGS

Heaven and earth last forever.
Why do heaven and earth last forever?
They are unborn,
So ever living.
The sage stays behind, thus he is ahead.
He is detached, thus at one with all.
Through selfless action, he attains fulfillment.

—Lao Zi, *Dao de Jing*

I N JANUARY OF 2003, I had the great opportunity to return to Egypt as a presenter at the "Mysteries of the Spirit" Conference held at the Mena House at the foot of the Giza Plateau. I had not seen Hakim since October of 1999 and there had been virtually no contact between us in the intervening three years. After checking into the Mena House, I rushed by cab to the village of Nazlet el Samman to see him again. It was a glorious reunion with much hugging and crying. I presented him with a signed copy of *The Land of Osiris* and he was very pleased with my written exposition of his preliminary teachings—this with his basic distrust of the written word.

Over the next six days I spent every possible free moment in extended discussions with him on many topics—such as the Cataclysm of 9500 BC, early dynastic religion, and Akhenaten and Moses and the rise of Judaism, all of which have found their way into the previous chapters of this book. But it was the profound conversations that we had in the last two days I was with him that became the basis, the *raison d'etre*, of this whole book.

Hakim had always emphasized to me the importance of certain numbers in his oral tradition, especially the numbers five and forty-two. Forty-two was the number of the original tribes of ancient Khemit, also reflected in the forty-two judges of Osiris in later dynastic funerary scenes, the forty-two declarations of the Negative Confession, the forty-two pieces that Osiris/Wizzer was torn into in the oldest versions of the Set-Osiris myth, the forty-two steps of stairs leading into temples, etc. The number five was reflected in the five stages of the Sun, five stages of consciousness, five stages of each cycle of human history, and the five Pers (houses). In *The Land of Osiris,* I mentioned four Pers; *Per-Aa,* The High House and the origin of the word Pharaoh; *Per-Ka,* the origin of the tomb; *Per-Ba,* the origin of the temple; and *Per-Neter,* the origin of the word pyramid. When we were on tour together at the site of Dahshur in October of 1999, Hakim mentioned to our group that there had been five Pers and he began to name them. He paused after the four just mentioned and seemed perplexed that he had forgotten the fifth one. He looked at me for help and I joked that he had not told me the fifth one—that it must be the hidden or secret one.

Later when we went to the Temple of Horus at Edfu, I found the fifth Per on the walls of the temple and showed it to Hakim and he was very pleased. It is *Per-Wir*, the House of the Wise Man or Teacher (see Figure 72). The Temple of Horus at Edfu had a section of it dedicated to the instruction of young priests—this was an early form of a university. Since the Temple at Efu was a relatively late Ptolemaic temple, and most of its inscriptions and reliefs were copied from much earlier temples and texts, the concept of Per-Wir was an ancient one going back to Old Kingdom times. The Per-Wir was the site of the original mystery schools or universities where detailed teaching and instruction of priests took place and was a separate section of the Per-Ba/Temple.

So in 1999 Hakim had given me the five Pers, and in 2003 he completed another important cycle of five for me. In 1992, when I had first met him, Hakim had given me two key pieces of his tradition, which he elaborated upon many years later. He had told me, according to his tradition, that there was no **time** and there was no **death**. Because of my metaphysical studies and initiations into several mystery school tradi-

Figure 72: Edfu. Temple of Horus. Glyph for *Per-Wir,* the House of the Wise Man or Teacher. Represents the first university. Photo by author 1999.

tions, these concepts were no great surprise to me—H. Spencer Lewis had written an article many years ago where he stated there was no absolute death—but Hakim's take on these ideas was unique. As I mentioned in *The Land of Osiris*, there was no word for death in prehistoric Khemit, only "Westing" or going to the West upon the end of the physical body. That there was no time was a teaching of many great masters and teachers—that the concepts of the past and future were illusions, that there was only the eternal now.

In 1997, Hakim returned to these themes with me and elaborated further, adding a third concept of there being no **separation**. This concept added a much deeper dimension to his teachings and I could see this thread in many other traditions. In fact, the oral tradition of the Khemitian wisdom keepers began to sound more and more like some of the tenets of Buddhism, the teachings of Siddharta of the Sakyamuni tribe, known as Gautam Buddha. No separation implies there is no real difference between the physical and non-physical worlds—indeed, that the physical is an illusion, as is taught in Vedantism, in the Vedas of the Hindu religion. These ideas have now found fruit in the latest theories of quantum and theoretical physics—that at the quantum and subatomic levels, all objects seem to be interconnected by what mystics have called "consciousness."

I have mentioned in earlier chapters the work of quantum physicist Dr. Fred Alan Wolf. Wolf discusses the great paradox in attempting to explain these concepts. He states: "For the Buddha our big illusion arises in our attaching significance to the I."[1] Hakim's teachings seem to be the foundation of much of the Buddha's thoughts—that if there is no separation, then there is no individual, no "I." Hakim returned to these ideas with me in 1998 and 1999, further stating that the early Hanuti/Priests of Khemit, realizing that there was no time, no death and no separation, used the fears of the people falling from high consciousness to create early religion based upon the illusory ideas of time, death and separation.

The fulfillment of these teachings was the basis of the profound conversations I had with Hakim in January of 2003. Upon seeing our early work now in print with *The Land of Osiris*, Hakim presented to me the last two pieces of this basic foundation of his teaching— that there is no **soul** and there is no **God.**

These last two concepts are truly the great paradox that I present in this book. They are also the reason I have presented all the material and ideas before this. Now, how to explain what can only be experienced directly and not understood through books or the written word? To say that there is no soul would tend to make one believe that there is nothing about us that remains or continues once we cease our physical existence— but, again, if there is no death, then that itself is another paradox. Hakim's insistence that there is no soul must be understood in how the word or concept of soul has been commonly understood. I wrote about the Per-Ba being the House of the Soul, the temple, but if there is no soul, how can there be a house for it?

Per-Ba is also translated as House of the Spirit, and that may be much closer to what Hakim means. I discussed the glyph *Nefer* in my first book and I return to it now for a deeper understanding. Nefer is Harmony, and the glyph itself actually represents the trachea, larynx, pharynx and lungs—the area of the human body in which we produce sound. This brings in the ancient Rosicrucian teaching that **All is Vibration,** and that understanding is the essence of this teaching. Hakim was clear to me that the tongue is not included in Nefer, that the "tongue can lie," but the vibrations produced as sound are pure, "The Truth." This area of the human body that can produce sound, Nefer, accentuates vibrations that are omnipresent throughout the universe, on all levels, from the gross to the subatomic, the visible and invisible. These vibrations of sound have now been demonstrated as being a physical definition of "God," not a being, but a quality of all there is—and these vibrations are neither created nor can they be destroyed, and continue to exist after we have dropped the body—this is the essence of Spirit.

Then the question arises—another paradox—is not Spirit the same as Soul? Hakim has stated to me that it is the way the word soul had been used by the early Hanuti/Priests, defined as individual spirit or consciousness, the "I" that his teachings say does not exist. This is a difficult understanding for many to achieve—not only for religious people, but also for many in the so-called New Age community—that there is no individual soul or consciousness. Again, this idea is compatible to the teachings of the Buddha; he stated that there is no such thing as an individual soul, only universal awareness.[2] It does come down to semantics for it is very popular in metaphysical circles in the present day to use terms such as "higher self," "soul personality," "soul retrieval," "oversoul." If there is no soul, then all these terms are illusions. But an important concept then to discuss would be that of reincarnation or past lives, another topic very popular in the present day—and another paradox.

Buddhism states there is no soul, but speaks of reincarnation, as does Vedantism. Hakim himself has spoken of "previous life cycles," but his tradition states that there is no individual soul—so **who** is it that reincarnates? It may be that people are accessing the Collective Unconscious of Carl Jung or the Akashic records of ancient India—where one can access the impressions, memories or vibrational energies of people who have lived before and one can believe they actually were that person in a past life. The Rosicrucians teach the concept of "projection," that one can project one's consciousness anywhere and to any time and "see" through the eyes of one who has lived before and believe they were that person. Barbara Hand Clow has even written about co-existing parallel lives—that our present consciousness may be inhabiting another physical form in another star system or dimension contiguous with our lives here on earth.

At one time, consistent with my metaphysical and mystical studies and initiations, I believed that I had many past lives—several as Egyptian priests, a Greek student of Socrates, a Knights Templar, a Rosicrucian both during the Renaissance in Europe and in the time of Sir Francis Bacon, a Mayan priest working with Crystal Skulls, a Samurai in ancient Japan, among others. But now the concept of reincarnation is not so clear-cut to me. If there is no I, no individual soul, then those thoughts were all some sort of ego projection, illusions, and I may have identified with certain individuals whose lives and time periods I was interested in or attracted to, or whose energies and lives were important for me in this time, or even some other reason unknown to my present consciousness.

It is still difficult to put these experiences in words—the true Tao cannot be written—and the continual use of the words "I," "individual" and "me" are artificial constructs that create a false separation and understanding. One has to have had the experience of realization that "we" are more than the body (or brain), that there is no separation of the physical and non-physical, or physics and metaphysics, that the I or ego is an illusion, and that "we" all have an essence that was never created and therefore cannot be destroyed. Only by experience can the concepts of no time, no death, no separation and no soul be comprehended and really understood.

The concept of no God is by far the most difficult to explain and fully understand. A first response would be to say that this idea is just Atheism, but this understanding would be simplistic and incorrect. It would also be incorrect to say this stance is one of Agnosticism—a stance I held for many years—that of not addressing the question of Deity. But we do address it. Again it comes down to semantics, the word "God" itself, and how it has been used and interpreted. In the dictionary god with a small "g" is defined as: "A being of more than human attributes and power; a deity." God with a capitol "G" is: "The Supreme Being, the eternal and infinite Spirit, Creator and Sovereign of the universe."[3]

It is obvious that if we accept the concept of no separation, then most of the previous definitions must be rejected—there cannot be a being separate from everything else, no Creator separate from Creation or the uncreated. Some past masters have stated that "God" is not a being but "beingness." The Rosicrucians use terms such as "Supreme Mind" and "The Cosmic," instead of the religiously loaded term of God. However, one part of the definition given above for God, "The eternal and infinite Spirit," does come closest perhaps to the concept I am trying to elucidate here. I must try to make it clear that what I am trying to say, to express the basis of the indigenous wisdom of ancient Khemit, is **not** atheism. I have said that the essence of Nefer, the omnipresent vibrations that we utilize to produce sound, is neither created nor can it be destroyed. As I previously mentioned, this can be thought of as a definition of Deity or God, not as a being but a quality. So it simply comes down to an understanding of what Hakim is saying by "there is no God"—that there is no being we call God, separate from humanity, all of creation, all of the uncreated, visible and invisible. But "Godness," "Spirit," "Consciousness," "Awareness," "Isness"—all is vibration, infinite without beginning or end, and cannot be defined by intellect but only experienced.

This may sound like philosophical meanderings or "New Age woo-woo" to the religiously entrenched minds stuck on the concept of a patriarchal grandfather figure, usually white, sitting on a throne in heaven, judging and directing his "children" in all things He has manifested from Himself. But this is the point; to continually accept, only on faith, the idea that we are separate from Spirit, from a "creator" or "God," will perpetually keep humanity as children and in the Age of Amen, in darkness.

When Hakim speaks of The Awakening, it is to state that we have been asleep, or rather he has said we are currently "crippled," only using five out of 360 senses because we have been taught that we have a limited consciousness with only five accessible senses, and remain stuck in mindsets brought on by the low end of the cycle, the Age of Amen. But it is without judgment or blame, just the fact of the natural cycles of existence. While the early Hanuti/Priesthood set about to create religions, and initiate and maintain a cycle of darkness and "hidden teachings," the masters of the oral tradition hid in caves—keeping themselves "hidden" from the persecution of those who wanted all humanity to remain in darkness—and perpetuated the Light in small, tight groups of adepts, sages and their initiates.

Just as the five cycles of the sun represent not only daily cycles, but cycles of human consciousness and awareness, cycles of prehistory and history, so do the five aspects of the indigenous oral tradition represent a totality of understanding. It cannot be enough to say there is no time and no death—it must also be stated and comprehended that there is no separation, which inevitably leads to the understanding that there is no soul or no God. But this is not a teaching of despair or pessimistic surrender to an empty existence. On the contrary, it is a teaching of hope, liberation, joy and fulfillment. In stating there is no death and no God, then it follows that there is no reason to fear—and no reason for the violence, prejudice and ignorance that has pervaded the last five thousand plus years of the current cycle as a result of the fall from total consciousness.. These teachings, given freely and openly now by masters such as Abd'El Hakim, give us a solid foundation to prepare for The Awakening, the new Dawn of Kheper finally upon us.

I had the great fortune to return to Egypt for another conference/tour in November 2004, which also featured as presenters my great friends and colleagues, Christopher Dunn, David Hatcher Childress and Mark Amaru Pinkham. I was able to stay on for five extra days after the tour was over and live in Hakim's village and spend extensive time with him and family in deep conversation covering the various topics in this book. Hakim was supremely confident that the cycle of Amen is coming to a close and that no one or nothing can stop or prevent the shift in consciousness that The Awakening will bring. Again, it seems "darkest before the dawn" is an adequate expression to represent the last couple of hundred years of humanity's history. Hakim said to me, "We are growing every day," to indicate that people are coming into consciousness at a continued rate all around the world, and current events like wars, plagues, earth changes such as major earthquakes, tsunamis, etc.—all apparent tragedies featuring great suffering and loss of lives— are events that will bring people together and raise consciousness and are indications of the end of a cycle and signal the coming Dawn.

We also discussed this book and the misunderstanding and criticism I fully expect to receive by those entrenched in religious fundamentalism, and those who cannot let go of the illusion of individual soul and a personality of "God." Hakim reassured me that there is also nothing to fear—indeed, if we truly believe there is no time or death, then there cannot be anything to fear—and our work and the indigenous oral tradition that we are presenting will be understood and provide a framework for

Figure 73: Giza. Abd'El Hakim Awyan in his home in the village of Nazlet el Samman, near the Giza Plateau. Photo by author 2004.

those actively seeking to raise their consciousness and welcome the new Dawn (see Figure 73)

The Dalai Lama, the spiritual and secular leader of Tibetan Buddhism, was once asked if he remembered all his past lives as the other thirteen Dalai Lamas before him. He responded by saying, "Of course I do, but this one now is the only one that is important." He then refused to discuss further the idea of past lives and reincarnation. The oral indigenous tradition of Khemit, as taught by Abd'El Hakim, is being reflected by many other masters teaching today and here is another example:

Thought for the Day

The cosmos does not exist. It is an illusion. It never is, has been or will be. The creation of the cosmos, the dissolution of the cosmos, these billions of individuals emerging and merging, all this is but a dream. There is no separation of individualized soul (Jivatma). How can there be billions of Jivatmas? There is only one Indivisible Complete Absolute. Like the one Sun reflected as a billion suns in a billion lakes and other water bodies, the Jivatmas are but reflections of the One in the minds that it shines upon.

Sri Sathya Sai Baba[4]

CHAPTER TWELVE

BACK TO THE DAWN

Stand before it and there is no beginning.
Follow it and there is no end.
Stay with the ancient Tao,
Move with the present.

—Lao Zi, *Dao de Jing*

N HIS BOOK *The Spiritual Universe,* physicist Fred Alan Wolf attempts to use the latest work in quantum and theoretical physics to address the topics of spirit, soul, matter and self. At the end of his book, he presents these definitions: spirit—the vibrations of nothing, soul—the reflection of spirit at nodes of time, matter—the reflections of spirit at nodes of space, and self—the reflection of soul in matter.[1] The interesting thing is that Wolf has been to Egypt and has had as his tour guide my teacher, Abd'El Hakim. He even mentions some of the teachings of Hakim in his book.

But with Hakim's presentations of the ancient Khemitian wisdom teachings that there is no time, no death, no separation, no soul and no God, almost all of Wolf's definitions fall away and only the definition of spirit remains—the vibrations of nothing. This definition itself is a paradox and the basis of the dilemma that Wolf addresses throughout his book—how something can be created out of nothing.

A paradox is defined in the dictionary as "a tenet contrary to received opinion, an assertion or sentiment seemingly contradictory, or opposed to common sense, but that may be true in fact."[2] The use of passages from the *Dao de Jing* in this book has exemplified the essence of paradox, attempting to put into writing that which cannot be written down.

Spirituality and religion are also a paradox, seemingly the same or at least similar, perceived as the same by the "received opinion" of academic theory, but in essence quite different. According to Wolf's definition, spirituality is the practice or study of the vibrations of nothing—a clear paradox that opposes common sense. Religion, defined as a system that binds together, back to God, has been responsible for more divisive thinking and actions among human beings than any other system—again a clear paradox. The history of almost all religions in the past five thousand years, especially that of Judaism, Christianity and Islam, has been that of wars, violence, torture, intolerance, ignorance, prejudice, racism, sexism, and cruelty—hardly the evidence of a system designed to bind people together.

But the paradox therein is that the underlying spirituality of all modern religions is an unassailable remnant of a previous time, a previous level of consciousness and awareness where these divisions did not exist. Therefore, I have found a need to create a separation between spirituality and religion, even knowing that separation itself is an illusion, because academic theory has seen the two as the same and inevitable facets of the human condition.

Religion was the descendant of spirituality, the descent of practices without rules, definitions and textual frameworks—the realization of spirit being the essence and matter being an illusion. The development of religion devolved spirituality into a business, a system of control and restrictions forced upon spirit. But even these statements I have made will be grossly misunderstood—for although, in my opinion, religion has done much more harm to people in the last five thousand years than it has done good, the good is very profound and significant. The systems based on the life experiences and teachings of enlightened masters, Christs and Messiahs, avatars and bodhisattvas, gurus and sages have provided sparks of light amidst the cycle of darkness, and provided access to the inexorable spirit/spirituality and led us to the verge of a new cycle of awareness.

My first book, *The Land of Osiris*, was an introduction to the indigenous tradition as taught to me by Abd'El Hakim Awyan, and the first opportunity to put into book form the results of my over 30 years of research into ancient Egypt. But this current work is actually the culmination of all the major interests I have personally followed throughout my whole life. It was Freud's *Moses and Monotheism* that I first discovered in 1968, which triggered the interest in the king Akhenaten and his possible connection to Moses and Judaism. My great interest in Akhenaten led me to the Rosicrucian Order, AMORC, in 1977, and their esoteric tradition of originating and connecting all the way back to the 18th Dynasty of New Kingdom Egypt.

German Egyptologist Jan Assman had characterized Akhenaten as a "man of history" and Moses as a "man of memory," but I believe Moses was also a man of history and we can see evidence of that history. Alternative Egyptologist Ahmed Osman believes that Akhenaten and Moses were one and the same person, and the mythology of Moses was based on the life of this extraordinary king of ancient Egypt. While I would agree that aspects of Akhenaten's teaching and life experiences were incorporated into the mythology of Moses, there may have been an actual "Moses." There is a tradition in mythology that certain individuals are a composite of several actual persons; the myth of Moses was such a case. Akhenaten had two viziers, two men, who were close to the king and avid followers of his teachings.

One of these viziers, with the title Ramose (Ra-Mesu) who had the "ear" of the king and was a close advisor and confidante of Akhenaten, may have been the source of the Greek name "Mosis" or Moses. The other vizier, with the title Egyptologists have recognized as Aper-El, translated by Hakim as Ibra-El, may also have been incorporated into the myth of Moses and may be the link to the Semitic "Moses," bringing the Hebrew tradition of ancient Khemit together with the Semitic tradition of El which led to a fusion with other traditions to form the modern religion of Judaism.

The Exodus, therefore, was not a "revolt of slaves" that has lingered in the popular imagination for thousands of years, nor were the Hebrews originally a Semitic people "sojourning" in Khemit for 400 some odd years. I agree with Gary Greenberg that the original Hebrews were an African, not Semitic or Asian, people—as stated in the oral tradition of Abd'El Hakim. The original Hebrews were not a part of the period of Khemitian history with the so-called Hyksos, "the Chieftains of a foreign hill country," thought to have been Semites linked to the Amorites of the Old Testament of the Bible. According to Abd'El Hakim and his tradition, the Hyksos were native Khemitians who may have adopted Semitic titles, but were known in the oral tradition as "metal-workers," early geologists. The Exodus was a political-spiritual expulsion of the followers of Akhenaten, the Hebrew-Atenists, who left Khemit partially after the death or downfall of Akhenaten, en mass after the death of the King Horemheb, the "Pharaoh of the Oppression," and during the brief reign and vigorous pursuit by the King Ramses I, the "Pharaoh of The Exodus."

The excellent scholarship of Ahmed Osman has established that Akhenaten's maternal grandfather, Yuya, was indeed Joseph, one of the Patriarchs of Judaism, and that a link was formed between the Hebrew-Aten tradition and the Semitic-El-Yahweh tradition during the 18th Dynasty of New Kingdom Egypt. This bond was further forced and strengthened in the almost one hundred years between The Exodus and the formation of the Kingdom of Israel—and the Seshu-Aten, the people of Aten, known by Egyptologists as the Shasu, became Isra-El, the Servants of El.

Many researchers have taken different stances as to the origins of advanced civilizations in prehistory. As I have mentioned, Hakim is a staunch Afrocentrist, his tradition orally records Africa as the birthplace of humanity and all races of humans, including Caucasians, or more correctly the white race. He states the beginning of the current full cycle started 65,000 years ago, with the contention that civilizations may go even further back in African prehistory. Other traditions speak of great ancient civilizations arising in Asia, India, Australia and Polynesia. Many current researchers maintain the myth of Lemuria was an actual ancient Asian or South Pacific continent that had advanced ancient civilization hundreds of thousands of years ago. The oral traditions of other indigenous people state that "they" or their ancestors were the "original" people or civilization—such as the Hopi of North America, or the Polynesians of the South Pacific, or the pre-Vedic and Tamil traditions of South India and Sri Lanka, or many different peoples of Central Asia or the Far East.

Whoever the "original" people or civilization were may be argued or debated for years, according to the biases of different researchers discovering all these various oral traditions, but what all of us would agree upon is the concept of diffusionism. The current accepted paradigm in academia of isolationism, that cultures arrived at similar technologies, inventions and development in relative "vacuums" without exchange and contact with one another, is in need of major revision or even total disregard. All oral traditions mention massive migrations, global exchange and travel of ancient peoples that occurred many thousands and tens of thousands of years ago.

Wherever ancient civilizations "originated," many major cataclysmic events such as the one proposed in this book as having occurred 11,500 years ago caused massive migrations of humans to all reaches of the earth with all these people taking their spiritual beliefs, cultural innovations or inventions, knowledge and technologies and freely sharing them with other indigenous cultures. As for ancient Khemit, the great cataclysm of 11,500 years ago greatly impacted the climate of Northern Africa, caused once adequate rainfall to greatly decrease and the great ancient Ur Nil, the river of the west, to dry up and disappear. Many indigenous Khemitian tribes migrated out of Africa and may have gone to the Middle East where they merged with the early Semitic tribes, to Central Asia, to the Far East, and to ancient Europe and the Americas. Some of these tribes may have migrated back to Africa when the early dynastic civilization, which Egyptologists think was ancient Egypt, arose around five to six thousand years ago.

It is obvious to me that early religion in dynastic Khemit was a fusion of many different ancient spiritual traditions. That there were at least two traditions of Horus (some authors state three), Horus the Elder and Horus the Son of Isis and Osiris, demonstrates this combining of several different traditions. The key understanding that I have wanted to convey

BACK TO THE DAWN

in this book is the distinct difference between spirituality and religion. I do not see religion being "hard-wired" into the human psyche as many others do. I believe because of our genetic and cultural evolution we are pre-disposed towards spirituality, but not religion.

To assume that humanity needed to "bind together back to God" pre-supposes that people were no longer or ever together in thought and practice, and that there was a "God" to bind back to. This bias, that their individual traditions are the only correct way to bind back to God, is universal among Judeo-Christian-Islamic scholars and staunch adherents of their respective religions, and each one is sure their "God" is the only true one. The early priesthoods, deriving from the ancient shamans who engaged in rituals involving psychoactive substances and other means to experience "other worlds" or levels of awareness, were the ones who created the first religions. At first a system developed for all to experience these different "doors of perception"; religion then evolved as an elaborate means of controlling the minds of people and, as consciousness "fell" into the present cycle of darkness, created a mythology to explain who the people were, where they came from and the supposed origin of existence.

That religion became a business with priesthoods becoming powerful and wealthy should be painfully obvious to anyone with an open mind. Aligning themselves with powerful families of conquerors, the early Hanuti/Priests of Khemit created texts and mythologies with elaborate stories of the Neters, divine principles of creation and aspects of consciousness that degenerated into polytheistic gods and goddesses who controlled the newly defined concepts of soul, death and an afterlife. The early Hanuti guaranteed this warrior royalty that only they (priests) had access to and an "in" with these Neters, and with ample support—economically and politically—they (priests) would provide for the bodies and souls of the royal class after their "death," and that the royals would not only have a happy and unfettered afterlife, but would be assured of reincarnation.

Figure 74: (above) Ushabti,
ca.1400 BC.

Figure 75: (top right) Ushabti,
ca.1400 BC.

Figure 76: (right) Figurine of
Akhenaten. Created by priests
of Aten to replace ushabtis
in tombs of his followers.
Ca.1350 BC.

That this early religion was indeed a political business can be seen in the powerful and influential role the priesthood played for three thousand years of the duration of dynastic Khemit. The practice of selling the guaranteed afterlife is clearly demonstrated by the presence of what are known as *Ushabtis* in the tombs of the royalty and upper class. Ushabtis, also known as *Shawabtis*, were little statues with the visage of the deceased that were placed in the tombs along with mummified bodies (see Figures 74, 75, and 76). These ushabtis were the original selling of indulgences, that is, each ushabti would "speak" for the deceased and be responsible for absolving a sin of the dead. The more ushabtis found in a tomb, the more wealthy and influential was the deceased person—the most found, obviously, were in the tombs of kings. That the king or the royal family paid for these ushabtis, and that this practice was well under way in Middle and New Kingdom dynastic Khemit, demonstrates how religion had become a thriving business in the very early days of historical Khemit.

The indigenous teachings that there was no death nor soul would have made the whole practice of mummification to preserve the body for reoccupation by an individual soul personality ludicrous and unnecessary—so for the business of religion to prosper and grow, the original spiritual teachings had to go "underground" and be suppressed, hidden and kept only in small circles of initiates. The whole Age of Amen, The Hidden, gave rise to the business of religion and a powerful clergy had to be maintained to prevent the religious business from being exposed to the light of true spirituality. The elaborate practices of spells and rituals to the Ba, the "soul," to the Ka, the "personality," and mummifying and protecting the body for future reoccupation, the statues and images to the Neters, feast days and celebrations at specific times of the year, the development of calendars for these events—all these detailed practices were created to perpetuate the system and insure the importance of the clergy for many years to come.

Again, if there had been universal understanding and awareness that there is no time, no death, no separation, no soul and no God, then the whole business of religion would have been unnecessary and meaningless. But it should be clearly understood that these conclusions are hindsight, that this has been a natural process, that religion—although an artificial construct—is a function of the cycle in which it has arisen, the Age of Amen, and has been a universal facet of all humanity—and this is another paradox. Although there has been a degeneration of the behavior and practices of humanity throughout the current age, it still has been a progression through the natural order of the five cycles. So, indeed, there is no one (or God) to blame, just an understanding of the cycles involved.

As I was preparing the first draft of this manuscript, I received a scathing criticism of my first book from an obviously religious fundamentalist. This person strongly objected to my use of the term "Amen" and the seemingly negative connotations I had put on the word. My first reaction was that if this person objected to *The Land of Osiris* and the definition of the Age of Amen, wait until he reads **this** current work and the discussions of the evolution of religion! But it was obvious from his later comments that he would never read this second book at all, or if he somehow did or heard of it, he would totally misunderstand what was being stated here.

This strong criticism did lead me to think deeply upon how to end this book and to attempt to make the ideas more clearly understood. This person had stated that I had "trashed all Christians" and also, amazingly, had stated that Amen was symbolic of the real name of the Judeo-Christian God, Yahweh or Jehovah. This last statement made me ponder over one of the major themes of this book, that even in the midst of thousands of years of darkness, the spark of light still existed and prevailed—that even with a scathing, negative reaction to my first book, this person had, quite unintentionally, presented a profound insight with which to summarize the ideas in this current work.

I must try to make it clear at this point that even with my seemingly strong condemnation of religion in general, and Judaism, Christianity and Islam in particular, this whole process has been a natural progression with many positive results and effects upon humanity. The most important understanding is that this whole process, the degeneration of spirituality into the big business of modern day religion, has been a natural progression through the cycles we have always experienced.

Therefore, although I speak of religion in general as being a degradation and exploitation of ancient spiritual beliefs and practices, there is a need to be more specific in this explanation. It is how religion has been used that should be stressed, as opposed to the pure spark of spirituality that still remains behind all modern religions. It is fundamentalism that I see as the real divisive and detrimental factor of the last five thousand years—that although religion is defined as a system "to bind people together," it has been fundamentalism that has caused people to engage in wars, violence, prejudice, ignorance, crusades, inquisitions and propagated separatism and misunderstanding in the present day. I would define fundamentalism as being the form of religion that is totally dependant on a literal interpretation and strict adherence to the "book," the written texts such as the Torah, Bible and Koran. This overemphasis on the written word and not one's own experience is the particular failure, in my opinion, of all modern religions.

Orthodox Judaism, with its core tenet of Jews being the "Chosen People" and The Torah having been given to Moses as being the **only** "word of God"; Fundamentalist Christianity, with its tenet of having to be "born again," implying that one's original birth was tainted and impure, and total submission to Jesus as personal savior and messiah or suffer eternal damnation, and acceptance of The New Testament as the true "word of God"; Fundamentalist Islam, with its tenets of being the only way, and The Koran as the true "word of God," and all non-Muslims are "infidels" that Allah would condemn and condone being killed, tor-

FROM LIGHT INTO DARKNESS

tured or maimed in His Name—these beliefs have been the source of all crusades, religious wars, unprovoked invasions of sovereign nations, and the incredible suffering that humanity has inflicted upon all life in the last few thousand years.

I have had personal experiences with two "movements" that arose around ancient teachings and /or a teacher or master. I have mentioned my connections with the Rosicrucian Order, AMORC, and employment with them as a Staff Research Scientist. Although I was greatly impressed with the teachings of the Order and the life and work of Harvey Spencer Lewis, I became disillusioned with the spiritual quality of the officers and people running the Order. I learned that there was an "outer" and "inner" element to the Rosicrucians—that the teachings were part of what had been termed "The Invisible College," "The Great White Brotherhood," the Inner Order. The outer Order was just the organization, the mechanics of spreading the teachings, often run by very ordinary people who were not very enlightened nor particularly shining examples of the Order's principles and history, or even mystics at all. I learned to separate the teachings, The Inner Order, from the administrators, The Outer Order.

I repeated this same lesson many years later when I was living in Colorado Springs, Colorado in the mid 1990s. I went to work for Maharishi Ayurved Products International, known as MAPI—an organization based on the work and teachings of Maharishi Mahesh Yogi, the founder of Transcendental Meditation, popularly known as TM. I had always been interested in TM and the science of Ayurved, but had never joined the movement. I learned from my experience of working for MAPI that the people running the business and the movement were not the best examples of balanced, spiritual people that they were supposed to be—but my previous experience with AMORC had prepared me for this.

I bring up these two examples in order to make the point that one needs to learn to separate the teachings of a master from the movements (or religions) that arise from the experiences and teachings of the master, usually created by people who have not had the same experiences as that master. Moses, Jesus, and Mohammed presented teachings and had experiences that resulted in the formation of the three dominant religions in the world today. One needs to learn to separate the Mosaic Tradition, especially the Aten teachings of Akhenaten, from the excesses of Orthodox Judaism—the stoning of "sinners" in ancient Israel, the wholesale slaughter of native Canaanites by the invading Israelites, the rampant sexism inherent in the Torah, and the Palestinian situation today. One needs to learn to separate the experiences and teachings of Jesus from the excesses of Fundamentalist Christianity and Orthodox Roman Catholicism—the wholesale slaughter of millions of people and abuse and torture of women, in particular, during the Inquisition, Christians murdering other Christians in the Albigensian (Cathars) Crusades, and the raping and pillaging of indigenous cultures in Jesus' name. One also needs to learn to separate the experiences and teachings of the Prophet Mohammed from the murder of millions of people, massive beheadings of non-Muslims, and wholesale torture and abuse of women that has been committed by Fundamentalist Islam in the name of Allah.

This brings me back to the harangue I received from a critic of my first book. In the midst of his negativity towards me for "trashing all Christians," he made an incredible statement. He said to me that by "demeaning" the Age of Amen, I was attacking "God" as he equated the true meaning of Amen as the Judeo-Christian Deity. I was amazed to read this statement, that in the midst of his negativity, there was a spark of light and truth—for that was how I had intended to end this book. Indeed, I find myself in total agreement with this critic—that Yahweh/El/Jehovah/Allah are only thinly disguised names of Amen, The Hidden One. Those supposed religious scholars who argue that there are vast differences between our modern religions, where God has "revealed Himself" to humanity, and the "pagan" polytheistic ancient religions, such as that of ancient Egypt, are only expressing their own Judeo-Christian-Islamic biases of their religions being the "true" ones, and are not demonstrating real objective scholarship.

To say that God revealed Himself to Abraham and Moses, that Jesus was the only begotten Son of God, and that Mohammed was the only true Prophet of God, and the texts therefore produced, The Torah, The Bible and The Koran were the revealed words of God and therefore more sacred than any other books, and that this is somehow much different than the religious practices of dynastic Egypt, reflects a misunderstanding of what occurred in Khemit. All texts and scrolls produced by the Hanuti/Priesthood of dynastic Khemit were considered to be the "words of the Neters," and many kings were portrayed as having direct contact with Amen, personally chosen by Him to rule. A famous example can be seen at the temple of the female King Hatshepsut at Deir el Bahri near Luxor in Upper Egypt where the priests produced a story that Amen Himself had appeared to and mated with Hatshepsut's mother, and that she was a "divine child" chosen by Amen to rule Khemit.

This motif was repeated many times in Greek and Roman mythology where both Zeus and Jupiter took human or animal form to mate with women to produce a "divine heir." Zecharia Sitchin takes such myths from ancient Sumer and Babylon to literally interpret these tales as extra-terrestrials mating with human women. The point here is that this is a recurring theme throughout ancient mythology and there is nothing original in the story of the divine birth of Jesus.

The most important thing for me to be able to leave in the minds and hearts of everyone reading this book is that Hakim's message, the ultimate aim of his coming forth in the last twelve years or so with his wisdom tradition, is one of hope and optimism. While so many alternative researchers have disclosed the lies, distortions and manipulations of the so-called power elite in the present day to continue the state of ignorance and darkness they have immersed the bulk of humanity in, they usually offer no solutions, no hope and only lead their readers into despair in believing that nothing will change, that this is the way it has always been. The clear consistency of Hakim's teachings to me have always been without judgment, without blame—that it has been the natural order and cycle of events that will shift in the next few years

The beauty of the work of Fred Alan Wolf in using the latest ideas in quantum physics to attempt to delve into the previously isolated realms of metaphysics, to even discuss whether there is a soul or not—a revelation in itself as "hard" or physical scientists in the past left these areas to theologians, philosophers or mystics—is a shining example that consciousness is shifting and changing. My friend and colleague, Dr. Volodymyr Krasnoholovets of Ukraine, a brilliant theoretical physicist who also brings a strong spiritual and metaphysical understanding to his revolutionary concepts of quantum theory, is another outstanding example of the current change in thought that is here and will continue in the physical sciences—the merging of spirituality and science. Dr. Krasnoholovets is bringing back the concept of aether, which he labels the "space-substrate" to avoid the ridiculous criticism some of his colleagues in physics have applied to the old metaphysical idea of aether, also written ether—the idea that there is no such thing as the vacuum of space, that there are energy waves throughout all there is. This elucidation of the quantum energy dynamics and interdependence of all levels of existence is the closest thing to a scientific definition of "God" that has ever before existed in all of science.

These are all examples of what Hakim has called The Awakening. The list I provided in an earlier chapter of great scientists who were Rosicrucians and mystics—and that was only a partial list—were all brave and courageous human beings who persevered in their research and illumination despite the rigorous suppression and persecution by so-called "religious men of God," and many of these scientists gave their lives in this struggle. These illumined men and women, and many of the women have not even been properly recognized, were proof that the true light of spirituality inherent within the basic essence of all humanity can never be completely extinguished.

Let The Dawn come, let the Light shine forth—for we are the ones that Jesus predicted would be here, that Imhotep, Tiye, Amenhotep called Hapi, Akhenaten, Moses, Buddha, Lao Zi, Mary Magdalene, Yeshua ben Yosef, Mohammed, Guru Nanak, Babaji, Sir Francis Bacon, Helena Blavatsky, H. Spencer Lewis, Parmahansa Yogananda, J. Krishnamurti, Bhagwan Shri Rajneesh (Osho), Maharishi Mahesh Yogi, Sri Sathya Sai Baba, the Dalai Lama and many, many other past and present lights of humanity have paved the way for. The cosmic wake-up call has been issued. May you all experience the eternal bliss of **Peace Profound.**

POSTCRIPT

S HAPPENED during the writing of my first book, many synchronistic events occurred as I was completing a first draft of this current work. In 2004 I had the opportunity to see an independently made, low-budget film entitled *What The Bleep Do We Know?* This extraordinary cinematic wonder, not widely distributed, featured interviews with several quantum and theoretical physicists and open-minded physicians discussing many of the same themes presented in this book. The film featured, among others, Dr. Fred Alan Wolf, mentioned often in these pages—and came to many of the same conclusions presented herein about the illusory nature of what we think is solid reality.

The great theme that I took away from the movie is that what we have long considered to be the bedrock foundation of all mechanistic theories of existence, that of the solid and fixed nature of matter, is a complete illusion. Matter, in general, and subatomic quantum particles in particular, are only **possibilities**, not actualities. By the time we measure the existence of an electron, for example, it is already gone from the location in which we measured it, and has apparently "blinked" out of the space/time continuum of supposed third dimensional reality.

So all these learned scientists and physicians (and Wolf was particularly great in the film) were saying is that all existence is just a series of **possibilities** and enforced the trend that quantum and theoretical physics has now moved inexorably into *metaphysics*, although the word metaphysics was not mentioned in the film. Hakim's tradition of the teachings of the ancient Khemitians, which valued quality instead of quantity, and is very similar to Native American and other indigenous teachings, now have a scientific basis for corroboration. The understanding that quality is more important than quantity was also the basis of Rosicrucian principles. There is no separation, and as the Rosicrucian tradition declares, **All Is Vibration**; the rest of what we perceive with our limited intellectual abilities is just infinite possibilities that we determine as reality.

Another synchronistic event in 2004 was an interview I heard with Dr. Leonard Horowitz. I have met Len on several occasions, having been a presenter at various conferences with him—at one time speaking after him, and another time speaking before him. Len has written a new book, *DNA: Pirates Of The Sacred Spiral*, in which he fuses medicine, quantum physics, history and spirituality. Among other things, Len discusses how the very essence of our physical existence, determined by the sacred spiral, double helix of the DNA molecule, is intrinsically connected to both sound and water—both major themes of my first book and integral parts of Hakim's wisdom teachings.

There are many events that will occur in the next few years that will continue to be examples of the inevitable progression to greater understanding and awareness as predicted by the wisdom tradition of Abd'El Hakim. It is this great journey of enfoldment that is in store for all humanity, The Awakening, which imbues the positive and optimistic conclusions for me to end this discourse. I leave this positive affirmation, given freely by Abd'El Hakim, for all of us.

YAKHINI, YAKHINI
May you all be protected by the power of your Positive Essence forever.

HYMN OF AKHENATEN TO ATEN

LONG HYMN

Your dawning is beautiful and harmonious in the horizon,
O living Aten, Beginning of Life!
When you rise in the Eastern Horizon,
You fill every land with your beauty.
You are harmony, beauty, great, shimmering high above every land,
Your rays, they encompass the lands, all that has been made.
You are one with Ra, and you carry them away captive,
You bind all with Love,
Though you appear far away, your rays are upon earth,
Though you are on high, your impressions create each day.

When you set in the western horizon of the sky,
The earth is in darkness as those in the West,
All sleep in their chambers,
Their heads are covered,
Their nostrils are stopped,
And no one sees another,
While all things are no more,
Which are under their minds,
And they know it not.
Every lion comes forth from his den,

All serpents and their sting,
Darkness.
The world is in silence,
For Creation then rests in the horizon.
Bright is the earth when Light rises in the horizon,
When it is fulfilled as Aten in the day.
You drive away the darkness,
You send forth your rays.
All lands are in rejoicing,
Awake and aware and on their feet.
You have raised all up,
The body is bathed and covered completely.
All uplift their spirits in adoration of the Dawn,
Then all are able to contemplate and fulfill each day.

All cattle rest in their pastures,
All trees and plants flourish.
All birds fly about in their marshes,
Their wings are uplifted in adoration.
All sheep dance in their fields,
All winged things fly in rejoicing.
They live when Light shines upon them,
The ships sail upstream and downstream.
Every highway is open because of the Light,
The fish in the river leap before the Light,
Your rays are in the midst of the great green sea.

Essence of the egg in women,
Maker of the seed in man.
Giver of life to the child in the body of his mother,
Soothing all that they may not weep.
Giving sustenance even in the womb,
Giver of the breath of life to all living things.
When one is born—on the day of birth,

The mouth is opened to cry out in joy,
All necessities are supplied to live.

When the fledgling in the egg sings out,
The breath of Life is given to begin life.
The energy is provided to begin life,
To burst forth from the egg,
To sing out with the joy of birth.

How manifold are the things of life,
Many are hidden from our eyes.
O sole principle of life, the powers of fulfillment,
The earth was created according to love.
When all was uncreated in essence,
All men, all cattle, large and small.
All that is upon the earth,
All go about with divine movement.
All that are on high,
That fly about with wings.
Even foreign lands such as Syria and Kush,
And the land of Khemit.
Every man has his place in the world,
All necessities are supplied in abundance.
Everyone has all their physical and spiritual needs,
All physical days are numbered.
People have diverse languages and speech,
There are various forms of physical appearance,
For variation is an aspect of creation.

There is a Nile above as there is a Nile below,
All exists according to Divine Plan.
Life continues amongst all peoples,
For life exists for its own meaning.
Light is the Lord of all, dwelling therein,

Light is the Lord of all lands, rising for everyone,
Light as the Sun, great in majesty.
All distant lands,
All experience Light for their lives.
There is a celestial Nile in the Cosmos,
It provides Light for all.
It makes waves upon the mountains,
Like the great green seas,
Providing the water of life for all villages.

How excellent are all the designs of creation,
For It is Eternal.
There is a Nile in the sky for all humanity,
And it sustains the cattle of all countries,
But our Nile comes from the Neters for Khemit.

The rays of pure light nourish every garden,
When Light appears all flourishes.
All grow and maintain with Divine Light,
The seasons come and go.
Divine Order of manifested creation,
Winter to cool the earth.
And the heat of summer to give warmth.

Each day with its divine cycles,
The glory of life is there to behold.
The shimmering Light as the form of Living Aten,
Dawning, shining, glowing—going and returning.
The beauty and harmony of millions of forms,
Emanating through Divine Light.
Cities, towns, and all tribes, highways and rivers,
The opened eyes can behold the Divine Light,
For the spirit of Aten is all over the earth.

The Light is in my heart,
No one seems to recognize this.
Save the one who is the Shadow of the Wiser,
He has achieved some degree of understanding.
He is able to perceive the Divine Plan,
The world is there for all to see.
For all are made accordingly,
For in the Light all shall live.
For in the darkness it is hidden,
The length of Life is eternal.
Men shall know it if they perceive it,
When men live in harmony, they shall know.
When they remain in darkness all deeds shall be in vain,
And remain hidden in the West.

This world has been established by Light,
And only exists for Children of Light.
All come forth by means of Divine Love,
The King; The Precious of All Lands.
Living in Divine Truth, Precious of All Lands,
Nefer-Khepru-Re—Harmony of Dawn and Noon.
Child of Light, dwelling in Truth, Holder of royal design,
Akhenaten, The Shadow of the Wiser, Reflection of Enlightenment who
has endured.
And for the Woman of Power, his Beloved,
Mistress of All Lands, Nefer-Nefru-Aten, Nefertiti.
Harmony upon Harmony of The Wiser, She who walks in Harmony,
She lives and flourishes forever.

Retranslated by the author—based on the translation by J.H.
Breasted in *Development of Religion and Thought in Ancient Egypt*,
324-328.

PSALM 104

Bless the Lord, O my soul, O Lord my God,
You are very great, you are clothed with honor and majesty;

Who covers yourself with light as with a garment;
Who stretches out the heavens like a curtain;

Who lays the beams of his chambers in the waters;
Who makes the clouds his chariot, who walks upon the wings of the wind;

Who makes his angels spirits; his ministers a flaming fire;

Who laid the foundations of the earth, that it should not be
removed forever;

You covered it with the deep as with a garment,
The waters stood above the mountains;

At your rebuke they fled; at the voice of
Your thunder they ran away;

They go up by the mountains; they go down
By the valleys into the place which you have created for them;

You have set a boundary that they may not pass over;
That they turn not again to cover the earth;

He sends the springs into the valleys, which run among the hills;

They give drink to every beast of the field;
The wild asses quench their thirst;

By them shall the birds of the heaven have their

Habitation, which sing among the branches;

He waters the hills from his chambers;
The earth is satisfied with the fruit of your works;

He causes the grass to grow for the cattle, and herbs for the service
of man, that he may bring forth food out of the earth;

And wine that makes glad the heart of man, and oil to make his face to
shine, and bread which strengthens men's heart;

And the trees of the Lord are full of sap; the cedars of Lebanon, which he
has planted;

Where the birds make their nests; as for the stork, the fir trees are her house;

The high hills are a refuge for the wild goats, and the rocks for the conies;

He appointed the moon for seasons, the sun knows his going down;

You made darkness and it is night, where in all the beasts of the forest
creep forth;

The young lions roar after their prey, and seek their meat from God.

The sun rises, they gather themselves together, and lay down in
their dens;

Man goes forth with his work and his labor until the evening;

O Lord, how manifold are thy works; in wisdom you have made the
earth full of your riches;

So is the great and wide sea, wherein are things creeping innumer
able, both small and great beasts;

There go the ships; there is that leviathan, whom you have made to
play therein;

There wait upon you, that you may give them their meat in due season;

That you give them that which they gather; you open your hand, they are filled with good;

You hide your face, they are troubled; you take away their breath, they die and return to their dust;

You send forth your spirit, they are created, and you renew the face of the earth;

The glory of the Lord shall endure forever;
The Lord shall rejoice in his works;

He looks upon the earth, and it trembles,
He touches the hills, and they smoke;

I will sing unto the Lord as long as I live,
I will sing praise to my God while I have my being,
My meditation of him shall be sweet,
I will be glad in the Lord;

Let the sinners be consumed out of the earth,
And let the wicked be no more,
Bless you the Lord, O my soul,
Praise be to the Lord.

Based on the translation in the Standard Gideons Bible.

THE JEWISH
PATRIARCHS

Many authors, such as Ralph Ellis, Gary Greenberg and Ahmed Osman, have attempted to link the Patriarchs and kings of Jewish mythology and history with personages of dynastic Khemitian history and mythology.

Ellis believes the Hebrew Kings David and Solomon were myths based on the lives of actual Khemitian kings.[1] Greenberg, as I have mentioned, believes the story of Jacob wrestling with an angel, or even God Himself, that is found in Genesis of The Torah was based on the mythology of Osiris and Set. Greenberg further believes that **all** the Jewish Patriarchs were myths based on Khemitian mythology and were not real Semitic people.[2]

I have discussed the theories of Ahmed Osman in this regard. Both Hakim and I believe that Osman is essentially correct in his assertions that the myth of the Patriarch Joseph was based on the life of Yuya, the maternal grandfather of King Akhenaten. Osman has further stated that he not only believes Akhenaten and Moses were the same person—which I personally partially support, but also believe there "was" a Moses (Akhenaten's Vizier Ramose=Greek "Mosis")—but Osman also believes that the story of Joshua, who succeeded Moses as the leader of the Israelites and led them into Canaan according to The Torah, was actually based upon the life of Tutankhamen, perhaps the younger brother or son of Akhenaten.[3]

Hakim agrees that many of the myths of the Patriarchs were based on the actual lives of the Khemitian kings or on Khemitian mythology. He further added to me that the king of ancient Khemit who had the title *Seshonk* was the basis of the name Yitzchak in Hebrew, Isaac in English.

But the most interesting information Hakim has presented to me concerns the first Jewish Patriarch, the supposed "father" of the Hebrew people, Abraham. In Hebrew the name is pronounced as "Av-ra-hum," supposedly related to *Abba*, father in Hebrew, *Abu* in Arabic. But the Arabic rendering of the name is *Ibrahim*, Ib-ra-him. Ib-ra is a title, as I mentioned in *The Land of Osiris*, and was also the Khemitian term for obelisk, "The Heart of Ra," a beam of light from the Sun at noon. But as I mentioned in an earlier chapter, the second Vizier of Akhenaten had the title *Ib-Ra-El* (Aper-el to Egyptologists). Was Ibra-El not only part of the basis for the myth of Moses, but also considered a "father" of the Israelites and, later, the Jewish people? Could the title Ib-Ra, combined with the Hebrew masculine plural ending *him*, be the basis for the Arabic name Ibrahim, Ibrahim=Abraham?

ALCHEMY
AND THE WHITE
POWDER GOLD

The definitive book on alchemy and its relationship to and derivation from ancient Khemit has yet to be written. As I mentioned in *The Land Of Osiris*, one of the modern Arabic terms for Egypt is "Al Khem," obviously the source of the term alchemy, the arts and sciences of *Khem*, the ancient term for Khemit.

Many people have become interested in the term "White Powder Gold," first mentioned by David Hudson and popularized by author Laurence Gardner. Gardner speaks of White Powder Gold being utilized by Khemitian kings for longevity, claiming it was produced in temples by alchemical processes.[1] Some people believe White Powder Gold was produced in the Great Pyramid, but we reject this idea as the energy produced in the pyramid, as per the Giza Power Plant theory of Christopher Dunn, would have been so powerful as to make it impossible for it to be used as a working laboratory. No one would have been able to enter inside while it was active.

Gardner speaks of a Khemitian term he believes to refer to the White Powder Gold; unable to read glyphs to any extent himself, he relies on the translation of Egyptologists and presents the words *Melfkat* or *Mefkat* as the word. In our discussions on the subject, Hakim rejected the idea that this term could refer to any form of gold. Hakim stated the term Gardner is referring to would be *Maskat*, which would refer to metal, but ground-up metal that was used to adorn the eyes in ancient Khemit, and this word is the source of the term "mascara."

Hakim is definite that the Khemitian term *Neb*, incorrectly translated by Egyptologists as "Lord," meant **precious** and also referred to gold. I mentioned in *The Land of Osiris* that the term *Neb Tawy*—one of the epithets for the king—has been mistranslated by Egyptologists to mean "Lord of the Two Lands," while Hakim maintains the meaning is "Precious of All Lands."

Hakim has taught me that Neb as precious would be a general term—all that was considered precious would fall under its rubric; therefore, gold as a precious metal would be Neb. Hakim further added that the area of ancient Khemit where most of its gold was found and mined, along with other items considered precious such as ivory and ebony, was called "Nebya"—today known as Nubia.

Gardner also talks about a temple in the Sinai region known as Serabit-el-Khadim, where in the 1880s Flinders Petrie found a large amount of white powder. Gardner has stated, without the material ever, to my knowledge, having been tested or analyzed, that this powder was White Powder Gold, produced in the temple for the kings. Hakim again denies this assertion, stating that according to his tradition that temple was a site for healing and the white powder found there by Petrie was lime, calcium hydroxide [$Ca(OH)_2$], a by product of the abundant limestone utilized by the ancient Khemitians. Hakim maintains the lime was used in the healing process of the temple. Interestingly, the temple at Serabit-el-Khadim is also mentioned by Ahmed Osman as a possible place Akhenaten stayed in refuge when he was exiled by the followers of Amen. Did he stay there because he knew it was a famous healing temple and an excellent haven for his exile?

ENDNOTES

CHAPTER ONE

[1] All the quotes from the *Dao de Jing* in this book are from *Tao Te Ching* translated by Gia Fu-Feng and Jane English.

[2] Robert Crawford, *What Is Religion?*, 3.

[3] Ibid, 3.

[4] Ibid, 7.

[5] Julien Ries, *The Origins of Religions*, 7.

[6] Ibid, 7.

[7] Ibid, 10.

[8] Geoffrey Parrinder, *World Religions*, 11.

[9] Ries, *The Origin of Religions*, 18.

[10] Ibid, 10.

CHAPTER TWO

[1] Michael Cremo and Richard Thompson, *The Hidden History of The Human Race*.

[2] Fred Alan Wolf, *The Spiritual Universe*, 72.

[3] Ibid, 72.

CHAPTER THREE

[1] Graham Hancock, *Fingerprints Of The Gods*, 423.

[2] D.S. Allan and J.B. Delair, *Cataclysm!*, 12.

[3] Barbara Hand Clow, *Catastrophobia*, 57.

CHAPTER FOUR

[1] Allan and Delair, *Cataclysm!*, x.

[2] Clow, *Catastrophobia*, 1.

[3] Ibid, 257.

[4] Christopher Dunn, *The Giza Power Plant*, 39-42.

[5] Peter Tompkins, *Secrets Of The Great Pyramid*, 101.

[6] Dunn, *The Giza Power Plant*, 165-167.

CHAPTER FIVE

[1] Andrew Collins, *Gods Of Eden*, 327-347.

[2] Allan and Delair, *Cataclysm!*, 17.

[3] Peter Bros, "The Case for the Flood", 67.

[4] Michael Hoffman, *Egypt Before The Pharaohs*, 16.

[5] Ibid, 17.

[6] Clow, *Catastrophobia*, 60-68.

CHAPTER SIX

[1] James H. Breasted, *Development of Religion And Thought In Ancient Egypt*, 4.

[2] Siegfried Morenz, *Egyptian Religion*, xv.

[3] Reis, *The Origin of Religions*, 106.

[4] See articles by Dr. Volodymyr Krasnoholovets on the Websites www.gizapyramid.com and www.inerton.cjb.net.

[5] Hakim has stated that the original term was *Her-Hor*, "The Face Of The Falcon". Hakim has further stated that his tradition does not support the idea of "invaders," foreign tribes who conquered Khemit, but rather a series of compromises of indigenous tribal families with migrating tribal families that led to kingship and the so-called "dynastic" time periods.

CHAPTER SEVEN

[1] R.A. Schwaller de Lubicz, *Sacred Science*, 178, 283-286.

[2] Stephen S. Mehler, "Lifting The Veil," 38-41.

[3] Margaret Murray, *The Splendor That Was Egypt*, 126.

CHAPTER EIGHT

[1] Those exceptions are noted in the text; some of them are *Son of the Sun* by Savitri Devi, *Moses And Akhenaten* by Ahmed Osman, *The Moses Mystery* by Gary Greenberg and *True Esoteric Traditions* by M. Dale Palmer.

[2] Erik Hornung, *Akhenaten and the Religion of Light*, 1-3.

[3] I would recommend Osman's *Moses And Akhenaten* for the best discussion of the co-regency between Akhenaten and his father, Amenhotep III.

[4] Ahmed Osman, *Moses And Akhenaten*, 150-154.

[5] Hornung, *Akhenaten and the Religion of Light*, 52.

[6] Ibid, 126.

[7] Ibid, 27.

[8] Ibid, 8, 15-18.

[9] Jan Assman, *Moses, The Egyptian*, 2.

[10] Sigmund Freud, *Moses and Monotheism*, 4-5.

[11] Assman, *Moses, The Egyptian*, 149.

[12] Ibid, 111.

[13] Gary Greenberg, *The Moses Mystery*, 167-206.

[14] It should be obvious to the reader that I have very low opinions of the views and writings of most Egyptologists about Akhenaten—the person that I feel is the most off is Donald Redford. In his book *True Esoteric Traditions*, M. Dale Palmer, who is a relative of the Masonic scholar Manly P. Hall, is very critical of Redford. Ahmed Osman, in *Moses And Akhenaten*, offers this very revealing quote of Redford concerning the writings of the "historian" Manetho: "Nor is it correct to imagine Manetho garnering **oral** traditions (emphasis mine) and committing them to writing. He would have had no use for, and probably despised, material circulating orally and not found formally represented by the temple scroll" (31). By putting his own opinion in Manetho's thoughts, Redford demonstrates his total dismissal of the indigenous oral tradtion-which characterizes Redford and his colleagues by their over-dependence on the Greek versions of the imaginary histories created by both Herodotus and Manetho. Flavius Josephus falls into the same category of creating imaginary histories to please a particular audience, the Romans.

[15] Assman, *Moses, The Egyptian*, 150.

[16] Greenberg, *The Moses Mystery*, 188.

CHAPTER NINE

[1] Greenberg, *The Moses Mystery*, 11.

[2] Peter A. Clayton, *Chronicle Of The Pharaohs*, 93.

[3] Ahmed Osman, *Stranger In The Valley Of The Kings*, 26-27.

[4] Ibid, 93, 118.

[5] Osman, *Moses And Akhenaten*, 49.

[6] Hornung, *Akhenaten and the Religion of Light*, 110-113.

[7] Greenberg, *The Moses Mystery*, 137.

[8] Ibid, 228-233.

[9] Ibid, 256.

[10] Assman, *Moses, The Egyptian*, 156.

[11] Hornung, *Akhenaten and the Religion of Light*, 12.

[12] Greenberg, *The Moses Mystery*, 144-146.

[13] Assman, *Moses, The Egyptian*, 23-24, 223.

[14] Osman, *Moses And Akhenaten*, 166-169.

[15] Greenberg, *The Moses Mystery*, 146.

[16] Osman, *Moses And Akhenaten*, 42-50, 193-197.

[17] Ibid, 47.

[18] Greenberg, *The Moses Mystery*, 152-156.

[19] Ibid, 254-255.

[20] Fabre D'Olivet, *The Hebraic Tongue Restored*, 79.

[21] Greenberg, *The Moses Mystery*, 28-29.

CHAPTER TEN

[1] I would include the books by Savitri Devi and M. Dale Palmer here.

[2] Christopher McIntosh, *The Rosy Cross Unveiled*.

[3] June Singer, *Androgyny*, 95.

[4] All historical information about H. Spencer Lewis is from *Cosmic Mission Fulfilled* by Ralph M. Lewis.

[5] H. Spencer Lewis, *Rosicrucian Questions and Answers*, 43-51.

[6] Ibid, 52-60.

[7] Ehrton, *Born of the Sun*, 254.

[8] Lewis, *Rosicrucian Questions and Answers*, 88-93.

[9] Many readers will recognize some of the individuals on Lewis' list from Dan Brown's popular novel *The Da Vinci Code*. The names Brown lists were from a document called "Les Dossiers Secret" (The Secret Dossiers) found in a French library in the 1960s. Many researchers have classified the document, which refers to a shadowy group known as "The Priory of Sion," as a modern forgery accomplished in the 1950s. Whatever the case may be concerning The Priory of Sion, Lewis' list of past Rosicrucians was first put into book form in 1928 and was presented in earlier writings of his that go back to 1918 that were based on ancient documents he was given in France in 1909.

[10] Some of the best books on The Templars, in my opinion, are David Hatcher Childress's *Pirates and The Lost Templar Fleet* and *Guardians of The Holy Grail* by Mark Amaru Pinkham.

CHAPTER ELEVEN
[1] Wolf, *The Spiritual Universe*, 142.
[2] Ibid, 144.
[3] Webster's *New Collegiate Dictionary* (second edition), 355.
[4] Posted on the official Website www.srisathyasai.org.in on Friday, July 30, 2004.

CHAPTER TWELVE
[1] Wolf, *The Spiritual Universe*, 271.
[2] Webster's *New Collegiate Dictionary* (second edition), 609.

APPENDIX C
[1] Ralph Ellis, *Solomon, Falcon of Sheba*.
[2] Greenberg, *The Moses Mystery*, 131-133, 256.
[3] Ahmed Osman, *The House of The Messiah*.

APPENDIX D
[1] Discussed in *Genesis of The Grail Kings and Lost Secrets of the Sacred Ark*.

SELECTED REFERENCES

Aldred, Cyril. *Akhenaten*. London: Abacus, 1968.

_____. *Akhenaten and Nefertiti*. London: Thames & Hudson, 1973.

Allan, D.S. and J.B. Delair. *Cataclsym!* Santa Fe: Bear & Company, 1997.

Assman, Jan. *Moses, The Egyptian*. London: Harvard University Press, 1997.

Bachofen, J.J. *Myth, Religion & Mother Right*. Princeton: Princeton University Press, 1973 (1954).

Baigent, Michael and Richard Leigh and Henry Lincoln. *Holy Blood, Holy Grail*. New York: Dell Publishing, 1983.

_____. *The Messianic Legacy*. New York: Dell Publishing, 1986.

_____ and Richard Leigh. *The Temple And The Lodge*. New York: Arcade Publishing, 1989.

_____. *The Dead Sea Scrolls Deception*. New York: Summit Books, 1991.

ben-Jochannan, Yosef. *African Origin Of The Major "Western Religions."* Baltimore: Black Classic Press, 1991 (1970).

Bentley, James. *Secrets of Mount Sinai*. New York: Doubleday & Company, 1986.

Bernard, Helene. *Great Women Initiates*. San Jose: AMORC, 1984.

Blavatsky, H.P. *The Secret Doctrine*. Vol. II. Pasadena: Theosophical University Press, 1970 (1888).

_____. *The Key To Theosophy*. Wheaton: Theosophical Publishing House, 1972 (1889).

Bloom, Harold. *The Book of J*. New York: Grove Weidenfeld, 1990.

Breasted, James H. *Development of Religion And Thought In Ancient Egypt.* Philadelphia: University of Penn. Press, 1972 (1912).

Brier, Bob. *Ancient Egyptian Magic.* New York: William Morrow & Company, 1980.

Bromage, Bernard. *The Occult Arts of Ancient Egypt.* New York: The Aquarian Press, 1960 (1953).

Bros, Peter. "The Case For The Flood." *Atlantis Rising Magazine.* No. 41, 42-43, 67-69.

Budge, E.A. Wallis. *The Egyptian Book of The Dead.* New York: Dover Publications, 1967 (1895).

_____. *Osiris.* Vol. I & II. New York:, Dover Publications, 1973 (1911).

Burgoyne Thomas H. *The Light of Egypt.* Vol. I & II. Denver: H.O. Wagner, 1965 (1889).

Ceram, C.W. *The Secret Of The Hittites.* New York: Alfred A. Knopf, 1956.

Childress, David Hatcher. *A Hitchhiker's Guide To Africa And Arabia.* Chicago: Chicago Review Press, 1984.

_____. *Lost Cities & Ancient Mysteries of Africa & Arabia.* Stelle: Adventures Unlimited Press, 1997 (1989).

_____. *Pirates & The Lost Templar Fleet.* Kempton: Adventures Unlimited Press, 2003.

Clayton, Peter A. *Chronicle of the Pharaohs.* London: Thames and Hudson, Ltd., 1994.

Clow, Barbara Hand. *Catastrophobia.* Rochester: Bear & Company, 2001.

Cohen, A. (editor). *The Soncino Chumash.* London: The Soncino Press, 1966 (1947).

Collins, Andrew. *Gods of Eden: Egypt's Lost Legacy and the Genesis of Civilization.* London: Headline, 1998.

Cottrell, Leonard. *Life Under The Pharaohs.* New York: Holt, Rinehart and Winston, 1960.

Cottrell, Maurice. *The Tutankhamen Prophecies*. Rochester: Bear & Company, 2001.

Crawford, Robert. *What Is Religion?* New York: Routledge, 2002.

Cremo, Michael and Richard Thompson. *The Hidden History of the Human Race*. Badger: Govardhan Hill Publishing, 1994.

David, Rosalie. *Cult Of The Sun*. New York: Barnes & Noble, Inc., 1980.

_____. *The Ancient Egyptians: Beliefs and Practices*. Portland: Sussex Academic Press, 1998.

Delaforge, Gaetan. *The Templar Tradition*. Putney: Threshold Books, 1987.

Desroches-Noblecourt, Christiane. *Tutankhamen*. Boston: New York Graphic Society, 1963.

Devi, Savitri. *Son of the Sun*. San Jose: Kingsport Press, 1981 (1946).

Diop, Cheikh Anta. *The African Origin of Civilization*. New York: Lawrence Hill, 1974.

D'Olivet, Fabre. *The Hebraic Tongue Restored*. York Beach: Samuel Weiser, Inc., 1981 (1921, 1815).

Dunn, Christopher. *The Giza Power Plant*. Santa Fe: Bear & Company, 1998.

Easwaren, Eknath. *The Bhagavad Gita*. Petaluma: Niliri Press, 1985.

Ehrton. *Born of the Sun*. Sedona: 1st Books, 2001.

El Mahdy, Christine. *Mummies, Myth and Magic*. London: Thames and Hudson, 1989.

Elkington, David. *In The Name Of The Gods*. Dorset: Green Man Press, 2001.

Ellis, Normandie. *Awakening Osiris*. Ann Arbor: Phanes Press, 1988.

Ellis, Ralph. *Tempest & Exodus*. Kempton: Adventures Unlimited Press, 2002.

_____. *Solomon, Falcon of Sheba*. Kempton: Adventures Unlimited Press, 2003.

Emory, Walter B. *Archaic Egypt*. New York: Penguin Books, 1962.

Fagan, Brian (editor). *Eyewitness To Discovery*. New York: Oxford University Press, 1996.

Feng, Giu-Fu and Jane English. *Tao Te Ching*. New York: Vintage Books, 1972.

Fox, Robin Lane. *Pagans and Christians*. San Francisco: Harper & Row, 1986.

Freud, Sigmund. *Moses And Monotheism*. New York: Vintage Books, 1939.

Gardner, Laurence. *Bloodline Of The Holy Grail*. New York: Barnes & Noble, 1996.

_____. *Genesis Of The Grail Kings*. New York: Fair Winds Press, 2002.

_____. *Lost Secrets Of The Sacred Ark*. London: Thorsons Publishing, 2003.

Gideons. *The Holy Bible*. Chicago: The Gideons International, 1959.

Gimbutas, Marija. *The Goddesses And Gods Of Old Europe*. Berkeley: University of California Press, 1982 (1974).

_____. *The Language Of The Goddess*. San Francisco: Harper & Row, 1989.

Goldman, Jonathan. *Healing Sounds*. Rockport: Element Books, 1992.

Gordon, Cyrus H. *Forgotten Scripts*. New York: Basic Books, Inc., 1968.

Graves, Robert. *The White Goddess*. New York: Farrar, Straus and Giroux, 1979 (1948).

Greenberg, Gary. *The Moses Mystery: The African Origins of The Jewish People*. Secaucus: Birch Lane Press, 1996.

Guilmot, Max. *The Initiatory Process In Ancient Egypt*. San Jose: AMORC, 1978.

Gurdjieff, G. I. *Meetings With Remarkable Men*. New York: Penguin Books, 1985 (1960).

Hancock, Graham. *The Sign And The Seal*. New York: Crown Publishers, 1992.

_____. *Fingerprints Of The Gods*. New York: Crown Publishers, 1995.

Harding, M. Esther. *Women's Mysteries*. New York: Harper Colophon Books, 1976 (1971).

Harner, Michael. *The Way of the Shaman*. San Francisco: Harper San Francisco, 1990 (1980).

Hertz, J.H. (editor). *Pentateuch & Haftorahs.* London: The Soncino Press, 1960 (1936).

Hoffman, Michael. *Egypt Before The Pharaohs.* London: Michael O'Mara Books Limited, 1991 (1979).

Hollenbach, Karl F. *Francis Rosicross.* Ekron: Dunsinane Hill Publications, 1996.

Hope, Murry. *Ancient Egypt: The Sirius Connection.* Dorset: Element Books, 1990.

_____. *The Ancient Wisdom of Egypt.* London: Thorsons, 1998 (1984).

Hornung, Erik. *Akhenaten and the Religion of Light.* Ithaca: Cornell University Press, 2001.

Ishbel. *The Secret Teachings of the Temple of Isis.* St. Paul: Llewellyn Publications, 1989.

Jairazbhoy, R.A. *Ancient Egyptian Survival In The Pacific.* London: Karnak House, 1990.

Jonas, Hans. *The Gnostic Religion.* Boston: Beacon Press, 1958.

Kirsch, Jonathan. *Moses: A Life.* New York: Ballantine Publishing Group, 1998.

Knight, Christopher and Robert Lomas. *The Hiram Key.* New York: Barnes & Noble, 1996.

Krishnamurti, J. *Think on These Things.* New York: Harper & Row, 1970 (1964).

Kueshana, Eklal. *The Ultimate Frontier.* Quinton: The Adelphi Organization, 1992 (1963).

Lamy, Lucie. *Egyptian Mysteries.* New York: Crossroad Publishing Company, 1981.

Lehner, Mark. *The Egyptian Heritage.* Virginia Beach: ARE Press, 1974.

_____. *The Complete Pyramids.* London: Thames and Hudson, 1997.

Lesko, Barbara S. *The Remarkable Women of Ancient Egypt.* Berkeley: B.C. Scribe Publications, 1978.

_____. *The Great Goddesses Of Egypt.* Norman: University of Oklahoma Press, 1999.

Lewis, H. Spencer. *Rosicrucian Questions and Answers with Complete History of The Rosicrucian Order*. San Jose: The Rosicrucian Press, Ltd., 1977 (1929).

_____. *Rosicrucian Manual*. San Jose: Kingsport Press, Inc., 1980 (1918).

Lewis, Ralph M. *Cosmic Mission Fulfilled*. San Jose: Kingsport Press, Inc., 1978 (1966).

MacQuitty, William. *Tutankhamun: The Last Journey*. New York: Crown Publishers, 1978.

McIntosh, Christopher. *The Rosy Cross Unveiled*. Wellingsborough: The Aquarian Press, Ltd., 1980.

Mead, G.R.S. *Thrice Greatest Hermes*. York Beach: Samuel Weiser, Inc., 1992 (1906).

Mehler, Stephen S. *The Land of Osiris*. Kempton: Adventures Unlimited Press, 2001.

_____. "Lifting The Veil: Speculation On The Face Of The Great Sphinx of Giza." *World Explorer Magazine*. Vol. 1, No. 6, 38-41, 1995.

_____. "Was There An Explosion in The Great Pyramid in Antiquity?" *World Explorer Magazine*. Vol. 3, No. 4, 27-29, 2003.

Melchizedek, Drunvalo. *The Ancient Secret Of The Flower Of Life*. Vol. I & II. Sedona: Light Technology Publishing, 1998, 2000.

Morenz, Siegfried. *Egyptian Religion*. Ithaca: Cornell University Press, 1973 (1960).

Murphy, John. *The Origins And History of Religions*. Manchester: Manchester University Press, 1949.

Murray, Margaret. *The Splendor That Was Egypt*. New York: Philosophical Library, 1961 (1949).

Neumann, Erich. *The Great Mother*. New York: Princeton University Press, 1974 (1965).

Osman, Ahmed. *Stranger in the Valley of the Kings*. San Francisco: Harper & Row, 1987.

_____. *The House Of The Messiah*. London: HarperCollins, 1992.

_____. *Moses And Akhenaten*. Rochester: Bear & Company. 2002 (1990).

Pagels, Elaine. *The Gnostic Gospels*. New York: Random House, 1979.

Palmer, M. Dale. *True Esoteric Traditions*. Plainsfield: Noetics Institute, Inc., 1994.

Parminder, Geoffrey (editor). *World Religions*. New York: Facts on File Publications, 1971.

Petrie, W.M. Flinders. *Religious Life In Ancient Egypt*. London: Constable & Company, Ltd., 1924.

Pickthall, Mohammed Marmaduke. *The Glorious Koran*. New York: Mentor Books, 1953.

Picknett, Lynn and Clive Prince. *The Templar Revolution*. Putney: Threshold Books, 1987.

Pinkham, Mark Amaru. *Guardians Of The Holy Grail*. Kempton: Adventures Unlimited Press, 2004.

Rajneesh, Bhagwan Shree. *Tao: The Pathless Path*. Vol. I & II. Poona: Rajneesh Foundation, 1978, 1979.

Redford, Donald B. *Akhenaten, The Heretic King*. Princeton: Princeton University Press, 1984.

Reed, Bika. *Rebel In The Soul*. New York: Inner Traditions International, Ltd., 1978.

_____. *The Field of Transformations*. Rochester: Inner Traditions International Ltd., 1987.

Reymond, E.A.E. *The Mythological Origin of the Egyptian Temple*. New York: Barnes & Noble, 1989.

Riemer, Jack (editor). *Jewish Reflections On Death*. New York: Schocken Books, 1976.

Ries, Julien. *The Origins of Religions*. Grand Rapids: William B. Eerdmaus Publishing Company, 1994.

Schoch, Robert M. *Voices Of The Rocks*. New York: Harmony Books, 1999.

_____ and Aquinas McNally. *Voyages Of The Pyramid Builders*. New York: Jeremy P. Tarcher, 2004.

Schwaller de Lubicz, Isha. *Her-Bak*. Vol. I & II. New York: Inner Traditions International Ltd., 1985 (1955).

Schwaller de Lubicz, R.A. *Sacred Science*. New York: Inner Traditions International, Ltd., 1982 (1961).

_____. *The Egyptian Miracle*. New York: Inner Traditions International, Ltd., 1985 (1963).

Sellers, Jane B. *The Death of Gods in Ancient Egypt*. London: Penguin Books, 1992.

Singer, June. *Androgyny*. New York: Anchor Press, 1976.

Singh, Ranbir. *Glimpses Of The Divine Masters*. New Delhi: International Traders Corporation, 1965.

Sitchin, Zecharia. *Divine Encounters*. New York: Avon Books, 1995.

Smith, Huston. *The Religions of Man*. New York: Harper & Row, 1958.

Sogyal, Rinpoche. *The Tibetan Book Of Living And Dying*. San Francisco: Harper SanFrancisco, 1992.

Sollberger, Edmund. *The Babylonian Legend of the Flood*. London: University Press, Oxford, 1971 (1962).

Steiner, Rudolf. *Egyptian Myths and Mysteries*. New York: Anthroposophic Press, Inc., 1971.

Stone, Merlin. *When God Was A Woman*. New York: Dial Press, 1976.

Suares, Carlo. *The Resurrection of the Word*. Berkeley: Shambhala Publications, 1975.

Suzuki, D.T. *Zen Buddhism*. New York: Doubleday & Company, Inc., 1956.

Tompkins, Peter. *Secrets of The Great Pyramid*. New York: Harper Colophon Books, 1978 (1971).

Vandenberg, Philipp. *Nefertiti*. New York: J.B. Lippencott Company, 1978.

Velikovsky, Immanuel. *Oedipus And Akhnaton*. New York: Abacus Books, 1982 (1960).

Wallace-Murphy, Tim and Marilyn Hopkins. *Rosslyn*. Boston: Element Books, 2000.

Weigall, Arthur. *The Life and Times of Akhenaten*. London: Thornton Butterworth, 1923 (1910).

Weed, Joseph J. *A Rosicrucian Speaks*. New York: The Chatsworth Press, 1965.

_____. *Wisdom Of The Mystic Masters*. New York: Parker Publishing Company, Inc., 1972 (1968).

West John Anthony. *Serpent In The Sky*. New York: Harper & Row, 1979.

_____. *The Travelers Key To Ancient Egypt*. Wheaton: Theosophical Publishing House, 1995 (1985).

White, John (editor). *What Is Enlightenment?* New York: Paragon House, 1995 (1985).

Wigoder, Geoffrey (editor). *Jewish Art and Civilization*. Vol. I & II. New York: Walker & Co., 1972.

Williams, Larry. *The Mount Sinai Myth*. New York: Wynwood Press, 1990.

Wolf, Fred Alan. *The Spiritual Universe*. Portsmouth: Moment Point Press, 1999.

Yogi, Maharishi Mahesh. *Enlightenment*. Berlin: Meru Press, 1978.

INDEX

Cataclysm, vi, 30-34, 41-42, 44, 46, 48-
50, 56-58, 66, 70-71, 75, 97, 170, 184,
209-210
Catastrophism, 57
Catastrophobia, 22, 31, 46, 209, 210, 215
Chaldea, Chaldeans, 143-144
Chester, Lynn, 14
Christianity, 3, 7, 11, 84, 97, 136, 140-141,
148, 168, 180, 189, 191
Church, 8, 97, 141, 151, 166-168
Clow, Barbara Hand, xiii, 22, 30-31, 46,
62, 174, 209
Collins, Andrew, 49, 210
Crawford, Robert, 8, 209
Cremo, Michael, 18, 209
Cycles, 3, 7, 10, 14-20, 22, 25, 51, 59,
60, 71, 100, 174, 176, 188-189, 200
D'Olivet, Fabre, 109, 143, 212
Dahshur, vi, 24, 27, 40-42, 170
Dao de Jing, see also Tao Te Ching, 180,
209, 217
Darwin, Charles, 11
David, 142, 177, 205, 207, 213, 215-216
Deity, 6-8, 10, 12, 64, 77, 95, 132-133,
138, 175-176, 191
Djehuti, see also Thoth, v-vi, 27, 52-53,
55, 71-73, 75, 80
Delair, J.B., 30-31, 33, 42, 44, 57-58,
209-210, 214
Deluge, see Flood, 30, 48-49
Dendara, vi, xii, 26, 53, 80
Descending Passage, 34
Devi, Savitri, 105, 210, 212, 216
Dirac, Paul A.M., 19
Dunn, Christopher, xiii, 24, 33-34, 37,
40-43, 177, 207, 210
Durkheim, Emile, 8
Edfu, v, x-xi, 25-26, 49, 150, 171
Ehrton 162, 212, 216
El Shaddai, x, 45
El, Eloh, 84, 132-133, 145
Elohim 132
Exodus, The, ix, 107, 109, 114, 116-118,
120, 122-125, 127-129, 132-133, 136,
138, 182-183
Explosion hypothesis, 39
Ezra, 123, 144

Fama Fraternitatis, 152
Flood, 30, 57, 143, 210, 215, 221
Franklin, Benjamin, 163-164
Freemasonry, see also Masonry, 3, 166
Freud, Sigmund, 88, 107, 110, 114, 124,
211
Gemini, 48, 51-52, 80
Giza Plateau, xi, 14, 39, 170, 178
Giza Power Plant, 33, 37, 207, 210, 216
Giza, xi, xiii, 14, 16, 18, 23, 27, 33, 35-39,
42, 61, 119, 161, 170, 178, 207, 210,
216, 219
God, x, 2-3, 8, 11, 64-65, 70, 72, 81-82,
84, 96-97, 120, 131-132, 135-141,
144-145, 149, 173, 175-177, 180, 185,
188-189, 191-193, 202-205, 221
Goldman, Jonathan, 141
Grand Gallery, v, 35-37, 39-40, 42
Great Mother, 19, 48, 58, 219
Great Pyramid, v-vi, xiii, 24, 27, 33-38,
40, 42-43, 49, 60-61, 207, 210, 219,
221
Greeks, 44, 56, 69, 80, 84, 109, 145, 163
Greenberg, Gary, 107, 117, 131, 182,
205, 210-211
Gurdjieff, G.I, 142, 217
Habiru, see also Apiru, 131
Hall, Manly P., 211
Hancock, Graham, 209
Hanut, Hanuti, 66, 68-70, 72, 75-78,
81-82, 84, 92, 94, 96 ,123, 136-137,
139, 143, 172, 174, 176, 185, 192
Hathor, vi, x, xii, 26, 53, 80, 134
Hatshepsut, vii, 68, 83, 159, 192
Hebis Temple, 26-27
Hebrew, ix, x, 50, 88, 99-100, 107-109,
120, 122, 124, 127-129, 131-132,
134-135, 139-140, 142-145, 182-183,
205-206
Hebrews, viii, 11, 108, 112, 114, 117,
123-125, 127, 129, 131-132, 136, 182
Heka (Hekau), 52, 55, 117, 131
Hekau-Khoswert, see Hyksos,
Helmholtz Resonators, 37
Herodotus, 211
Hick, John, 8

INDEX

ABOUT THE AUTHOR

Stephen S. Mehler's fascination with Egypt, which began at the age of eight, has guided his education and spiritual work all his life. Born in Brooklyn and raised in the Bronx, Mehler studied physiology and anatomy at Hunter College of the City University of New York. He holds two masters degrees from San Jose State University in the natural and social sciences. Pursuing metaphysical as well as scientific truth, Mehler served as a staff research scientist for the Rosicrucian Order, AMORC, from 1978 to 1980. Mehler has researched material about ancient Egypt for over 37 years.

In his first book, *The Land of Osiris*, Mehler introduced his tutelage and collaboration with Egyptian-born Egyptologist and indigenous wisdom keeper, Abd'El Hakim Awyan. Mehler presented Hakim's mastery of the oral traditions of his country, and together they introduced concepts and paradigms for a whole new discipline that they define as Khemitology, not Egyptology. In this current work, Mehler presents further teachings of Hakim and Mehler's own research concerning the origins of religion and its evolution in ancient Khemit, the teachings of the king Akhenaten and his influence upon Judaism and the Rosicrucian tradition. The presentation of the wisdom tradition of the ancient Khemitians is again being offered to help prepare for the new cycle of the coming Dawn, the Awakening.

ANCIENT SCIENCE

THE LAND OF OSIRIS
An Introduction to Khemitology
by Stephen S. Mehler

Was there an advanced prehistoric civilization in ancient Egypt? Were they the people who built the great pyramids and carved the Great Sphinx? Did the pyramids serve as energy devices and not as tombs for kings? Independent Egyptologist Stephen S. Mehler has spent over 30 years researching the answers to these questions and believes the answers are yes! Mehler has uncovered an indigenous oral tradition that still exists in Egypt, and has been fortunate to have studied with a living master of this tradition, Abd'El Hakim Awyan. Mehler has also been given permission to present these teachings to the Western world, teachings that unfold a whole new understanding of ancient Egypt and have only been presented heretofore in fragments by other researchers. Chapters include: Egyptology and Its Paradigms; Khemitology—New Paradigms; Asgat Nefer—The Harmony of Water; Khemit and the Myth of Atlantis; The Extraterrestrial Question; 17 chapters in all.
272 PAGES. 6x9 PAPERBACK. ILLUSTRATED. COLOR SECTION. BIBLIOGRAPHY. $18.95. CODE: LOOS

A HITCHHIKER'S GUIDE TO ARMAGEDDON
by David Hatcher Childress

With wit and humor, popular Lost Cities author David Hatcher Childress takes us around the world and back in his trippy finalé to the Lost Cities series. He's off on an adventure in search of the apocalypse and end times. Childress hits the road from the fortress of Megiddo, the legendary citadel in northern Israel where Armageddon is prophesied to start. Hitchhiking around the world, Childress takes us from one adventure to another, to ancient cities in the deserts and the legends of worlds before our own. Childress muses on the rise and fall of civilizations, and the forces that have shaped mankind over the millennia, including wars, invasions and cataclysms. He discusses the ancient Armageddons of the past, and chronicles recent Middle East developments and their ominous undertones. In the meantime, he becomes a cargo cult god on a remote island off New Guinea, gets dragged into the Kennedy Assassination by one of the "conspirators," investigates a strange power operating out of the Altai Mountains of Mongolia, and discovers how the Knights Templar and their off-shoots have driven the world toward an epic battle centered around Jerusalem and the Middle East.
320 PAGES. 6x9 PAPERBACK. ILLUSTRATED. BIBLIOGRAPHY. INDEX. $16.95. CODE: HGA

CLOAK OF THE ILLUMINATI
Secrets, Transformations, Crossing the Star Gate
by William Henry

Thousands of years ago the stargate technology of the gods was lost. Mayan Prophecy says it will return by 2012, along with our alignment with the center of our galaxy. In this book: Find examples of stargates and wormholes in the ancient world; Examine myths and scripture with hidden references to a stargate cloak worn by the Illuminati, including Mari, Nimrod, Elijah, and Jesus; See rare images of gods and goddesses wearing the Cloak of the illuminati; Learn about Saddam Hussein and the secret missing library of Jesus; Uncover the secret Roman-era eugenics experiments at the Temple of Hathor in Denderah, Egypt; Explore the duplicate of the Stargate Pillar of the Gods in the Illuminists' secret garden in Nashville, TN; Discover the secrets of manna, the food of the angels; Share the lost Peace Prayer posture of Osiris, Jesus and the Illuminati; more. Chapters include: Seven Stars Under Three Stars; The Long Walk; Squaring the Circle; The Mill of the Host; The Miracle Garment; The Fig; Nimrod: The Mighty Man; Nebuchadnezzar's Gate; The New Mighty Man; more.
238 PAGES. 6x9 PAPERBACK. ILLUSTRATED. BIBLIOGRAPHY. INDEX. $16.95. CODE: COIL

LEY LINE & EARTH ENERGIES
An Extraordinary Journey into the Earth's Natural Energy System
by David Cowan & Anne Silk

The mysterious standing stones, burial grounds and stone circles that lace Europe, the British Isles and other areas have intrigued scientists, writers, artists and travellers through the centuries. They pose so many questions: Why do some places feel special? How do ley lines work? How did our ancestors use Earth energy to map their sacred sites and burial grounds? How do ghosts and poltergeists interact with Earth energy? How can Earth spirals and black spots affect our health? This exploration shows how natural forces affect our behavior, how they can be used to enhance our health and well being, and ultimately, how they bring us closer to penetrating one of the deepest mysteries being explored. A fascinating and visual book about subtle Earth energies and how they affect us and the world around them.
368 PAGES. 6x9 PAPERBACK. ILLUSTRATED. BIBLIOGRAPHY. INDEX. $18.95. CODE: LLEE

THE ORION PROPHECY
Egyptian & Mayan Prophecies on the Cataclysm of 2012
by Patrick Geryl and Gino Ratinckx

In the year 2012 the Earth awaits a super catastrophe: its magnetic field reverse in one go. Phenomenal earthquakes and tidal waves will completely destroy our civilization. Europe and North America will shift thousands of kilometers northwards into polar climes. Nearly everyone will perish in the apocalyptic happenings. These dire predictions stem from the Mayans and Egyptians—descendants of the legendary Atlantis. The Atlanteans had highly evolved astronomical knowledge and were able to exactly predict the previous world-wide flood in 9792 BC. They built tens of thousands of boats and escaped to South America and Egypt. In the year 2012 Venus, Orion and several others stars will take the same 'code-positions' as in 9792 BC! For thousands of years historical sources have told of a forgotten time capsule of ancient wisdom located in a mythical labyrinth of secret chambers filled with artifacts and documents from the previous flood. We desperately need this information now—and this book gives one possible location.
324 PAGES. 6x9 PAPERBACK. ILLUSTRATED. BIBLIOGRAPHY. $16.95. CODE: ORP

THE CHILDREN OF THE SUN
A Study of the Egyptian Settlement of the Pacific
by W.J. Perry

A reprint of the groundbreaking work of Professor W.J. Perry, an early diffusionist who believed that civilization spread through-out the world via transoceanic voyaging—an idea that most historians still fail to accept, even in the face of mounting evidence. First published in 1923, this classic presents the fascinating evidence that envoys of the ancient Sun Kingdoms of Egypt and India travelled into Indonesia and the Pacific circa 1500 BC, spreading their sophisticated culture. Perry traces the expansion of mega-lithic building from its origin in Egypt through Indonesia and across the Pacific all the way to the Americas. These early mariners searched for gold, obsidian, and pearls in their incredible explorations from island to island—they were the Children of the Sun! Includes: The Coming of the Warriors; Rulers and Commoners; The Sky World; The Indo-Egyptian Alliance of Builders; The Oceania-Indonesian Alliance of Explorers; more.
554 PAGES. 6x9 PAPERBACK. ILLUSTRATED. BIBLIOGRAPHY. INDEX. $18.95. CODE: CSUN

24 hour credit card orders—call: 815-253-6390 fax: 815-253-6300
email: auphq@frontiernet.net   www.adventuresunlimitedpress.com   www.wexclub.com

ANCIENT SCIENCE

THE GIZA DEATH STAR
The Paleophysics of the Great Pyramid & the Military Complex at Giza
by Joseph P. Farrell

Physicist Joseph Farrell's amazing book on the secrets of Great Pyramid of Giza. *The Giza Death Star* starts where British engineer Christopher Dunn leaves off in his 1998 book, *The Giza Power Plant*. Was the Giza complex part of a military installation over 10,000 years ago? Chapters include: An Archaeology of Mass Destruction, Thoth and Theories; The Machine Hypothesis; Pythagoras, Plato, Planck, and the Pyramid; The Weapon Hypothesis; Encoded Harmonics of the Planck Units in the Great Pyramid; High Freqquency Direct Current "Impulse" Technology; The Grand Gallery and its Crystals: Gravito-acoustic Resonators; The Other Two Large Pyramids; the "Causeways," and the "Temples"; A Phase Conjugate Howitzer; Evidence of the Use of Weapons of Mass Destruction in Ancient Times; more.
290 PAGES. 6x9 PAPERBACK. ILLUSTRATED. $16.95. CODE: GDS

THE GIZA DEATH STAR DEPLOYED
The Physics & Engineering of the Great Pyramid
by Joseph P. Farrell

Physicist Joseph Farrell's amazing sequel to *The Giza Death Star* which takes us from the Great Pyramid to the asteroid belt and the so-called Pyramids of Mars. Farrell expands on his thesis that the Great Pyramid was a chemical maser, designed as a weapon and eventually deployed—with disastrous results to the solar system. Includes: Exploding Planets: The Movie, the Mirror, and the Model; Dating the Catastrophe and the Compound; A Brief History of the Exoteric and Esoteric Investigations of the Great Pyramid; No Machines, Please!; The Stargate Conspiracy; The Scalar Weapons; Message or Machine?; A Tesla Analysis of the Putative Physics and Engineering of the Giza Death Star; Cohering the Zero Point, Vacuum Energy, Flux: Synopsis of Scalar Physics and Paleophysics; Configuring the Scalar Pulse Wave; Inferred Applications in the Great Pyramid; Quantum Numerology, Feedback Loops and Tetrahedral Physics; and more.
290 PAGES. 6x9 PAPERBACK. ILLUSTRATED. BIBLIOGRAPHY. INDEX. $16.95. CODE: GDSD

TECHNOLOGY OF THE GODS
The Incredible Sciences of the Ancients
by David Hatcher Childress

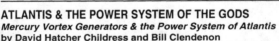

Popular *Lost Cities* author David Hatcher Childress takes us into the amazing world of ancient technology, from computers in antiquity to the "flying machines of the gods." Childress looks at the technology that was allegedly used in Atlantis and the theory that the Great Pyramid of Egypt was originally a gigantic power station. He examines tales of ancient flight and the technology that it involved; how the ancients used electricity; megalithic building techniques; the use of crystal lenses and the fire from the gods; evidence of various high tech weapons in the past, including atomic weapons; ancient metallurgy and heavy machinery; the role of modern inventors such as Nikola Tesla in bringing ancient technology back into modern use; impossible artifacts; and more.
356 PAGES. 6x9 PAPERBACK. ILLUSTRATED. BIBLIOGRAPHY. $16.95. CODE: TGOD.

MAPS OF THE ANCIENT SEA KINGS
Evidence of Advanced Civilization in the Ice Age
by Charles H. Hapgood

Charles Hapgood's classic 1966 book on ancient maps produces concrete evidence of an advanced world-wide civilization existing many thousands of years before ancient Egypt. He has found the evidence in the Piri Reis Map that shows Antarctica, the Hadji Ahmed map, the Oronteus Finaeus and other amazing maps. Hapgood concluded that these maps were made from more ancient maps from the various ancient archives around the world, now lost. Not only were these unknown people more advanced in mapmaking than any people prior to the 18th century, it appears they mapped all the continents. The Americas were mapped thousands of years before Columbus. Antarctica was mapped when its coasts were free of ice.
316 PAGES. 7x10 PAPERBACK. ILLUSTRATED. BIBLIOGRAPHY & INDEX. $19.95. CODE: MASK

ATLANTIS & THE POWER SYSTEM OF THE GODS
Mercury Vortex Generators & the Power System of Atlantis
by David Hatcher Childress and Bill Clendenon

Atlantis and the Power System of the Gods starts with a reprinting of the rare 1990 book *Mercury: UFO Messenger of the Gods* by Bill Clendenon. Clendenon takes on an unusual voyage into the world of ancient flying vehicles, strange personal UFO sightings, a meeting with a "Man In Black" and then to a centuries-old library in India where he got his ideas for the diagrams of mercury vortex engines. The second part of the book is Childress' fascinating analysis of Nikola Tesla's broadcast system in light of Edgar Cayce's "Terrible Crystal" and the obelisks of ancient Egypt and Ethiopia. Includes: Atlantis and its crystal power towers that broadcast energy; how these incredible power stations may still exist today; inventor Nikola Tesla's nearly identical system of power transmission; Mercury Proton Gyros and mercury vortex propulsion; more. Richly illustrated, and packed with evidence that Atlantis not only existed—it had a world-wide energy system more sophisticated than ours today.
246 PAGES. 6x9 PAPERBACK. ILLUSTRATED. $15.95. CODE: APSG

PATH OF THE POLE
Cataclysmic Pole Shift Geology
by Charles Hapgood

Maps of the Ancient Sea Kings author Hapgood's classic book *Path of the Pole* is back in print! Hapgood researched Antarctica, ancient maps and the geological record to conclude that the Earth's crust has slipped in the inner core many times in the past, changing the position of the pole. *Path of the Pole* discusses the various "pole shifts" in Earth's past, giving evidence for each one, and moves on to possible future pole shifts. Packed with illustrations, this is the sourcebook for many other books on cataclysms and pole shifts.
356 PAGES. 6x9 PAPERBACK. ILLUSTRATED. $16.95. CODE: POP.

24 hour credit card orders—call: 815-253-6390 fax: 815-253-6300
email: auphq@frontiernet.net   www.adventuresunlimitedpress.com   www.wexclub.com

ANCIENT SCIENCE

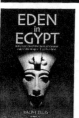

EDEN IN EGYPT
by Ralph Ellis

The story of Adam and Eve from the Book of Genesis is perhaps one of the best-known stories in circulation, even today, and yet nobody really knows where this tale came from or what it means. But even a cursory glance at the text will demonstrate the origins of this tale, for the river of Eden is described as having four branches. There is only one river in this part of the world that fits this description, and that is the Nile, with the four branches forming the Nile Delta. According to Ellis, Judaism was based upon the reign of the pharaoh Akhenaton, because the solitary Judaic god was known as Adhon while this pharaoh's solitary god was called Aton or Adjon. But what of the identities of Adam and Eve? The Israelites were once the leaders of Egypt and would originally have spoken Egyptian (Joseph, according to the Bible, was prime minister of all Egypt). This discovery allows us to translate the Genesis story with more confidence, and the result is that it seems that Adam and Eve were actually Pharaoh Akhenaton and his famous wife Queen Nefertiti. Includes 16 page color section.
320 PAGES. 6X9 PAPERBACK. ILLUSTRATED. BIBLIOGRAPHY. INDEX. $20.00. CODE: EIE

SOLOMON: FALCON OF SHEBA
The Tomb and Image of the Queen of Sheba Discovered
by Ralph Ellis

The Queen of Sheba, King Solomon and King David are still household names in much of the Western and Middle Eastern world, so how is it possible that all of these influential monarchs are completely missing from the archaeological record? The reality of this omission has perplexed theologians and historians for centuries, but maverick archeologist Ralph Ellis, author of *Jesus, Last of the Pharaohs* and *Tempest & Exodus*, has rediscovered their lost tombs and sarcophagi. The reason that Ralph has succeeded where generations of archaeologists have failed is that the latter were looking in the wrong location—surprisingly enough, the tombs of these monarchs are not to be found in either Israel, Ethiopia or Yemen. While the discovery of the tombs of King Solomon, King David, Hiram Abif and the Queen of Sheba may in itself be a startling and dramatic revelation, the precise historical identities of these monarchs serves to completely rewrite the whole of the Biblical Old Testament and much of our secular history, too. In short, history was not as we know it...
360 PAGES. 6X9 PAPERBACK. ILLUSTRATED. BIBLIOGRAPHY. $20.00. CODE: SFOS

THOTH
Architect of the Universe
by Ralph Ellis

This great book, now available in paperback, is on sacred geometry, megalithic architecture and the worship of the mathematical constant pi. Ellis contemplates Stonehenge; the ancient Egyptian god Thoth and his Emerald Tablets; Atlantis; Thoth's Ratios; Henge of the World; The Secret Gate of Knowledge; Precessional Henge; Royal Planisphere; Kufu's Continents; the Ma'at of the Egyptians; ancient technological civilizations; the Ark of Tutankhamen; Pyramidions; the Pyramid Inch and Pi; more. Well illustrated with color photo sections.
236 PAGES. 6X9 PAPERBACK. ILLUSTRATED. BIBLIOGRAPHY. $16.00. CODE: TOTH

K2—QUEST OF THE GODS
by Ralph Ellis

This sequel to *Thoth, Architect of the Universe* explains the design of the Great Pyramid in great detail, and it appears that its architect specified a structure that contains a curious blend of technology, lateral thinking and childish fun—yet this design can also point out the exact location of the legendary 'Hall of Records' to within a few meters! The 'X' marks the spot location has been found at last. Join the author on the most ancient quest ever devised, a dramatic journey in the footsteps of Alexander the Great on his search for the legendary Hall of Records, then on to the highest peaks at the top of the world to find the 'The Great Pyramid in the Himalayas'; more.
280 PAGES. 6X9 PAPERBACK. ILLUSTRATED. COLOR SECTION. BIBLIOGRAPHY. $16.00. CODE: K2QD

TEMPEST & EXODUS
by Ralph Ellis

Starts with the dramatic discovery of a large biblical quotation on an ancient Egyptian stele which tells of a conference in Egypt discussing the way in which the biblical Exodus should be organized. The quotation thus has fundamental implications for both history and theology because it explains why the Tabernacle and the Ark of the Covenant were constructed, why the biblical Exodus started, where Mt. Sinai was located, and who the god of the Israelites was. The most dramatic discovery is that the central element of early Israelite liturgy was actually the Giza pyramids, and that Mt. Sinai was none other than the Great Pyramid. Mt. Sinai was described as being both sharp and the tallest 'mountain' in the area, and thus the Israelite god actually resided deep within the bowels of this pyramid. Furthermore, these new translations of ancient texts, both secular and biblical, also clearly demonstrate that the Giza pyramids are older than the first dynasty—the ancestors of the Hyksos were writing about the Giza pyramids long before they are supposed to have been constructed! Includes: Mt. Sinai, the Israelite name for the Great Pyramid of Egypt; the biblical Exodus inscribed on an Egyptian stele of Ahmose I; the secret name of God revealed; Noah's Ark discovered, more.
280 PAGES. 6X9 PAPERBACK. ILLUSTRATED. COLOR SECTION. BIBLIOGRAPHY & INDEX. $16.00. CODE: TEXO

JESUS, LAST OF THE PHARAOHS
Truth Behind the Mask Revealed
by Ralph Ellis

This book, with 43 color plates, traces the history of the Egyptian royal family from the time of Noah through to Jesus, comparing biblical and historical records. Nearly all of the biblical characters can be identified in the historical record—all are pharaohs of Egypt or pharaohs in exile. The Bible depicts them as being simple shepherds, but in truth they were the Hyksos, the Shepherd Kings of Egypt. The biblical story that has circulated around the globe is simply a history of one family, Abraham and his descendants. In the Bible he was known as Abram; in the historical record he is the pharaoh Maybra—the most powerful man on Earth in his lifetime. By such simple sleight of hand, the pharaohs of Egypt have hidden their identity, but preserved their ancient history and bloodline. These kings were born of the gods; they were not only royal, they were also Sons of God.
320 PAGES. 6X9 PAPERBACK. ILLUSTRATED. $16.00. CODE: JLOP

STRANGE SCIENCE

UNDERGROUND BASES & TUNNELS
What is the Government Trying to Hide?
by Richard Sauder, Ph.D.
Working from government documents and corporate records, Sauder has compiled an impressive book that digs below the surface of the military's super-secret underground! Go behind the scenes into little-known corners of the public record and discover how corporate America has worked hand-in-glove with the Pentagon for decades, dreaming about, planning, and actually constructing, secret underground bases. This book includes chapters on the locations of the bases, the tunneling technology, various military designs for underground bases, nuclear testing & underground bases, abductions, needles & implants, military involvement in "alien" cattle mutilations, more. 50 page photo & map insert.
201 PAGES. 6X9 PAPERBACK. ILLUSTRATED. $15.95. CODE: UGB

UNDERWATER & UNDERGROUND BASES
Surprising Facts the Government Does Not Want You to Know
by Richard Sauder
Dr. Sauder lays out the amazing evidence and government paper trail for the construction of huge, manned bases offshore, in mid-ocean, and deep beneath the sea floor! Bases big enough to secretly dock submarines! Official United States Navy documents, and other hard evidence, raise many questions about what really lies 20,000 leagues beneath the sea. Many UFOs have been seen coming and going from the world's oceans, seas and lakes, implying the existence of secret underwater bases. Dr. Sauder also adds to his incredible database of underground bases. New, breakthrough material reveals the existence of additional clandestine underground facilities as well as the surprising location of one of the CIA's own underground bases. Plus, new information on tunneling and cutting-edge, high speed rail magnetic-levitation (MagLev) technology.
264 PAGES. 6X9 PAPERBACK. ILLUSTRATED. BIBLIOGRAPHY. INDEX. $16.95. CODE: UUB

REICH OF THE BLACK SUN
Nazi Secret Weapons and the Cold War Allied Legend
by Joseph P. Farrell
Why were the Allies worried about an atom bomb attack by the Germans in 1944? Why did the Soviets threaten to use poison gas against the Germans? Why did Hitler in 1945 insist that holding Prague could win the war for the Third Reich? Why did US General George Patton's Third Army race for the Skoda works at Pilsen in Czechoslovakia instead of Berlin? Why did the US Army not test the uranium atom bomb it dropped on Hiroshima? Why did the Luftwaffe fly a non-stop round trip mission to within twenty miles of New York City in 1944? *Reich of the Black Sun* takes the reader on a scientific-historical journey in order to answer these questions. Arguing that Nazi Germany actually won the race for the atom bomb in late 1944, *Reich of the Black Sun* then goes on to explore the even more secretive research the Nazis were conducting into the occult, alternative physics and new energy sources. The book concludes with a fresh look at the "Nazi Legend" of the UFO mystery by examining the Roswell Majestic-12 documents and the Kecksburg crash in the light of parallels with some of the super-secret black projects being run by the SS.
352 PAGES. 6X9 PAPERBACK. ILLUSTRATED. BIBLIOGRAPHY. $16.95. CODE: ROBS

QUEST FOR ZERO-POINT ENERGY
Engineering Principles for "Free Energy"
by Moray B. King
King expands, with diagrams, on how free energy and anti-gravity are possible. The theories of zero point energy maintain there are tremendous fluctuations of electrical field energy embedded within the fabric of space. King explains the following topics: Tapping the Zero-Point Energy as an Energy Source; Fundamentals of a Zero-Point Energy Technology; Vacuum Energy Vortices; The Super Tube; Charge Clusters: The Basis of Zero-Point Energy Inventions; Vortex Filaments, Torsion Fields and the Zero-Point Energy; Transforming the Planet with a Zero-Point Energy Experiment; Dual Vortex Forms: The Key to a Large Zero-Point Energy Coherence. Packed with diagrams, patents and photos. With power shortages now a daily reality in many parts of the world, this book offers a fresh approach very rarely mentioned in the mainstream media.
224 PAGES. 6X9 PAPERBACK. ILLUSTRATED. $14.95. CODE: QZPE

HITLER'S FLYING SAUCERS
A Guide to German Flying Discs of the Second World War
by Henry Stevens
Learn why the Schriever-Habermohl project was actually two projects and read the written statement of a German test pilot who actually flew one of these saucers; about the Leduc engine, the key to Dr. Miethe's saucer designs; how U.S. government officials kept the truth about foo fighters hidden for almost sixty years and how they were finally forced to "come clean" about the foo fighter's German origin. Learn of the Peenemuende saucer project and how it was slated to "go atomic." Read the testimony of a German eyewitness who saw "magnetic discs." Read the U.S. government's own reports on German field propulsion saucers. Read how the post-war German KM-2 field propulsion "rocket" worked. Learn details of the work of Karl Schappeller and Viktor Schauberger. Learn how their ideas figure in the quest to build field propulsion flying discs. Find out what happened to this technology after the war. Find out how the Canadians got saucer technology directly from the SS. Find out about the surviving "Third Power" of former Nazis. Learn of the U.S. government's methods of UFO deception and how they used the German "Sonderbueroll" as the model for Project Blue Book.
388 PAGES. 6X9 PAPERBACK. ILLUSTRATED. INDEX. $18.95. CODE: HFS

THE TIME TRAVEL HANDBOOK
A Manual of Practical Teleportation & Time Travel
edited by David Hatcher Childress
In the tradition of *The Anti-Gravity Handbook* and *The Free-Energy Device Handbook*, science and UFO author David Hatcher Childress takes us into the weird world of time travel and teleportation. Not just a whacked-out look at science fiction, this book is an authoritative chronicling of real-life time travel experiments, teleportation devices and more. *The Time Travel Handbook* takes the reader beyond the government experiments and deep into the uncharted territory of early time travellers such as Nikola Tesla and Guglielmo Marconi and their alleged time travel experiments, as well as the Wilson Brothers of EMI and their connection to the Philadelphia Experiment—the U.S. Navy's forays into invisibility, time travel, and teleportation. Childress looks into the claims of time travelling individuals, and investigates the unusual claim that the pyramids on Mars were built in the future and sent back in time. A highly visual, large format book, with patents, photos and schematics. Be the first on your block to build your own time travel device!
316 PAGES. 7X10 PAPERBACK. ILLUSTRATED. $16.95. CODE: TTH

24 hour credit card orders—call: 815-253-6390 fax: 815-253-6300
email: auphq@frontiernet.net   www.adventuresunlimitedpress.com   www.wexclub.com

TESLA TECHNOLOGY

THE FANTASTIC INVENTIONS OF NIKOLA TESLA
Nikola Tesla with additional material by David Hatcher Childress

This book is a readable compendium of patents, diagrams, photos and explanations of the many incredible inventions of the originator of the modern era of electrification. In Tesla's own words are such topics as wireless transmission of power, death rays, and radio-controlled airships. In addition, rare material on German bases in Antarctica and South America, and a secret city built at a remote jungle site in South America by one of Tesla's students, Guglielmo Marconi. Marconi's secret group claims to have built flying saucers in the 1940s and to have gone to Mars in the early 1950s! Incredible photos of these Tesla craft are included. The Ancient Atlantean system of broadcasting energy through a grid system of obelisks and pyramids is discussed, and a fascinating concept comes out of one chapter: that Egyptian engineers had to wear protective metal head-shields while in these power plants, hence the Egyptian Pharoah's head covering as well as the Face on Mars!
•His plan to transmit free electricity into the atmosphere. •How electrical devices would work using only small antennas mounted on them. •Why unlimited power could be utilized anywhere on earth. •How radio and radar technology can be used as death-ray weapons in Star Wars.
•Includes an appendix of Supreme Court documents on dismantling his free energy towers. •Tesla's Death Rays, Ozone generators, and more...
342 PAGES. 6x9 PAPERBACK. ILLUSTRATED. BIBLIOGRAPHY AND APPENDIX. $16.95. CODE: FINT

THE TESLA PAPERS
Nikola Tesla on Free Energy & Wireless Transmission of Power
by Nikola Tesla, edited by David Hatcher Childress

David Hatcher Childress takes us into the incredible world of Nikola Tesla and his amazing inventions. Tesla's rare article "The Problem of Increasing Human Energy with Special Reference to the Harnessing of the Sun's Energy" is included. This lengthy article was originally published in the June 1900 issue of *The Century Illustrated Monthly Magazine* and it was the outline for Tesla's master blueprint for the world. Tesla's fantastic vision of the future, including wireless power, anti-gravity, free energy and highly advanced solar energy.
Also included are some of the papers, patents and material collected on Tesla at the Colorado Springs Tesla Symposiums, including papers on:
•The Secret History of Wireless Transmission •Tesla and the Magnifying Transmitter
•Design and Construction of a half-wave Tesla Coil •Electrostatics: A Key to Free Energy
•Progress in Zero-Point Energy Research •Electromagnetic Energy from Antennas to Atoms
•Tesla's Particle Beam Technology •Fundamental Excitatory Modes of the Earth-Ionosphere Cavity
325 PAGES. 8X10 PAPERBACK. ILLUSTRATED. $16.95. CODE: TTP

THE ENERGY MACHINE OF T. HENRY MORAY
by Moray B. King

In the 1920s T. Henry Moray invented a "free energy" device that reportedly output 50 kilowatts of electricity. It could not be explained by standard science at that time. The electricity exhibited a strange "cold current" characteristic where thin wires could conduct appreciable power without heating. Moray suffered ruthless suppression, and in 1939 the device was destroyed. Frontier science lecturer and author Moray B. King explains the invention with today's science. Modern physics recognizes that the vacuum contains tremendous energy called the zero-point energy. A way to coherently activate it appears surprisingly simple: first create a glow plasma or corona, then abruptly pulse it. Other inventors have discovered this approach (sometimes unwittingly) to create novel energy devices, and they too were suppressed. The common pattern of their technologies clarified the fundamental operating principle. King hopes to inspire engineers and inventors so that a new energy source can become available to mankind.
192 PAGES. 6x8 PAPERBACK. ILLUSTRATED. REFERENCES. $14.95. CODE: EMHM

TAPPING THE ZERO POINT ENERGY
Free Energy & Anti-Gravity in Today's Physics
by Moray B. King

King explains how free energy and anti-gravity are possible. The theories of the zero point energy maintain there are tremendous fluctuations of electrical field energy imbedded within the fabric of space. This book tells how, in the 1930s, inventor T. Henry Moray could produce a fifty kilowatt "free energy" machine; how an electrified plasma vortex creates anti-gravity; how the Pons/Fleischmann "cold fusion" experiment could produce tremendous heat without fusion; and how certain experiments might produce a gravitational anomaly.
190 PAGES. 5X8 PAPERBACK. ILLUSTRATED. $12.95. CODE: TAP

HAARP
The Ultimate Weapon of the Conspiracy
by Jerry Smith

The HAARP project in Alaska is one of the most controversial projects ever undertaken by the U.S. Government. Jerry Smith gives us the history of the HAARP project and explains how works, in technically correct yet easy to understand language. At best, HAARP is science out-of-control; at worst, HAARP could be the most dangerous device ever created, a futuristic weapon that is everything from super-beam weapon to world-wide mind control device. Topics include Over-the-Horizon Radar and HAARP, Mind Control, ELF and HAARP, The Telsa Connection, The Russian Woodpecker, GWEN & HAARP, Earth Penetrating Tomography, Weather Modification, Secret Science of the Conspiracy, more. Includes the complete 1987 Eastlund patent for his pulsed super-weapon that he claims was stolen by the HAARP Project.
256 PAGES. 6x9 PAPERBACK. ILLUSTRATED. $14.95. CODE: HARP

HARNESSING THE WHEELWORK OF NATURE
Tesla's Science of Energy
by Thomas Valone, Ph.D., P.E.

Chapters include: Tesla: Scientific Superman who Launched the Westinghouse Industrial Firm by John Shatlan; Nikola Tesla—Electricity's Hidden Genius, excerpt from The Search for Free Energy; Tesla's History at Niagara Falls; Non-Hertzian Waves: True Meaning of the Wireless Transmission of Power by Toby Grotz; On the Transmission of Electricity Without Wires by Nikola Tesla; Tesla's Magnifying Transmitter by Andrija Puharich; Tesla's Self-Sustaining Electrical Generator and the Ether by Oliver Nichelson; Self-Sustaining Non-Hertzian Longitudinal Waves by Dr. Robert Bass; Modification of Maxwell's Equations in Free Space; Scalar Electromagnetic Waves; Disclosures Concerning Tesla's Operation of an ELF Oscillator; A Study of Tesla's Advanced Concepts & Glossary of Tesla Technology Terms; Electric Weather Forces: Tesla's Vision by Charles Yost; The New Art of Projecting Concentrated Non-Dispersive Energy Through Natural Media; The Homopolar Generator: Tesla's Contribution by Thomas Valone; Tesla's Ionizer and Ozonator: Implications for Indoor Air Pollution by Thomas Valone; How Cosmic Forces Shape Our Destiny by Nikola Tesla; Tesla's Death Ray plus Selected Tesla Patents; more.

288 PAGES. 6x9 PAPERBACK. ILLUSTRATED. $16.95. CODE: HWWN

24 hour credit card orders—call: 815-253-6390 fax: 815-253-6300
email: auphq@frontiernet.net   www.adventuresunlimitedpress.com   www.wexclub.com

CONSPIRACY & HISTORY

PIRATES & THE LOST TEMPLAR FLEET
The Secret Naval War Between the Templars & the Vatican
by David Hatcher Childress

Childress takes us into the fascinating world of maverick sea captains who were Knights Templar (and later Scottish Rite Free Masons) who battled the Vatican, and the Spanish and Italian ships that sailed for the Pope. The lost Templar fleet was originally based at La Rochelle in southern France, but fled to the deep fiords of Scotland upon the dissolution of the Order by King Phillip. This banned fleet of ships was later commanded by the St. Clair family of Rosslyn Chapel (birthplace of Free Masonry). St. Clair and his Templars made a voyage to Canada in the year 1298 AD, nearly 100 years before Columbus! Later, this fleet of ships and new ones to come, flew the Skull and Crossbones, the symbol of the Knights Templar. They preyed on the ships of the Vatican coming from the rich ports of the Americas and were ultimately known as the Pirates of the Caribbean. Chapters include: 10,000 Years of Seafaring; The Knights Templar & the Crusades; The Templars and the Assassins; The Lost Templar Fleet and the Jolly Roger; Maps of the Ancient Sea Kings; Pirates, Templars and the New World; Christopher Columbus—Secret Templar Pirate?; Later Day Pirates and the War with the Vatican; Pirate Utopias and the New Jerusalem; more.
320 PAGES. 6X9 PAPERBACK. ILLUSTRATED. BIBLIOGRAPHY. $16.95. CODE: PLTF

CLOAK OF THE ILLUMINATI
Secrets, Transformations, Crossing the Star Gate
by William Henry

Thousands of years ago the stargate technology of the gods was lost. Mayan Prophecy says it will return by 2012, along with our alignment with the center of our galaxy. In this book: Find examples of stargates and wormholes in the ancient world; Examine myths and scripture with hidden references to a stargate cloak worn by the Illuminati, including Mari, Nimrod, Elijah, and Jesus; See rare images of gods and goddesses wearing the Cloak of the illuminati; Learn about Saddam Hussein and the secret missing library of Jesus; Uncover the secret Roman-era eugenics experiments at the Temple of Hathor in Denderah, Egypt; Explore the duplicate of the Stargate Pillar of the Gods in the Illuminati' secret garden in Nashville; Discover the secrets of manna, the food of the angels, Jesus and the Illuminati; more. Chapters include: Seven Stars Under Three Stars; The Long Walk; Squaring the Circle; The Mill of the Host; The Miracle Garment; The Fig; Nimrod: The Mighty Man; Nebuchadnezzar's Gate; The New Mighty Man; more.
238 PAGES. 6X9 PAPERBACK. ILLUSTRATED. BIBLIOGRAPHY. INDEX. $16.95. CODE: COIL

GUARDIANS OF THE HOLY GRAIL
by Mark Amaru Pinkham

Although the Templar Knights had been schooled in the legend of Jesus Christ and his famous chalice while in their homeland of France, during their one hundred years in the Holy Land they discovered that Jesus's Holy Grail was but one of a long line of Holy Grail manifestations, and that a lineage of Guardians of the Holy Grail had existed in Asia for thousands of years prior to the birth of the Messiah. This book presents this extremely ancient Holy Grail lineage from Asia and how the Knights Templar were initiated into it. It also reveals how the ancient Asian wisdom regarding the Holy Grail became the foundation for the Holy Grail legends of the west while also serving as the bedrock of the European Secret Societies, which included the Freemasons, Rosicrucians, and the Illuminati. Also: The Fisher Kings; The Middle Eastern mystery schools, such as the Assassins and Yezidhi; The ancient Holy Grail lineage from Sri Lanka and the Templar Knights' initiation into it; The head of John the Baptist and its importance to the Templars; The secret Templar initiation with grotesque Baphomet, the infamous Head of Wisdom; more.
248 PAGES. 6X9 PAPERBACK. ILLUSTRATED. BIBLIOGRAPHY. $16.95. CODE: GOHG

RETURN OF THE SERPENTS OF WISDOM
by Mark Amaru Pinkham

According to ancient records, the patriarchs and founders of the early civilizations in Egypt, India, China, Peru, Mesopotamia, Britain, and the Americas were the Serpents of Wisdom—spiritual masters associated with the serpent—who arrived in these lands after abandoning their beloved homelands and crossing great seas. While bearing names denoting snake or dragon (such as Naga, Lung, Djedhi, Amaru, Quetzalcoatl, Adder, etc.), these Serpents of Wisdom oversaw the construction of magnificent civilizations within which they and their descendants served as the priest kings and as the enlightened heads of mystery school traditions. Pinkham recounts the history of these "Serpents"—where they came from, why they came, the secret wisdom they disseminated, and why they are returning now.
400 PAGES. 6X9 PAPERBACK. ILLUSTRATED. REFERENCES. $16.95. CODE: RSW

THE STONE PUZZLE OF ROSSLYN CHAPEL
by Philip Coppens

Rosslyn Chapel is revered by Freemasons as a vital part of their history, believed by some to hold evidence of pre-Columbian voyages to America, assumed by others to hold important relics, from the Holy Grail to the Head of Christ, the Scottish chapel is a place full of mystery. The history of the chapel, its relationship to freemasonry and the family behind the scenes, the Sinclairs, is brought to life, incorporating new, previously forgotten and heretofore unknown evidence. Significantly, the story is placed in the equally enigmatic landscape surrounding the chapel, which includes features from Templar commanderies to enigmatic markings, from an ancient kingly site to the South to Arthur's Seat directly north of the chapel. The true significance and meaning of the chapel is finally unveiled: it is a medieval stone book of esoteric knowledge "written" by the Sinclair family, one of the most powerful and wealthy families in Scotland, chosen patrons of Freemasonry.
124 PAGES. 6X9 PAPERBACK. ILLUSTRATED. $12.00. CODE: SPRC

THE HISTORY OF THE KNIGHTS TEMPLARS
by Charles G. Addison, introduction by David Hatcher Childress

Chapters on the origin of the Templars, their popularity in Europe and their rivalry with the Knights of St. John, later to be known as the Knights of Malta. Detailed information on the activities of the Templars in the Holy Land, and the 1312 AD suppression of the Templars in France and other countries, which culminated in the execution of Jacques de Molay and the continuation of the Knights Templars in England and Scotland; the formation of the society of Knights Templars in London; and the rebuilding of the Temple in 1816. Plus a lengthy intro about the lost Templar fleet and its North American sea routes.
395 PAGES. 6X9 PAPERBACK. ILLUSTRATED. $16.95. CODE: HKT

SAUNIER'S MODEL AND THE SECRET OF RENNES-LE-CHATEAU
The Priest's Final Legacy
by André Douzet

Berenger Saunière, the enigmatic priest of the French village of Rennes-le-Château, is rumored to have found the legendary treasure of the Cathars. But what became of it? In 1916, Sauniere created his ultimate clue: he went to great expense to create a model of a region said to be the Calvary Mount, indicating the "Tomb of Jesus." But the region on the model does not resemble the region of Jerusalem. Did Saunière leave a clue as to the true location of his treasure? And what is that treasure? After years of research, André Douzet discovered this model—the only real clue Saunière left behind as to the nature and location of his treasure—and the possible tomb of Jesus.
116 PAGES. 6X9 PAPERBACK. ILLUSTRATED. BIBLIOGRAPHY. $12.00. CODE: SMOD

PHILOSOPHY & RELIGION

THE CHRIST CONSPIRACY
The Greatest Story Ever Sold
by Acharya S.

In this highly controversial and explosive book, archaeologist, historian, mythologist and linguist Acharya S. marshals an enormous amount of startling evidence to demonstrate that Christianity and the story of Jesus Christ were created by members of various secret societies, mystery schools and religions in order to unify the Roman Empire under one state religion. In developing such a fabrication, this multinational cabal drew upon a multitude of myths and rituals that existed long before the Christian era, and reworked them for centuries into the religion passed down to us today. Contrary to popular belief, there was no single man who was at the genesis of Christianity; Jesus was many characters rolled into one. These characters personified the ubiquitous solar myth, and their exploits were well known, as reflected by such popular deities as Mithras, Heracles/Hercules, Dionysos and many others throughout the Roman Empire and beyond. The story of Jesus as portrayed in the Gospels is revealed to be nearly identical in detail to that of the earlier savior-gods Krishna and Horus, who for millennia preceding Christianity held great favor with the people. *The Christ Conspiracy* shows the Jesus character as neither unique nor original, not "divine revelation." Christianity re-interprets the same extremely ancient body of knowledge that revolved around the celestial bodies and natural forces.

436 PAGES. 6X9 PAPERBACK. ILLUSTRATED. $16.95. CODE: CHRC

SUNS OF GOD
Krishna, Buddha and Christ Unveiled
by Acharya S

From the author of the controversial and best-selling book *The Christ Conspiracy: The Greatest Story Ever Sold* comes this electrifying journey into the origins and meaning of the world's religions and popular gods. Over the past several centuries, the Big Three spiritual leaders have been the Lords Christ, Krishna and Buddha, whose stories and teachings are so remarkably similar as to confound and amaze those who encounter them. As classically educated archaeologist, historian, mythologist and linguist Acharya S thoroughly reveals, these striking parallels exist not because these godmen were "historical" personages who "walked the earth" but because they are personifications of the central focus of the famous and scandalous "mysteries." These mysteries date back thousands of years and are found globally, reflecting an ancient tradition steeped in awe and intrigue. In unveiling the reasons for this highly significant development, the author presents an in-depth analysis that includes fascinating and original research based on evidence both modern and ancient—captivating information kept secret and hidden for ages.

428 PAGES. 6X9 PAPERBACK. ILLUSTRATED. BIBLIOGRAPHY. INDEX. $16.95. CODE: SUNG

THE TRUTH BEHIND THE CHRIST MYTH
The Redemption of the Peacock Angel
by Mark Amaru Pinkham

The Peacock Angel of the Catholic Church is Murrugan's symbol, the peacock, a bird native to southeast Asia. Murrugan evolved into the Persian Mithras who evolved into Jesus Christ. Saint Paul came from Tarsus, the center of Mithras worship in Asia Minor; he amalgamated the legend of the Persian Son of God onto Jesus' life story. Topics include: The Three Wise Men were Magi priests who believed that Jesus was an incarnation of Mithras; While in India, Saint Thomas became a peacock before he died and merged with Murrugan, the Peacock Angel; The myth of the One and Only Son of God originated with Murrugan and Mithras; The Peacock Angel has been worshipped by many persons world-wide as The King of the World; Hitler, the Knights Templar, and the Illuminati sought to use the power of the Peacock Angel to conquer the world; more.

174 PAGES. 6X9 PAPERBACK. ILLUSTRATED. BIBLIOGRAPHY. $14.95. CODE: TBCM

THE AQUARIAN GOSPEL OF JESUS THE CHRIST
Transcribed from the Akashic Records
by Levi

First published in 1908, this is the amazing story of Jesus, the man from Galilee, and how he attained the Christ consciousness open to all men. It includes a complete record of the "lost" 18 years of his life, a time on which the New Testament is strangely silent. During this period Jesus travelled widely in India, Tibet, Persia, Egypt and Greece, learning from the Masters, seers and wisemen of the East and the West in their temples and schools. Included is information on the Council of the Seven Sages of the World, Jesus with the Chinese Master Mencius (Meng Tzu) in Tibet, the ministry, trial, execution and resurrection of Jesus.

270 PAGES. 6X9 PAPERBACK. INDEX. $14.95. CODE: AGJC

THE BOOK OF ENOCH
The Prophet
translated by Richard Laurence

This is a reprint of the Apocryphal *Book of Enoch the Prophet* which was first discovered in Abyssinia in the year 1773 by a Scottish explorer named James Bruce. In 1821 *The Book of Enoch* was translated by Richard Laurence and published in a number of successive editions, culminating in the 1883 edition. One of the main influences from the book is its explanation of evil coming into the world with the arrival of the "fallen angels." Enoch acts as a scribe, writing up a petition on behalf of these fallen angels, or fallen ones, to be given to a higher power for ultimate judgment. Christianity adopted some ideas from Enoch, including the Final Judgment, the concept of demons, the origins of evil and the fallen angels, and the coming of a Messiah and ultimately, a Messianic kingdom. The *Book of Enoch* was ultimately removed from the Bible and banned by the early church. Copies of it were found to have survived in Ethiopia, and fragments in Greece and Italy.

224 PAGES. 6X9 PAPERBACK. ILLUSTRATED. INDEX. $16.95. CODE: BOE

THE WORLD'S SIXTEEN CRUCIFIED SAVIORS
Christianity Before Christ
by Kersey Graves, foreword by Acharya S.

A reprint of Kersey Graves' classic and rare 1875 book on Christianity before Christ, and the 16 messiahs or saviors who are known to history before Christ! Chapters on: Rival Claims of the Saviors; Messianic Prophecies; Prophecies by the Figure of a Serpent; Virgin Mothers and Virgin-Born Gods; Stars Point Out the Time and the Saviors' Birthplace; Sixteen Saviors Crucified; The Holy Ghost of Oriental Origin; Appollonius, Osiris, and Magus as Gods; 346 Striking Analogies Between Christ and Krishna; 25th of December as the birthday of the Gods; more. 45 chapters in all.

436 PAGES. 6X9 PAPERBACK. ILLUSTRATED. $19.95. CODE: WSCS

One Adventure Place
P.O. Box 74
Kempton, Illinois 60946
United States of America
•Tel.: 1-800-718-4514 or 815-253-6390
•Fax: 815-253-6300
Email: auphq@frontiernet.net
http://www.adventuresunlimitedpress.com
or www.adventuresunlimited.nl

10% Discount when you order 3 or more items!

ORDERING INSTRUCTIONS

➤➤ Remit by USD$ Check, Money Order or Credit Card

➤➤ Visa, Master Card, Discover & AmEx Accepted

➤➤ Prices May Change Without Notice

➤➤ 10% Discount for 3 or more Items

SHIPPING CHARGES

United States

➤➤ Postal Book Rate { $3.00 First Item
50¢ Each Additional Item

➤➤ Priority Mail { $4.50 First Item
$2.00 Each Additional Item

➤➤ UPS { $5.00 First Item
$1.50 Each Additional Item

NOTE: UPS Delivery Available to Mainland USA Only

Canada

➤➤ Postal Book Rate { $6.00 First Item
$2.00 Each Additional Item

➤➤ Postal Air Mail { $8.00 First Item
$2.50 Each Additional Item

➤➤ Personal Checks or Bank Drafts MUST BE
USD$ and Drawn on a US Bank

➤➤ Canadian Postal Money Orders in US$ OK

➤➤ Payment MUST BE US$

All Other Countries

➤➤ Surface Delivery { $10.00 First Item
$4.00 Each Additional Item

➤➤ Postal Air Mail { $14.00 First Item
$5.00 Each Additional Item

➤➤ Checks and Money Orders MUST BE US $
and Drawn on a US Bank or branch.

➤➤ Payment by credit card preferred!

SPECIAL NOTES

➤➤ RETAILERS: Standard Discounts Available

➤➤ BACKORDERS: We Backorder all Out-of-
Stock Items Unless Otherwise Requested

➤➤ PRO FORMA INVOICES: Available on Request

➤➤ VIDEOS: NTSC Mode Only. Replacement only.

➤➤ For PAL mode videos contact our other offices:

European Office:
Adventures Unlimited, Pannewal 22,
Enkhuizen, 1602 KS, The Netherlands
http: www.adventuresunlimited.nl
Check Us Out Online at:
www.adventuresunlimitedpress.com

Please check: ☑

☐ This is my first order   ☐ I have ordered before   ☐ This is a new address

Name _____

Address _____

City _____

State/Province _____   Postal Code _____

Country _____

Phone day _____   Evening _____

Fax _____   Email _____

Item Code	Item Description	Price	Qty	Total

Please check: ☑

☐ Postal-Surface

☐ Postal-Air Mail
(Priority in USA)

☐ UPS
(Mainland USA only)

Subtotal ➤	
Less Discount-10% for 3 or more items ➤	
Balance ➤	
Illinois Residents 6.25% Sales Tax ➤	
Previous Credit ➤	
Shipping ➤	
Total (check/MO in USD$ only) ➤	

☐ Visa/MasterCard/Discover/Amex

Card Number _____

Expiration Date _____

10% Discount When You Order 3 or More Items!

Comments & Suggestions	Share Our Catalog with a Friend